NEVER ENOUGH

NEVER ENOUGH

AMERICA'S LIMITLESS WELFARE STATE

WILLIAM VOEGELI

Encounter Books  New York · London

First American edition published in 2010 by Encounter Books,
an activity of Encounter for Culture and Education, Inc.,
a nonprofit, tax exempt corporation.
Encounter Books website address: www.encounterbooks.com

Manufactured in the United States and printed on
acid-free paper. The paper used in this publication meets
the minimum requirements of ANSI/NISO Z39.48 1992
(R 1997) (*Permanence of Paper*).

FIRST AMERICAN EDITION

LIBRARY OF CONGRESS CATALOGING-IN-PUBLICATION DATA

Voegeli, William J., 1954-
Never enough: America's limitless welfare state / by William Voegeli.
p. cm.
Includes bibliographical references and index.
ISBN-13: 978-1-59403-376-6 (hardcover : alk. paper)
ISBN-10: 1-59403-376-5 (hardcover : alk. paper)
1. Public welfare—United States—History. 2. Welfare state—United States—
History. 3. United States—Social policy. 4. Liberalism—United States—History.
5. United States—Appropriations and expenditures. I. Title.
HV91.V59 2010
361.6'50973—dc22
2009044438

10 9 8 7 6 5 4 3 2 1

for
Bailey and Martha

CONTENTS

FOREWORD

Thirty years after the arrival of the Reagan Revolution was thought to have ushered in the end of the New Deal era, 16 years after the Gingrich Revolution arrived in Washington to continue the job, and 14 years after President Bill Clinton capitulated in "ending welfare as we know it," Americans find themselves on the cusp of a vast expansion of their welfare state to near-European dimensions. Liberals understandably revel in their good fortune while it lasts, while conservatives are bewildered: "What happened"?

This circumstance makes *Never Enough* all the more timely and important. But even more than timeliness is its original contribution to serious reflection about the American welfare state. William Voegeli has produced a work that achieves a rare intellectual triple play: *Never Enough* is theoretical, empirical, and—readable. I am tempted to stop here and suggest readers skip the rest of this foreword, as I have little original to add to his thorough analysis. But I shall at least try to adumbrate a few key themes and suggest some ways in which Voegeli has shown true intellectual courage in shining a necessary light of self-criticism at the cherished axioms of opponents of the welfare state. Few people—myself included—have wanted to go very far down this road.

In discussing the "hundred years' war" Voegeli describes between left and right over the growth of the welfare state—a war the left has been slowly winning—it is useful to recall the premises and main arguments both sides have rolled out onto the political battlefield. For many decades the right complained variously of the high cost of the welfare state and occasionally its injustice, that is, it is wrong in principle to take from one person to give to another. When private citizens do this, it is called "theft," but when the government does it, it's called a "transfer payment," "income security," or some other euphemism. The latter argument has had only marginal appeal beyond doctrinaire libertarians, while the former argument has, so far at least, failed to be borne out by the fact that the prodigious growth of the American economy has enabled us to afford a continuously more generous welfare state. (Yes, yes, entitlements such as Medicare look to be catastrophically unsustainable, but that day is still ahead of us.)

The whole matter took a stunning turn in the 1960s when liberalism's claims that applied social science and massive funding would end poverty and solve social problems hit the wall in a way that discredited liberalism for nearly a generation. Who cannot look back now without a smirk at War on Poverty czar Sargent Shriver's 1966 declaration that the U.S. was on its way to the total elimination of poverty in ten years? Beyond the intractability of poverty was the visible decay of urban areas, which were becoming increasingly unlivable when they were not erupting into flames. Voters drew the simple correlation that the worst conditions correlated with liberal governance. Following the Detroit riots of 1967, Daniel Patrick Moynihan noted that "ravaged Detroit was, as it were, liberalism's city."

But the nation's turn to the right in the 1970s and 1980s merely slowed the growth of the welfare state, and did not reverse it. One of the virtues of Voegeli's book is that it confronts head-on the failure of Ronald Reagan's stated aim "to curb the size and influence of the federal establishment." This is not to deny Reagan's substantial successes. As Voegeli discusses and shows in his historical data tables, Reagan's record in restraining the growth of the welfare state is the most impressive of any modern president by almost an order of magnitude. "For welfare state spending to have grown less than 1% a year for eight years was an exceptional achievement," Voegeli observes, "whether we compare Reagan to other presidents or to other nations' governments." But it proved temporary; we couldn't re-elect Reagan forever, and as Voegeli argues, to confuse relative restraint with success "amounts to defining effectuality down." Conservatives who rightly celebrate Reagan's greatness often slide into what might be called Reagan triumphalism, and thereby do a disservice to Reagan's memory, and their mutual cause. Reagan triumphalists have tended to avert their gaze from reckoning with the seeming permanence of the New Deal revolution, which was the central political aim of the New Deal. Since the New Deal, conservatives have merely slowed the advance of the welfare state, but seldom reversed it. Voegeli will annoy Reagan triumphalists, but his bracing honesty should not be confused with chronic pessimism, all the more so when one compares the debilitations of liberalism's political weaknesses that Voegeli also enters on his thorough balance sheet. Liberalism may not have a limiting principle, but markets and voters periodically construct some sharp speed bumps on the path of the further growth of the welfare state. Hence the mutual frustration of left and right: the left can't get the freewheeling Rawlsian-scale redistribution it lusts for in its heart, while the right cannot abolish the welfare state.

Liberalism's irrepressible drive for an ever larger welfare state without limit arises from at least two premises upon which the left no longer reflects: the elevation of compassion to a political principle (albeit with other people's money), and the erosion of meaningful constitutional limits on government on account of the imperatives of the idea of Progress. Voegeli explains here the Progressive/New Deal deformation of our constitutional order—a story not all conservatives grasp in its fullness, let alone most citizens—and its crucial relation to the steady expansion of the welfare state, both in its social insurance functions and in its regulatory functions. "The political success of liberalism is that people are generally very receptive to the tangible benefits the welfare state delivers," Voegeli concludes, "and have largely forgotten their qualms about the propriety of the government dispensing such benefits." To this cogent theoretical excursion Voegeli presents the numbers about the growth of welfare state spending in simple but alarming fashion. Not since Ronald Reagan has the outsized expansion of the welfare state been stated in such clear and compelling terms.

It is important to grasp that the egalitarian urge of the left goes beyond merely the passion for equalizing incomes or insuring against misfortune. Kenneth Minogue's penetrating 1963 book, *The Liberal Mind,* reminded us that modern liberalism "is rather like the legend of St. George and the dragon." Unlike St. George, however, the modern liberal is unable to retire:

> The more he succeeded, the more he became bewitched with
> the thought of a world free of dragons, and the less capable
> he became of returning to private life. He needed his dragons.
> He could only live by fighting for causes—the people, the
> poor, the exploited, the colonially oppressed, the underprivi-
> leged and the underdeveloped. As an ageing warrior, he grew
> breathless in his pursuit of smaller and smaller dragons—for
> the big dragons are harder to come by.

Having slain most of the big dragons of Depression-era destitution, the liberal's anguish over "suffering situations" (as Minogue called the liberals' chief compass point) now extends to the self-esteem of elementary school children, whose team games sometimes go deliberately un-scored to spare the tender feelings of impressionable youth on the losing end.

Score-free kids' games are not the frivolous outliers they might seem from their obvious absurdity, for in the logic of limitless liberalism the individual's pursuit of happiness has been transformed into the government's burden of delivering it. Recall the woman who told a television reporter shortly before the 2008 election that "Obama will pay my mortgage and my gas bill." The San Francisco Board of Supervisors in 2005 declared free Internet access to be a "human right" which the city was obligated to provide (when it became apparent that universal free Internet access cost real money, the Board said "never mind" about this "human right"). Because liberalism has increasingly defined the means to happiness as basic human rights, Voegeli asks "on what basis can we tell people who repeatedly demand additions to the honor roll that some things are indeed conducive to a decent life but, at the same time, are not rights?"

Most Americans have a healthy distaste for the illogical but inexorable end-point of such liberalism for reasons liberals refuse or are unable to see, namely, that the European-style welfare states they so prize as models don't fit the American character, chiefly because the European welfare states are a legacy of Europe's ancient feudalism. An earlier generation of liberals (Louis Hartz most prominently) understood this, but contemporary liberalism has become so unreflective about its premises that this essential difference is outside their field of view. This is why the language of America's welfare state liberalism is the attenuated language of individual rights more than the mutual obligations of community (though this strain has a constituency on the left). Hence Franklin Roosevelt's compelling argument that a needy man cannot be a free man. That the welfare state was necessary to secure the promise of individual liberty was a clever and effective way to blunt the political liabilities of egalitarianism.

   This background puts the one undeniable conservative policy triumph in reforming the welfare state in the last generation into a different light, and turns up an irony and a crucial tacit concession that confirms the way in which FDR's formula turned the correlation of forces in the favor of liberalism. During the Reagan years the intellectual case deepened (most especially with Charles Murray's book, *Losing Ground*) that current federal welfare programs were actually *harmful* to most recipients—an argument Reagan made from instinct back in the 1960s. The new welfare state of the 1960s, Murray wrote, bestowed on the poor new rules that "make it profitable for the poor to behave in the short term in ways that were destructive in the long term. . . . We tried to remove the barriers to escape from poverty, and inadvertently built a trap." Murray called it "the generous revolution," and made a powerful empirical case about how it had backfired. The welfare state was not helping individuals achieve their pursuit of happiness.

   This was new: a conservative argument about the welfare state that said it failed to achieve its objectives, rather than being too expensive or in violation of some fundamental principle of limited government. This turned out to be the political basis for the sweeping welfare reform of 1996, which ended welfare as an open-ended entitlement of the previous Aid to Families with Dependent Children (AFDC) and replaced it with Temporary Assistance to Needy Families (TANF), with the emphasis on "temporary"—time limits for program eligibility were adopted for the first time, along with work requirements for the able-bodied and job training for those without skills. The results were dramatic: a nearly 50 percent decline in the nation's welfare caseload over the following decade. The object of TANF was now to lift people out of poverty, not to enable them to remain dependents of the state, one generation after another.

But this signal triumph of "ending welfare as we know it" represented hoisting liberals by their own petard; conservative critics of welfare succeeded by turning the compassion argument against welfare. This explains why the success of the 1996 welfare reform has not been replicable to any other large entitlement program such as Social Security or Medicare, let alone housing or food stamps. And some of the key features of the 1996 act, such as time limits for eligibility, are under attack in Congress. While conservatives argued that their next reform ideas, such as private retirement and medical savings accounts, would ensure greater benefits than the present configurations, they could not carry the day for the simple reason that the current programs cannot be said to suffer from a compassion gap as did AFDC, along with the fact that these other entitlements flow to a broader middle-class base.

So we are left with a stalemate in which a majority of Americans desire a welfare state, but not too much of one. It may be that the ever larger pool of independent swing voters, who are now the bane of partisan strategists in both parties, want Democrats to design the welfare state, but Republicans to run it. Conservatives and libertarians avert their gaze from this uncongenial circumstance, too often reacting with the equivalent of a child's temper tantrum, thinking if the denunciation of the welfare state is shouted louder the people will change their mind. Voegeli asks us to embrace the seeming paradox that conservatives' only hope of limiting the welfare state is to overcome their categorical opposition to it.

While the ambivalence of public opinion has favored liberals' "brick by brick" construction of an ever larger welfare state, there are ominous signs that this is ultimately an unstable rather than dynamic equilibrium. To keep the welfare state solvent as the baby boomers crash the rope line of eligibility will require tax increases far larger than Americans are likely willing to bear. One might almost say that the welfare state is the next bubble waiting to collapse. Voegeli proposes a grand bargain: major program benefits should be means-tested so that they are directed at the truly needy, in exchange for defined limits on the extent of the welfare state. It is a bargain that will be a tough sell to all points on the political compass, and Voegeli is under no illusions that this bargain will be simple to accomplish, even though it would still leave both sides plenty to fight over in the aftermath. The outlines of such a deal on Medicare and Social Security were tentatively struck in 1997 between then-President Bill Clinton and then-Speaker Newt Gingrich. Clinton's impeachment crisis derailed the idea before it could even leave the station; in retrospect, Clinton's impeachment may have been a multi-trillion dollar catastrophe.

Ultimately what is at stake is not money or prosperity as much as self-government itself. Voegeli explains: "The danger liberalism poses to the American experiment comes from its disposition to deplete rather than replenish the capital required for self-government." And the main use of that capital was not material comfort alone, as the Founders understood, but happiness. As James Madison explained in Federalist #62: "A good government implies two things: first, fidelity to the object of government, which is the happiness of the people; secondly, a knowledge of the means by which that object can be best attained." One of the most salient features of European welfare states, Charles Murray points out, is not that they retard material prosperity significantly (the European nations are generally very comfortable places to live) but that, according to survey data, contemporary Europeans are the least happy—happy in terms of deep satisfaction with jobs and family life—among peoples of wealthy nations. A people that are genuinely happy replenish the capital required for self-government, while a dependent people suffer a diminished capacity for happiness and slowly lose the ability to self-rule.

This is why *Never Enough* is much more than a policy trea-
tise. It is about nothing less than the meaning and character of
modern America.

Steven F. Hayward
January 2010

THE SEARCH FOR SUFFICIENCY

The book you are reading is not the one I set out to write. The finished product differs from the original concept, which was to find the answer to a question posed by American liberals in thousands of articles, speeches and books. All those polemics insist that government must do more—*much* more—to help the poor, to increase economic security, to promote social justice and solidarity, to reduce inequality and mitigate the harshness of capitalism. Consider:

- "Of course we will continue to seek to improve working conditions for the workers of America—to reduce hours overlong, to increase wages that spell starvation, to end the labor of children, to wipe out sweatshops. Of course we will continue every effort to end monopoly in business, to support collective bargaining, to stop unfair competition, to abolish dishonorable trade practices. For all these we have only just begun to fight.

  "Of course we will continue to work for cheaper electricity in the homes and on the farms of America, for better and cheaper transportation, for low interest rates, for sounder home financing, for better banking, for the regulation of security issues, for reciprocal trade among nations, for the wiping out of slums. For all these we have only just begun to fight. . . .

  "Of course we will provide useful work for the needy unemployed; we prefer useful work to the pauperism of a dole. . . .

"Of course we will continue our efforts for young men and women so that they may obtain an education and an opportunity to put it to use. Of course we will continue our help for the crippled, for the blind, for the mothers, our insurance for the unemployed, our security for the aged. Of course we will continue to protect the consumer against unnecessary price spreads, against the costs that are added by monopoly and speculation. We will continue our successful efforts to increase his purchasing power and to keep it constant.

"For these things, too, and for *a multitude of others like them*, we have only just begun to fight." Franklin D. Roosevelt, October 31, 1936 (emphasis added).[1]

■ There should be "more government spending in blighted areas, even if it could not be done in a better way than scattering dollar bills from airplanes." *The Nation*, 1964.[2]

■ "A society such as ours is disgraced by the plight of our elderly, and the resources of the entire nation should be mobilized to help provide a decent standard of living upon retirement." *The New Republic*, 1965.[3]

■ "[The] Poverty War, like military ones, needs vast supplies of money. These are a necessary component of the power which must be exerted to raise the poor from their poverty." *The New Republic*, 1965.[4]

■ "[The] realization of common opportunities for all within a single society . . . will require a commitment to national action—compassionate, massive and sustained, backed by the resources of the most powerful and the richest nation on this earth. From every American it will require new attitudes, new understanding, and, above all, new will. The vital needs of the nation must be met; hard choices must be made, and, if necessary, new taxes enacted." Report of the National Advisory Commission on Civil Disorders (the "Kerner Commission"), 1968.[5]

- "[While] it is true that the generosity of some of the new rich is extraordinary, it is also true that charity is not economic justice. (It is the absence of economic justice that makes charity necessary.)" *The New Republic*, 2007.[6]
- "Democrats want to give health coverage to kids, and Republicans want kids to go without health coverage." *The American Prospect*, 2007.[7]

The 1964 *Nation* editorial quoted on page two was titled, "Not Enough." For nearly a century, "Not Enough" has been the liberal position on domestic policy. The premise of the book I didn't write was that all the bitter accusations about the insufficiency of our social programs must point to a criterion of sufficiency, defining a completely adequate welfare state. The cost and scope of America's social welfare programs have grown dramatically since 1933. The nation has grown steadily, and vastly, more prosperous. All the while, no matter how large the welfare state, liberal politicians and writers have accused it of being shamefully small. A fair supposition would be that one could follow the trajectory of these relentless complaints to determine the coordinates of the Platonic ideal of the welfare state, one that has every single program and resource it needs and deserves, and consequently requires no further expansion.

My original goal was to examine the liberal account of *that* welfare state, a project that had to be abandoned when I realized it had no subject matter. Liberal rhetoric never engages this issue: What would be the size and nature of a welfare state that was not contemptibly austere, that did not urgently need a larger budget and a broader agenda?

The answer to this question is . . . well, that there is no answer to this question. Liberals could tackle the problem at the macro-level, describing the boundaries beyond which the welfare state need not and should not expand. They never do. Alternatively, they could suggest the welfare state's limits by concentrating on the micro-level, offering instructive examples of social programs that are too expensive, too intrusive or demand too much of government and too little of their beneficiaries. They don't do that, either. In 1964 Lyndon Johnson said, "We're in favor of a lot of things and we're against mighty few."[8] That's about as rigorous as the liberal theory of the welfare state ever gets.

The situation resembles the story about the cattle baron who insisted he didn't want to acquire all the land in Texas—only those acres adjacent to the land he already owns. Liberals don't want the government to grow indefinitely. They just want it to be bigger than it is right now. The corollary of this stance is liberals' refusal even to entertain questions on the dimensions of a welfare state that is exactly the right size.

IDEAS, BIG AND SMALL

This book tries to make sense of why that other volume was impossible. Its subject will be what "liberalism's lack of a limiting principle" means for the long-standing dispute between liberals and conservatives over the welfare state.[9] The first step toward addressing that question is to get a clear idea about how big the American welfare state really is, how much and how rapidly it has grown, and how it compares in these respects with welfare states in other modern industrial societies. Chapter One will undertake that task by examining data from the Office of Management and Budget, and the Organisation for Economic Co-Operation and Development.

Though lacking a limiting principle, liberalism has an animating one. Progressives and New Dealers established its theoretical foundations by reinterpreting—some say rewriting—the American founding. Chapter Two describes the intellectual labors of those who supplanted a government kept on a short leash to protect liberty, with a government able to lay claim to all the powers it needs, or thinks it needs, to promote welfare.

The absence of a limiting principle requires examining, in Chapter Three, modern liberalism's elucidation of, and disagreements about, the welfare state. For one thing, liberals disagree about whether they need a "big idea." Its proponents say that liberalism suffers from being a themeless grab bag of policy proposals held together by no larger purpose. Those skeptical about such theorizing, however, insist that it is not only possible but necessary for liberalism to move from issue to issue without forging a philosophy that links all of its policy prescriptions.

The central belief of those who favor a big idea is that intellectual coherence will make liberalism more politically dynamic. A big idea that explained what liberalism is supposed to do, however, would have the unintended but unavoidable consequence of making clear what it is *not* supposed to do. As it turns out, this danger is largely hypothetical—the big ideas actually offered by those who insist on them are too paltry and confused to tell us the specifications of a welfare state in need of no additional expansion or improvement.

The logical consequence of the alternate approach, explicitly disdaining big ideas, is the belief that every problem deserves a program. The corollary is that liberalism has no authoritative way to tell anyone who's dissatisfied, either with the contours of his own life or the condition of society, that his grievance does not deserve to be taken seriously and alleviated through a program of its own. Turning away people with problems, after all, is why God (or Satan) created conservatism.

The gaps in the liberal argument for the welfare state, though serious, have done more to help than harm liberalism's cause. Many people really do have problems, and many others have gripes. The defining victory of the New Deal was not the individual programs it created, but the evisceration of the principle that government, especially the federal government, had no rightful business undertaking a whole range of social improvements, no matter how gratifying the beneficiaries might find them. Once this "legitimacy barrier" was demolished, liberals could frame the politics of the welfare state as a contest between the compassionate party that wants the government to give things to people and do things for them, and the mean-spirited party that wants to deprive people of all those indispensable and beneficial things.

MONEY, MONEY, MONEY

The demise of the belief that there is such a thing as a social welfare program that would provide some people with tangible assistance, but which also lies beyond the legitimate scope of the government's powers and must not, therefore, be undertaken, means that the only remaining constraint on the growth of the welfare state is the problem of paying for it. Though the tax collector will never be a beloved folk hero, liberals could, if they chose, make a simple, direct and seemingly powerful argument: The welfare state is good and necessary. The taxes it requires are not fun to pay, but they fund programs that improve the quality of life for everyone by strengthening and uniting our nation. We should accept and even embrace those taxes as a fair price we pay for the essential benefits they buy.

In reality, liberals have avoided this argument in favor of any and every alternative they can find. They have made this choice out of the fear that voters' enthusiasm for welfare state programs will never be sufficient to win their support for the taxes to pay for them. Rather, liberals have tried to establish an adequate political foundation for the welfare state by indulging the voters' wish that someone or something other than they themselves will pay for its programs.

To encourage this hope rather than disabuse voters of it, liberals have performed heroic contortions. The results, to be examined in Chapter Four, are a cluster of arguments relying on non-Euclidean economics. One is that welfare state programs will pay for themselves. Indeed, according to a phrase near the top of many sales pitches for expanding the welfare state, new programs will pay for themselves many times over. Voters, therefore, needn't worry their pretty little heads about the price tags. Alternatively, the programs, yes, need to be paid for, but very, very, very rich people and giant corporations will pick up the tab; the rest of us only have to chip in to cover the tip. Finally, by blackening the skies with criss-crossing dollars, the welfare state manages people's perceptions of its costs and benefits to encourage them to believe an impossibility: that every household can be a net importer of the wealth redistributed by the government.

THE INSUFFICIENT CONSERVATIVE RESPONSE

Once it became clear that the New Deal was not just an ambitious effort to end the Depression, but an ambitious effort to expand the scope of government—dramatically, endlessly and permanently—conservative activists and writers began complaining bitterly that Republicans were more interested in accommodating than reversing this radical revision of the Jeffersonian republic established 150 years before. They accused "me-too" presidential candidates like Wendell Willkie, Thomas Dewey and Dwight Eisenhower of depriving the leading opponent of the New Deal, Robert Taft, the GOP nomination by limiting their critique of Big Government to the need for it to be managed honestly and competently—by Republicans, in other words, not Democrats.

The rationale of Barry Goldwater's 1964 presidential campaign was that the voters wanted and deserved a choice between perpetuating and dismantling the New Deal, rather than Republicans who merely echoed the arguments put forward by New Deal Democrats.

Lyndon Johnson's crushing defeat of Goldwater seemed, at the time, to demonstrate beyond doubt that the question conservatives had insisted on posing had been answered—in a way guaranteeing that the era of liberal hegemony begun in 1932 would never end. In reality, that election, and the numerous Great Society programs enacted by Congress in its aftermath, marked the "high tide of liberalism," to borrow from the title of a collection of scholarly essays.[10] One factor explaining this surprising reversal is the large number of voters who became dubious and even bitterly cynical about liberals' assurances that the benefits from the welfare state would be considerable while its costs were negligible. The opposite seemed to be true during the 1960s and '70s. The problems Great Society programs were supposed to alleviate—crime, welfare dependency, racial tensions—became worse, while inflation and unlegislated tax increases from "bracket creep" eroded families' purchasing power and economic security. These jolts caused middle-class Americans "to withdraw their pledges of trust from a liberal state depleted of credibility," according to Jonathan Rieder's *Canarsie*, and left them unwilling "to give the government a blank check. . . ."[11]

The Great Society's extravagant promises, and unintended, undesired consequences, presented conservatives with their best political opportunity in half a century. They took advantage, winning victories, especially in 1980 and 1994, that would have been dismissed as fantasies the day after LBJ's landslide. In another sense, however, conservatives' efforts to capitalize on the skepticism about taxes and government programs accomplished little.

Conservatives hoped, and liberals feared, that the tax revolt begun in 1978 when California passed Proposition 13 would lead to the welfare state's contraction. In reality, conservatives have neither reversed nor halted but merely slowed the welfare state's growth. Adjusted for inflation, per capita federal welfare state spending was 77% higher in 2007 than it was when Pres. Reagan took office.

Conservatives have made the least of their good situation. Chapter Five examines why the conservative case against the welfare state has been unavailing. America's competing ideologies are locked in a futile symmetry. No matter how big the welfare state is, liberals say it's too small; no matter how small it is, conservatives say it's too big. All the liberal arguments point to a welfare state even bigger than Sweden's; all the conservative ones to a welfare state smaller than pre-New Deal America's. The welfare state we actually have limps along, lacking enthusiastic support and a compelling rationale that could explain how to improve it without making it radically larger or smaller. Liberals and conservatives are both in the awkward position of reassuring voters that they don't really mean what all of their arguments clearly *do* mean. As a result, neither of them can muster the syllogisms or the votes to change the welfare state we're stuck with.

This political gridlock brings us to a second way this book turned out to be different from the one I thought I was going to write. Important questions are at stake in the argument over the welfare state, questions about the type of polity, economy and society America should be. Nevertheless, the argument has been going on for three-quarters of a century without any important point being settled or conceded. Liberals and conservatives, that is, have been making pretty much the same accusations about each other's shameful motives and the dire consequences of implementing each other's agendas ever since the New Deal. As this same argument is reenacted, election cycle after election cycle, it becomes increasingly clear that there is a Hatfields-and-McCoys quality to the whole enterprise: It's imperative to go on doing all we can to thwart the wicked, stupid designs of those other, bad people because, well, that's who we are and that's what we do.

I originally thought this book would be the next volley in that long war. In my Walter Mitty moments, I imagined it would be the decisive attack that won the war on conservatives' terms. I ultimately realized, however, that neither I nor any other conservative is likely to come up with a new argument that wins, ends or even changes the debate over the welfare state. It has been a long time since *any* liberal or conservative has come up with something genuinely new to say about the welfare state. Saying all the old things again, but louder, isn't worth the trouble.

The final chapter of this book attempts, instead, to get past the Hatfields-and-McCoys fight. For the argument over the welfare state to change from being a consumer of political energy to a producer of political clarity, liberals and conservatives will both have to leave their comfort zones and seriously consider the possibility that some of the ideas that need to be reconsidered are their own, not just their adversaries'.

For liberals, this will mean acknowledging that it is impossible to sell the American people more welfare state than they are willing to buy, and reckless to pretend otherwise. Intellectually dishonest arguments about how taxing the corporations and the rich, or ingeniously structuring social insurance programs, will make it possible for scarcely noticeable taxes to pay for generous social benefits are exercises in governmental malpractice. Unless liberals discover an argument that will make a majority of the electorate feel good about passing much higher taxes in order to fund a much more ambitious welfare state, they will have to come to terms with the reality that a welfare state comparable to those in Western Europe is politically infeasible, even unimaginable, in America. The full meaning of this coming to terms would be for liberals to finally grapple with the question of the welfare state's optimal size. The minimum requirement of coming to terms with the realities on the ground is to accede to the necessity to use the resources the American people *are* willing to devote to the welfare state to best advantage, by reducing or eliminating the least urgent welfare state expenditures in order to maximize the most urgent.

Conservatives have their own thoughts on that question. They cannot, however, discuss in good faith how to make social welfare programs better, smarter and fairer if their ultimate goal is the withering away of the welfare state. "America is in peril," said the 1936 Republican platform. "To a free people, these actions [of the New Deal] are insufferable." Many of the platform's specific criticisms of the New Deal remain ones that conservatives can make against Big Government today. "The New Deal Administration constantly seeks to usurp the rights reserved to the States and to the people," "has been guilty of frightful waste and extravagance, using public funds for partisan political purposes" and "has bred fear and hesitation in commerce and industry, thus discouraging new enterprises, preventing employment and prolonging the depression."

The beginning of the 21st century, however, would be a good opportunity for conservatives to accept that even the perfect candidate and endless determination will not secure the victory that eluded Alf Landon. Conservatives cannot sell the American people a smaller welfare state than they are certain to demand, no matter how unpopular the corresponding taxes will be. The 1936 election is not going to be reversed, and the time and energy conservatives devote to that unattainable goal is time and energy they divert from valuable changes they actually could effect.

Conservatives, in other words, need to take the position that America is going to have a welfare state, should have a welfare state, and it's not part of the conservative project to bring about the disappearance of the welfare state, even in the distant future. The question is whether we are going to have a welfare state that uses its finite resources intelligently, concentrating on helping the people who need it most, or one that distributes benefits in an undisciplined and nearly random fashion. Conservatives should contend that any nation wealthy enough to have a welfare state will also have a majority of people wealthy enough not to need most of what the welfare state provides. Instead of talking constantly about the evils of Big Government, conservatives need to make the argument that our existing welfare state embodies too many attributes of Bad Government.

In the unlikely event liberals and conservatives both make these concessions, American politics will not become stupefyingly dull, or embark on a new Era of Good Feelings. This resulting framework leaves liberals and conservatives ample room to disagree about what it means for the welfare state to have sufficient resources, and to put them to their best use. What it does not allow them to pursue are plans to make America a Scandinavian social democracy or a night-watchman state. There is no prospect that America's welfare state will become either a multiple or a fraction of what it is now, and no justification for pursuing either goal. Such romantic visions of political transformation are not what the exigencies of domestic governance call for. We "are in a painful period," James Q. Wilson wrote in 1986, and it has grown more painful over the past quarter-century.

> [W]hat people want from government vastly exceeds what
> they are willing to pay for. Politicians encouraged people to
> take this view and now must find a way to persuade them to

take a different view. To modify and rationalize public policy will take a lot longer than it took to whoop through Congress the spending and taxing programs that got us into this fix. It will be a life's work for some dedicated, patient, and determined people willing to stay the course.[12]

CHAPTER ONE

AMERICA'S WELFARE STATE IN NUMBERS

MEASURING ITS GROWTH

In 2004 *The American Prospect* staged an online "debate" over whether Pres. Clinton's domestic policy had been sufficiently liberal. Ann Lewis defended the proposition that Clinton's presidency had been "good for our country," an argument the former communications director in the Clinton White House could have made under sedation. Disputing her claim was Max Sawicky, an economist at the Economic Policy Institute, a liberal think tank. His central accusation was that Clinton had failed to "rehabilitate the reputation of the welfare state by proposing well-founded expansions. This, I submit, is the mission of the Democratic Party; otherwise, it has little purpose."[1]

Lewis responded with Clintonian triangulation, asserting that while government programs *can* be the best tools to promote social goals, "more government is not an end in itself." In rebuttal, Sawicky called more government for the sake of more government a red herring. He insisted that abstract objections to expanding government were trivial compared to concrete realities that require a bigger welfare state, which "offers obvious solutions to fundamental problems."

> There are huge gaps in our social safety net, giving rise to major sources of economic insecurity for working people: displacement, ill health, workplace injury, destitution in old age, inability to finance long-term care, and an increasingly rapacious Wal-Mart-style labor market. There is no mystery about how to fill these gaps: with social insurance.[2]

If the expansion of the welfare state is the reason liberals get up and go to work in the morning, its contraction is the reason conservatives do. Ronald Reagan made this clear in his 1981 inaugural address: "In this present crisis, government is not the solution to our problem; government is the problem. . . . It is my intention to curb the size and influence of the Federal establishment and to demand recognition of the distinction between the powers granted to the Federal Government and those reserved to the States or to the people."[3] He made the point repeatedly during the course of his presidency. To pick just one example, Reagan told the American Bar Association in 1983, "It's time to bury the myth that bigger government brings more opportunity and compassion. . . . In the name of fairness, let's stop trying to plunder family budgets with higher taxes, and start controlling the real problem—Federal spending."[4]

WHAT BIG GOVERNMENT ENCOMPASSES

It is worthwhile, before diving into the data, to make a distinction between the welfare state and the more encompassing idea of "Big Government." As used in conservative rhetoric, Big Government is a catchall term that is usually disparaging but rarely precise. The term amalgamates three different but related efforts of modern government: 1) macro-economic regulation, to keep inflation low, employment high and economic growth steady; 2) micro-economic regulation of individual industries and companies; and 3) welfare state programs to promote individuals' economic opportunities and security, and enhance the quality of their lives.

All three aspects of Big Government work to correct what liberals see as the defects of capitalism. The first two undertakings, economic policy and the regulatory state, work to modify capitalism's processes. For the entire economy, the problem liberals perceive and set out to solve is that capitalism, left to its own devices, is susceptible (or even doomed) to debilitating boom-and-bust cycles. The workings of the market economy are more often self-aggravating than self-correcting. When bad economic trends engender worse ones, the government must step in to moderate the business cycle. As Franklin Roosevelt said in 1932, "We must build toward the time when a major depression cannot occur again; and if this means sacrificing the easy profits of infla-tionist booms, then let them go; and good riddance."[5]

The regulatory state concerns itself with those capitalistic processes held to be unacceptably harsh, risky, unscrupulous, or to have harmful effects on third parties. The government estab-lishes and enforces standards of conduct for participants in the market when it wants to remedy these problems. Examples of the resulting activities include the protections given to labor unions, regulations of pollutants, the government's efforts to assure the safety of a wide range of consumer goods and services—cars, food, drugs, airline travel—and the transparency and integrity of financial transactions carried out by banks, brokers and insurance companies.

We should be careful not to make the line between regulating an entire economy and regulating components of it more dis-tinct for the purposes of our analysis than it is in reality. Macro-economic regulations will have micro-economic consequences, and vice versa. The line is blurred in another sense: Leftist thought and rhetoric, going back to Marx, has come down on both sides of this question: Are macro-economic dislocations caused by the impersonal workings of the inner logic of the capitalistic system or the follies and depredations of capitalists? Much of the polit-ical energy of the New Deal was directed against "malefactors of wealth" and "economic royalists," phrases meant to resonate with those who believed villains in top hats were the primary cause of the Depression. One New Dealer told the Senate in 1933, "We have reached a stage in the development of human affairs where it has

become intolerable to have our primitive capitalistic system operated by selfish individualists engaged in ruthless competition."[6]

As Alan Brinkley chronicles in *The End of Reform*, this belief
"that something was wrong with capitalism and that government
should find a way to repair it" was supplanted in the late 1930s
and the decades to follow by "a set of liberal ideas essentially rec-
onciled to the existing structure of the economy and committed
to using the state to compensate for capitalism's inevitable flaws."
This transformation owes, in part, to frustrations with the New
Deal's protracted failure to restore the standards of living Americans had enjoyed in the 1920s. The unexpected recession that
began in 1937 was particularly dispiriting. Another cause was that
the economic theories of John Maynard Keynes had few followers
in the U.S. before 1938, either in economics departments or in
government. Thereafter, however, the idea that government could
abbreviate and moderate economic downturns by fiscal policies
that stimulated aggregate demand was embraced enthusiastically
by liberals in and out of Washington.[7]

This focus on extending the benefits of capitalism rather than
correcting its evils proved to be more harmonious with the welfare
state, which concerns itself with how capitalism works out rather
than how it works. It attends to the results of capitalism by trying
to make them conform more closely to some notion of "distributive justice." If some people wind up with too much and others
too little, the welfare state redistributes income through policies
of taxation, transfer payments, and by providing or subsidizing
certain goods and services. The intention is to secure more for
those who have too little, as the sensibilities of the welfare state's
architects and advocates define a minimum level of decency.

Sometimes these advocates are also motivated by ideas about a
maximum level of decency. According to James MacGregor Burns,
FDR "astonished" Treasury officials in 1941 by "averring that he
favored taxing all personal income above $100,000 a year at 99½

or 100 percent. 'Why not?' he asked. 'None of us is ever going to make $100,000 a year. How many people report on that much income?' But he did not press his confiscatory idea." An income of $100,000 in 1941 would have had about the same purchasing power as $1,459,000 in 2009.[8] Heavy taxation on those above the level of maximum decency may be simply a means to the end of helping the poor, or may additionally be an end in itself, curtailing and even punishing those deemed guilty of extravagance and greed.

The arguments between liberals and conservatives over the proper size and scope of government include disputes about economic policy, the regulatory state and the welfare state, often without distinguishing between them. While these arguments raise many related questions about the proper roles of government and markets, this book will concentrate on the welfare state, saying considerably less about government regulation of business, industries or the entire economy.

DEFINING AND MEASURING THE WELFARE STATE

Sawicky pronounces the growth rate of the welfare state under Clinton "pathetic," but he arrives at that conclusion by using a measure—inflation-adjusted, discretionary federal spending on everything except national defense—that's more rough than ready. This category, used by the Office of Management and Budget (OMB) in its historical tables accompanying each year's federal budget, includes government endeavors no one thinks of as components of the welfare state, such as programs for international affairs, science, space and technology. At the same time, it excludes the social insurance programs Sawicky says are vital: Social Security, Medicare, Medicaid and food stamps, among others.[9]

A better yardstick can be fashioned to keep score of the Hundred Years' War between the welfare state's expanders and its reducers. OMB's historical tables track annual federal outlays beginning in 1940, using enormous categories ("superfunctions") composed of smaller but still vast "functions." One of these superfunctions, Human Resources, is made up of the following six functions:

- Education, Training, Employment and Social Services
- Health (excluding Medicare, but including health care services, health research and training, and consumer and occupational health and safety)
- Medicare
- Income Security (excluding Social Security, but including general retirement and disability insurance, federal employee retirement and disability insurance, unemployment compensation, housing assistance, food and nutrition assistance, and other income security programs)
- Social Security
- Veterans' Benefits and Services

For our purposes, we'll treat federal outlays on Human Resources as a proxy for the welfare state. The functions listed above cover the range of governmental activities liberals advocate, conservatives oppose and both treat as the things we talk about when we talk about the welfare state. Liberals want America's welfare state to be significantly larger, but all the additions they endorse could be easily accommodated by the OMB's existing delineation of Human Resource outlays without establishing any additional categories of government activities.

The OMB tables, which go back to 1940, make it possible to separate veterans' programs from the other five Human Resources functions. That's an excision worth making in order to describe a welfare state that approximates as closely as possible the one debated by liberals and conservatives. Veterans' benefits and services constitute a sort of parallel welfare state in America, but one that differs from the welfare state proper by making benefits contingent on military service rather than need or past financial contributions to social insurance programs. The questions about how to thank, honor and support the people who have served in the military should be treated separately from questions about how to promote economic security and alleviate suffering. Generally speaking, they are.

What's left is an imperfect but useable approximation of the welfare state. There are some things inside the circle defined by the five remaining Human Resources functions that, ideally, should be left outside. The Income Security function includes the Federal Employee Retirement and Disability "subfunction," which has more to do with the federal government's conduct as an employer than with the welfare state. The Education, Training, Employment and Social Services function includes federal outlays to the Library of Congress, Smithsonian Institutions and public broadcasting, programs liberals and conservatives have argued about, but ones that either might regard as collateral to the dispute over welfare state. The OMB's historical data is not available at a level of detail that would make it possible to take a scalpel and separate these outlays from the rest of the Human Resources expenditures.

The programs we would remove, if we could, represent a small portion of federal government spending on human resources. (The biggest item, Federal Employee Retirement and Disability outlays, accounts for 7.74% of all Human Resources outlays from 1962 through 2007, as measured in constant dollars.) On the other hand, our proxy for the welfare state examines only the federal government's outlays, excluding state and local spending on education, social services, health and income security. The reasons for doing so are partly technical—the historical data would be difficult to compile, since records of state outlays are in 50 different places, and local outlays in thousands.

Even if the numbers were easy to assemble, they would be hard to interpret. According to the OMB data on aggregate government spending, America's states and localities spent $1.59 trillion in 2007, an amount equal to 11.6% of the national Gross Domestic Product. Much of this money was spent on governmental housekeeping clearly unrelated to the welfare state: building and maintaining roads and bridges; operating courts, police departments, jails and prisons; public and state parks; offices that provide driver's licenses and building permits; etc. Much of it was spent on efforts that clearly *are* part of the welfare state, and could easily fit into the functions OMB uses to define federal outlays on Human Resources. Indeed, many of these expenditures were for Medicaid, unemployment compensation and other programs where federal funds supplement state and local expenditures.

Finally, much of the money spent by state and local governments falls in a gray area that isn't unambiguously part of, or distinct from, the welfare state. American states and cities were spending money on schools, hospitals, public health programs and relief efforts for the destitute for many decades prior to the New Deal, the Depression, or the Progressive Era. Had none of those historical developments occurred, a significant portion of state and local spending for these purposes would still be taking place. It seems impossible, however, to say *how* significant a portion, to devise a line that divides spending by states and localities that should be considered part of the welfare state from the portion that shouldn't.

Confining ourselves, then, to federal outlays on Human Resources, other than veterans' programs and benefits, the OMB totals yield Table 1.1.

This table shows that the welfare state, as we've defined it, was 472 times as big in 2007 as in 1940, which is about what you'd expect if you listen to a lot of conservative talk-radio. We need to clarify the picture by removing the distorting effects of inflation. The OMB "Total Nondefense Composite Outlay Deflator" allows us to do this by expressing the amount the federal government spent on Human Resources in constant dollars, reflecting the dollar's value in fiscal year 2000. The change matters enormously—federal government expenditures of $11,962 in 2000 would have had the same impact as an outlay of $1,000 on

TABLE 1.1   Federal Spending on Human Resources (Excluding Veterans' Programs), 1940–2007, In Billions of Dollars

1940	3.57	1963	28.00	1986	455.27
1941	3.60	1964	29.62	1987	475.45
1942	3.01	1965	30.86	1988	504.02
1943	2.38	1966	37.34	1989	538.66
1944	2.05	1967	44.54	1990	590.29
1945	1.75	1968	52.34	1991	658.39
1946	3.03	1969	58.78	1992	738.42
1947	3.57	1970	66.68	1993	791.92
1948	3.41	1971	82.13	1994	831.90
1949	4.21	1972	96.49	1995	885.96
1950	5.39	1973	107.52	1996	921.35
1951	5.48	1974	122.41	1997	963.13
1952	6.40	1975	156.66	1998	991.76
1953	7.32	1976	185.18	1999	1,014.66
1954	8.46	1977	203.87	2000	1,068.58
1955	10.23	1978	223.37	2001	1,149.60
1956	11.16	1979	247.66	2002	1,266.68
1957	13.16	1980	292.21	2003	1,360.92
1958	16.94	1981	339.05	2004	1,426.09
1959	19.45	1982	364.74	2005	1,515.97
1960	20.74	1983	401.18	2006	1,602.23
1961	24.13	1984	406.46	2007	1,685.64
1962	26.01	1985	445.56		

TABLE 1.2   Federal Spending on Human Resources (Excluding Veterans' Programs), 1940–2007, In Billions of Constant, Fiscal Year 2000 Dollars

1940	40.6	1963	137.7	1986	663.6
1941	41.1	1964	143.5	1987	670.6
1942	40.9	1965	146.8	1988	685.8
1943	34.9	1966	175.2	1989	705.1
1944	29.8	1967	203.8	1990	747.0
1945	20.7	1968	232.2	1991	799.4
1946	26.6	1969	245.9	1992	865.6
1947	30.3	1970	265.1	1993	903.0
1948	24.3	1971	308.7	1994	929.9
1949	30.8	1972	348.5	1995	966.0
1950	37.6	1973	374.4	1996	984.8
1951	35.9	1974	392.8	1997	1,010.2
1952	39.2	1975	458.3	1998	1,030.6
1953	44.1	1976	504.6	1999	1,039.7
1954	47.4	1977	516.0	2000	1,068.6
1955	59.9	1978	531.3	2001	1,123.8
1956	65.3	1979	543.0	2002	1,218.8
1957	73.9	1980	580.6	2003	1,282.3
1958	89.9	1981	610.2	2004	1,310.0
1959	103.7	1982	614.9	2005	1,347.9
1960	106.6	1983	646.0	2006	1,379.3
1961	121.8	1984	628.5	2007	1,421.9
1962	132.0	1985	667.4		

nondefense programs in 1940. Expressing all the values in Table 1.1 in terms of constant dollars yields Table 1.2.

Adjusting for inflation makes a difference. In constant dollars, federal spending on Human Resources was 35 times as high in 2007 as it had been in 1940.

We'll get a still more accurate picture if we adjust not only for inflation but population growth; the population in 2007 was 301.6 million, 2.28 times as many Americans as the 132.1 million there were in 1940. Ignoring this fact makes it impossible to distinguish the growth caused by a stronger political commitment to the welfare state from the growth attributable to a larger popula-

TABLE 1.3 Per Capita Federal Spending on Human Resources (Excluding Veterans' Programs), 1940–2007, In Constant, Fiscal Year 2000 Dollars

1940	308	1963	728	1986	2,763
1941	308	1964	748	1987	2,768
1942	303	1965	756	1988	2,805
1943	256	1966	891	1989	2,857
1944	215	1967	1,026	1990	2,994
1945	148	1968	1,157	1991	3,170
1946	188	1969	1,213	1992	3,394
1947	210	1970	1,293	1993	3,503
1948	166	1971	1,486	1994	3,572
1949	206	1972	1,660	1995	3,676
1950	247	1973	1,767	1996	3,713
1951	232	1974	1,837	1997	3,772
1952	249	1975	2,122	1998	3,814
1953	275	1976	2,314	1999	3,813
1954	291	1977	2,343	2000	3,787
1955	361	1978	2,387	2001	3,942
1956	386	1979	2,413	2002	4,234
1957	430	1980	2,555	2003	4,415
1958	514	1981	2,659	2004	4,468
1959	583	1982	2,654	2005	4,555
1960	590	1983	2,763	2006	4,617
1961	663	1984	2,665	2007	4,714
1962	707	1985	2,805		

tion receiving the same bundle of benefits formerly bestowed on fewer people. Dividing the annual outlays given in Table 1.2 by the Census Bureau's annual population estimates yields Table 1.3.

Adjusting for changes in population as well as inflation reduces the growth of the welfare state from mind-boggling to merely huge. By this metric, the federal government spent 15.3 times as much on Human Services programs in 2007 as in 1940. Whatever else it may reveal, this 1,431% increase is one more demonstration of the power of compound interest. You achieve that huge expansion over 67 years with an annual growth rate of 4.14%, which doesn't sound so formidable. (Strictly speaking, the increase takes place over 67¼ years. There was a "transitional quarter" before FY 1977 to permit the government to switch from a July 1 to an October 1 fiscal year.)

THE BIGGER PICTURE

To better understand the growth of the welfare state, we need to look outside the data presented in Table 1.3, and then look inside those numbers.

The growth of the welfare state depends on the interaction of two trends. The first, changes in per capita gross domestic product, is demographic and economic. The second, the portion of economic output that is directed to the federal government's Human Resources outlays, is political. The 4.14% annual growth rate of real, per capita Human Resources outlays could, at one extreme, reflect the decision to devote a constant portion of economic output to federal Human Resources spending over a 67-year period when per capita GDP grew by 4.14% annually. That way, a pie growing at the annual rate of 4.14% would have a slice representing exactly the same proportion for Human Resources every year. At the other extreme, the pie could remain the same size, and the slice devoted to Human Resources could get 4.14% bigger every year.

The reality, predictably, is a mixture of both trends. America's economy has been getting steadily bigger since 1940, and the portion of economic output devoted to federal Human Resources outlays has been growing steadily, too. Table 1.4, using OMB's data on Gross Domestic Product since 1940, its "GDP (Chained) Price Index" to factor out inflation, and the Census Bureau population data, shows real, per capita GDP.

The 406% increase shown in Table 1.4 from 1940 to 2007 means the underlying annual growth rate is 2.44%. At that pace, real, per capita economic output doubles roughly every 29½ years.

TABLE 1.4   Per Capita Gross Domestic Product, 1940–2007, In Constant, Fiscal Year 2000 Dollars

Year	GDP	Year	GDP	Year	GDP
1940	7,491	1963	14,506	1986	25,789
1941	8,435	1964	15,122	1987	26,234
1942	9,826	1965	15,752	1988	27,165
1943	11,338	1966	16,705	1989	27,930
1944	12,503	1967	17,259	1990	28,296
1945	12,770	1968	17,616	1991	27,921
1946	11,861	1969	18,261	1992	28,312
1947	11,037	1970	18,262	1993	28,862
1948	10,871	1971	18,324	1994	29,620
1949	10,947	1972	18,889	1995	30,240
1950	10,965	1973	19,886	1996	30,877
1951	12,014	1974	20,229	1997	31,966
1952	12,347	1975	19,674	1998	32,998
1953	12,756	1976	20,224	1999	34,140
1954	12,537	1977	21,177	2000	34,408
1955	12,772	1978	22,046	2001	34,464
1956	13,235	1979	22,760	2002	34,554
1957	13,204	1980	22,599	2003	34,965
1958	12,889	1981	22,834	2004	35,919
1959	13,320	1982	22,367	2005	36,698
1960	13,650	1983	22,628	2006	37,418
1961	13,566	1984	24,146	2007	37,903
1962	14,126	1985	24,999		

Before detailing the portion of per capita GDP absorbed by federal expenditures on Human Resources, it's worth remembering that this amount is a portion of a portion. That is, it depends on the percentage of GDP that winds up being spent by the federal government, and then it depends on the percentage of federal spending that is directed to Human Resources programs as opposed to all other governmental purposes.

We can see that, after escalating dramatically during World War II and plunging dramatically after the war, federal outlays have absorbed a remarkably stable portion of GDP for the past six decades. Table 1.5 is interesting by virtue of how little is going on.

TABLE 1.5   Federal Spending as a Percentage of Gross Domestic Product, 1940–2007

1940	9.78%	1963	18.59%	1986	22.45%
1941	11.97%	1964	18.51%	1987	21.61%
1942	24.35%	1965	17.21%	1988	21.25%
1943	43.57%	1966	17.87%	1989	21.18%
1944	43.64%	1967	19.40%	1990	21.85%
1945	41.88%	1968	20.56%	1991	22.31%
1946	24.80%	1969	19.36%	1992	22.14%
1947	14.79%	1970	19.33%	1993	21.44%
1948	11.63%	1971	19.46%	1994	21.00%
1949	14.32%	1972	19.58%	1995	20.69%
1950	15.59%	1973	18.79%	1996	20.28%
1951	14.20%	1974	18.71%	1997	19.57%
1952	19.42%	1975	21.29%	1998	19.16%
1953	20.41%	1976	21.41%	1999	18.65%
1954	18.78%	1977	20.73%	2000	18.43%
1955	17.35%	1978	20.69%	2001	18.52%
1956	16.54%	1979	20.16%	2002	19.38%
1957	17.01%	1980	21.67%	2003	19.99%
1958	17.89%	1981	22.20%	2004	19.94%
1959	18.74%	1982	23.11%	2005	20.20%
1960	17.80%	1983	23.49%	2006	20.40%
1961	18.41%	1984	22.18%	2007	19.98%
1962	18.82%	1985	22.85%		

Near the middle of the century, war was the proximate cause of the growth of government. "National Defense" is another superfunction used by OMB to categorize federal outlays. It peaked at 89.5% of federal outlays and 37.5% of GDP in FY 1945, which began on July 1, 1944, 3½ weeks after D-Day. This level of expenditure receded, but as the Cold War, which became manifest in 1948, turned into the Korean War in 1950, National Defense outlays increased again, peaking at 69.5% of federal outlays and 13.1% of GDP in 1954.

After the armistice ending the Korean War, federal outlays as a percentage of GDP settled into a narrow range, where they have stayed for more than half a century, falling short of 17% just once (1956) and exceeding 23% twice (1982 and 1983). One reason for this is that America's wars since Korea have been more important historically than fiscally. National Defense outlays were 46.0% of federal spending and 9.5% of GDP in FY 1968, at the height of the Vietnam War. These figures, however, are not appreciably different from the costs of Cold War vigilance generally—National Defense accounted for 50.8% of federal outlays and 9.3% of GDP in 1961, when there were many tensions but few shots fired.

National Defense outlays began a long, steady decline after 1968, reaching 22.7% of federal outlays and 4.9% of GDP in 1980. The Reagan military buildup partially and temporarily reversed this trend; National Defense spending reached 6.2% of GDP in 1986 and 28.1% of federal spending in 1987 before resuming its decline as the Cold War ended. By 1999, National Defense accounted for 16.1% of federal outlays and 3.0% of GDP. The costs of the subsequent wars in Afghanistan and Iraq have been quite modest, compared to the fiscal impact of previous wars, and in the context of the size of the federal budget and national economy. National Defense outlays in 2007 accounted for 20.2% of federal spending and 4.0% of GDP, figures lower than in 1980, when there were many tensions with the USSR and Iran, but the only actual military operation was the failed attempt to rescue the Iranian hostages.

The steady growth of America's economy means that military spending presents the polity with choices between guns and butter that are far smaller dilemmas than formerly. Using OMB's "Total Defense Composite Outlay Deflator," National Defense spending was $426 billion in 2007, measured in FY 2000 dollars, more than in any year since 1945, 2.5% more than in 1953, when the constant-dollar costs of National Defense reached their highest point during the Korean War, and 1.5% higher than in

1968, at the height of the Vietnam War. The key is that real, per capita GDP was 197% higher in 2007 than in 1953, and 115% higher than it was in 1968.

What is true of National Defense is even truer of Human Resources: Economic growth has made rapid expansion possible. Table 1.6 shows the increase in Human Resources outlays relative to GDP.

To get from 3.69% to 12.33% over 67.25 years (including the transitional quarter preceding FY 1977) entails an annual growth rate of 1.81%. The 4.14% annual growth of real per capita Human Resources outlays shown in Table 1.3 reflects the interaction of the 2.44% annual growth of real per capita GDP shown in Table 1.4, with the 1.81% annual increase of Human Resources outlays as a portion of GDP shown in Table 1.5. The pie got steadily bigger, as did the portion of the pie devoted to the welfare state. As a consequence, the slice of the economic pie that is the welfare state grows, in absolute terms, not only steadily but quasi-rapidly, doubling approximately every 17.4 years.

We can look at the changing composition of federal outlays to unpack the data showing the growth of Human Resources outlays a little further. Besides Human Resources and National Defense, the other superfunctions OMB uses to categorize federal outlays are:

- Physical Resources (e.g., Energy, the Environment)
- Other Functions (e.g., Science, International Affairs, Agriculture, General Government and the Administration of Justice)
- Net Interest on the National Debt

Let's lump these final superfunctions, along with expenditures on Veterans' Benefits and Services, as "Everything Else," and then chart the changing makeup of the federal budget since 1940 (Figure 1.1).

TABLE 1.6 Human Resources Outlays (Excluding Veterans' Programs) As a Percentage of Gross Domestic Product, 1940–2007

1940	3.69%	1963	4.68%	1986	10.32%
1941	3.15%	1964	4.63%	1987	10.23%
1942	2.15%	1965	4.49%	1988	10.06%
1943	1.32%	1966	4.96%	1989	9.97%
1944	0.98%	1967	5.49%	1990	10.29%
1945	0.79%	1968	6.04%	1991	11.09%
1946	1.36%	1969	6.20%	1992	11.83%
1947	1.53%	1970	6.59%	1993	12.04%
1948	1.33%	1971	7.61%	1994	11.95%
1949	1.55%	1972	8.19%	1995	12.09%
1950	1.97%	1973	8.22%	1996	11.97%
1951	1.71%	1974	8.50%	1997	11.77%
1952	1.84%	1975	10.04%	1998	11.49%
1953	1.96%	1976	10.66%	1999	11.12%
1954	2.24%	1977	10.33%	2000	11.01%
1955	2.59%	1978	10.08%	2001	11.43%
1956	2.61%	1979	9.90%	2002	12.21%
1957	2.92%	1980	10.72%	2003	12.59%
1958	3.68%	1981	11.10%	2004	12.40%
1959	3.96%	1982	11.30%	2005	12.39%
1960	4.01%	1983	11.66%	2006	12.31%
1961	4.55%	1984	10.58%	2007	12.33%
1962	4.58%	1985	10.76%		

We can see that Human Resources programs have become the primary thing the federal government does. Human Resources outlays, excluding veterans' programs, surpassed National Defense spending in 1971, for the first time since 1940, as Vietnam was winding down and the Great Society was ramping up. These outlays accounted for more than 40% of all federal spending for the first time in 1972, and have never since dropped below that level. They exceeded 50% for the first time in 1992 and stayed above that level for the subsequent 15 years. They surpassed 60% for the first time in 1997, and stayed above *that* level for eight of the subsequent ten years.

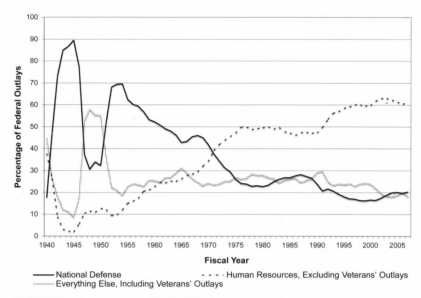

FIGURE 1.1   Composition of Federal Outlays, By Superfunction, From 1940–2007

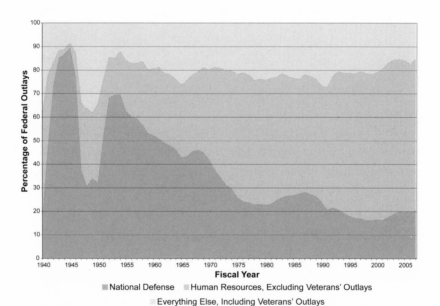

FIGURE 1.2   Federal Outlays by Superfunction, Relative to Total Federal Outlays, From 1940–2007

National Defense and all the federal government's other activities have been pushed to the periphery, as shown in Figure 1.2.

Thus, even though federal outlays have been very stable as a percentage of GDP, Human Resources outlays account for a steadily growing portion of the federal government's claim on the nation's economic output. We can see the same trend shown in Figure 1.2 at work in Figure 1.3.

If we look at the 52-year period from 1955 to 2007, after the spending surges for World War II and Korea had worked their way through the fiscal system, we see that total federal outlays, as a percentage of GDP, increased at the modest annual rate of 0.27%; they were 17.35% of GDP in 1955 and 19.98% in 2007. National Defense spending as a portion of GDP fell at an annual rate of 1.87%, from 10.83% in 1955 to 4.04% in 2007. Our makeshift Everything Else category fell at the slight annual rate of 0.16%, from 3.92% in 1955 to 3.60% in 2007. Human Resources spending (leaving aside outlays for veterans) has grown, as a percentage of

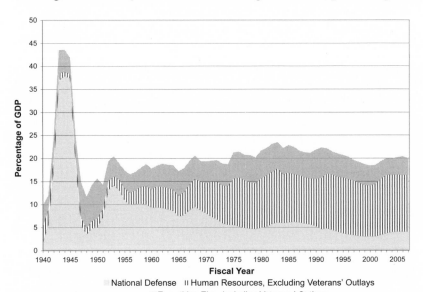

FIGURE 1.3   Composition of Federal Outlays, Relative to GDP, 1940–2007

GDP, at an annual rate of 3.03%, from 2.59% of GDP in 1955 to 12.33% in 2007.

THE SMALLER PICTURE

As Human Resources outlays have grown, both in relation to the nation's population and its economic output, they have also changed in composition. The following chart shows the changing mix of the five Human Resources functions that make up the superfunction, after excluding outlays for veterans' benefits and programs. Note that Medicare did not spend its first dollar until fiscal year 1966 (Figure 1.4).

If we add together the outlays on all five Human Resources functions over this 67-year period, measured in constant dollars, the percentages for each are as follows:

Social Security	39.50%
Income Security	26.62%
Medicare	15.21%
Health	11.57%
Education, Training, etc.	7.10%

If we confine our view to the years from 1966 to 2007, after Medicare began to function, we get the following percentages:

Social Security	39.35%
Income Security	25.59%
Medicare	16.05%
Health	11.94%
Education, Training, etc.	7.05%

The very slight change in the overall percentage caused by ignoring the first 26 years of Human Resources outlays reflects

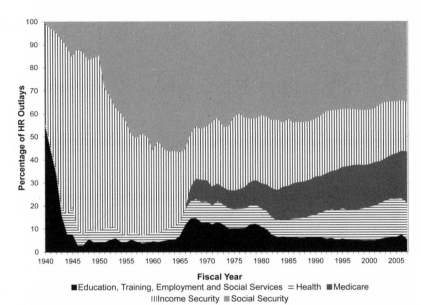

FIGURE 1.4   Human Resources Functions as Percentages of Human Resources Outlays, Excluding Veterans' Outlays, 1940–2007

how much the welfare state has grown since the beginning of the Great Society. Only 5.19% of all federal Human Resources outlays from 1940 to 2007, measured in constant FY 2000 dollars, were spent in the first 26 years of this 67-year period. Figure 1.5, showing the five functions over time in constant dollars, makes this clear.

As is true of the growth of total spending on Human Resources, the growth of the individual functions that constitute it is less dramatic in the context of America's growing economic output (Figure 1.6).

We can get a better sense of how the five individual components of federal Human Resources outlays have changed by comparing their annual growth rates. Table 1.7 compares real per capita outlays in 1940, 1966 and 2007, then shows two annual growth rates, one for the entire 67-year period and one for 1966 to 2007.

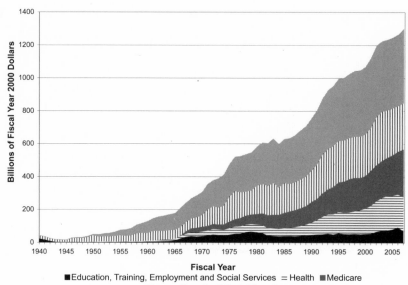

FIGURE 1.5   Human Resources Outlays, By Function, in Fiscal Year 2000 Dollars

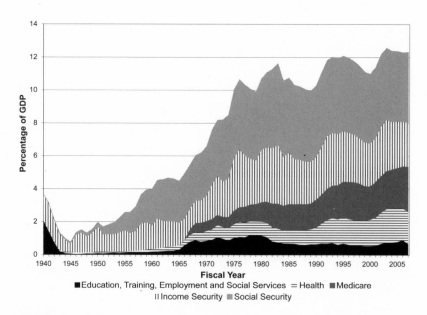

FIGURE 1.6   Outlays on Individual Human Resources Functions, in Relation to GDP, 1940–2007

TABLE 1.7   Human Resources Functions: 1940, 1966 and 2007

Function	1940 per capita outlays in FY 2000 $	1966 per capita outlays in FY 2000 $	2007 per capita outlays in FY 2000 $	Annual growth rate, 1940–2007	Annual growth rate, 1966–2007
Social Security	2.41	494.04	1,639.26	10.18%	2.95%
Income Security	130.51	231.05	1,023.50	3.11%	3.67%
Medicare	0	1.53	1,049.88		17.16%
Health	4.74	60.71	745.11	7.81%	6.27%
Education, Training, etc.	169.99	104.16	256.38	0.61%	2.21%
Total	307.66	891.47	4,714.14	4.14%	4.12%

America's welfare state is preoccupied with the welfare of old people. If we measure all the Human Resources spending since 1940 in FY 2000 dollars, Social Security and Medicare account for 54.76% of the total, despite Medicare's late arrival at the party. OMB classifies the outlays of these programs as "mandatory," as opposed to "discretionary." In the vernacular, Medicare and Social Security are the biggest "entitlement" programs, though there are several others (Medicaid, food stamps, and unemployment compensation).

The terms "mandatory" and "entitlement" describe the same political reality from different vantage points. From the federal government's point of view, spending on such programs is mandatory instead of discretionary because Congress does not have the power to appropriate a defined amount that the government will spend on them in a fiscal year. Federal outlays on food stamps, for example, will be determined by the number of people who apply for the program and are determined to be eligible for its benefits, multiplied by the formulas determining how much each recipient should get. The outlays, then, are a function of laws Congress enacted in the past—sometimes decades ago—as they apply to the realities that obtain at the moment. If Congress wants to change the amount of money the government spends on this program, it either has to change the eligibility standards, the benefits formulas, or the procedures by which the Department of Agriculture applies them.

From the citizen's point of view, the disbursements from Social Security, Medicare, etc., are entitlements because they fulfill promises the government has made to the people. These promises were not conditional commitments, ones where the government said, "We'll help you . . . if we can, and to the extent we can." Congress cannot, therefore, appropriate a fixed amount for food stamps and hope that the eligible beneficiaries don't run through that allotment before the end of the fiscal year. The people's insistence that the government fulfill its promises to the dollar is not, of course, unrelated to the fact that the promises are beneficial to the individuals who receive what the entitlement programs disburse.

INCREASING AT A DECREASING RATE

The 4.14% annual growth of the welfare state over the past 67 years has not been a constant, of course. Measured by the federal government's constant-dollar, per capita outlays on Human Resources, there were ten occasions since 1940 when welfare state spending declined from the previous year and 16 where it increased by more than 10%. Table 1.8 breaks the growth of the welfare state into presidential terms, and presidencies.

Note that although presidents are inaugurated in the midst of a fiscal year, their budget proposals, and the decisions made by Congress about spending, taxing and borrowing, are almost always directed to the ensuing rather than current fiscal year. For example, Pres. Carter took office in 1977, but the fiscal years shaped by his budget proposals were 1978, 1979, 1980 and 1981. The 1977 budget had been determined by Congress and President

TABLE 1.8 Growth Rates of Real, Per Capita Human Resources Outlays (Excluding Veterans' Benefits) By Presidential Term and Presidency

Presidential Term; Presidency	First and Final Years	Number of Years	Total Increase in Real, Per Capita Human Resources Outlays	Annual Growth Rate of Real, Per Capita Human Resources Outlays
FDR III	1941–45	4	−51.84%	−16.70%
FDR IV/Truman	1945–49	4	39.09%	8.60%
Truman	1949–53	4	33.35%	7.46%
FDR IV/Truman	**1945–53**	**8**	**85.48%**	**8.03%**
Eisenhower I	1953–57	4	56.27%	11.81%
Eisenhower II	1957–61	4	54.32%	11.46%
Eisenhower	**1953–61**	**8**	**141.15%**	**11.63%**
Kennedy/Johnson	1961–65	4	13.93%	3.31%
Johnson	1965–69	4	60.60%	12.57%
Kennedy/Johnson	**1961–69**	**8**	**82.97%**	**7.84%**
Nixon I	1969–73	4	45.59%	9.85%
Nixon II/Ford	1973–77	4	32.62%	6.87%
Nixon/Ford	**1969–77**	**8**	**93.08%**	**8.30%**
Carter	**1977–81**	**4**	**13.51%**	**3.22%**
Reagan I	1981–85	4	5.48%	1.34%
Reagan II	1985–89	4	1.85%	0.46%
Reagan	**1981–89**	**8**	**7.43%**	**0.90%**
George H.W. Bush	**1989–93**	**4**	**22.61%**	**5.23%**
Clinton I	1993–97	4	7.70%	1.87%
Clinton II	1997–2001	4	4.49%	1.10%
Clinton	**1993–01**	**8**	**12.53%**	**1.49%**
George W. Bush I	2001–05	4	15.57%	3.68%
George W. Bush II	2005–07	2	3.49%	1.73%
George W. Bush	**2001–07**	**6**	**19.60%**	**3.03%**

Ford in 1976. This chart takes Human Resources outlays in FY 1977 as the baseline for measuring spending under Carter.

Furthermore, the "transitional quarter" between the 1976 and 1977 fiscal years means that annual growth rates for periods including the quarter have been calculated to take into account the additional three months. The Nixon/Ford presidency, for example, saw an annual growth rate of 8.30%. That rate, however, applied to 99 months rather than 96.

The discovery that real, per capita Human Resources outlays expanded almost eight times as fast under Pres. Eisenhower as under Pres. Clinton is decidedly counterintuitive. We need to place that fact in context. The chart shows that the general trend is for the growth rate of the American welfare state to decline. Every one of the 16 occasions where year-to-year welfare state outlays increased by more than 10%, for example, occurred prior to 1976. Conservatism's political advances account for some of this slowdown, but much of it is better explained by a mathematical tautology: It's easier for small things than for big things to grow rapidly. The small American welfare state grew rapidly in the 1940s and '50s, while the big one grew slowly in the final quarter of the 20th century.

It's important to note that real, per capita Human Resources outlays declined by 52% between 1941 and 1945 as Dr. Win the War supplanted Dr. New Deal, in FDR's phrase. It took until 1955 for those outlays to surpass the level of 1940, making the years dominated by World War II and Korea a lost era for liberals' ambitions to expand the welfare state. The engine driving the growth of the welfare state between the end of World War II and the advent of the Great Society was the maturation of the Social Security program, which issued its first benefit check in 1940. Social Security outlays accounted for only 15% of Human Resources outlays in 1945 but more than 50% for nine out of the ten fiscal years from 1957 through 1966.

Important components of the welfare state were added, one by one, as it matured. Congress enacted disability insurance in 1956. It created a number of new programs in 1965, including

Medicare, Medicaid, the Elementary and Secondary Education Act, and the Higher Education Act.

Medicare and Medicaid have been the primary engines driving the growth of Human Resources outlays since 1966. Still using constant dollars, outlays for Medicare and Health, which is dominated by Medicaid, combined to account for 11% of Human Resources outlays under Kennedy and Johnson, 17% under Nixon and Ford, 18% under Carter, 23% under Reagan, 26% under George H.W. Bush, 32% under Clinton, and 36% under George W. Bush.

INTERNATIONAL COMPARISONS

According to the late Seymour Martin Lipset, it is "impossible to understand a country without seeing how it varies from others. Those who know only one country know no country."[10] Those who know only one country, in other words, have no way to be sure if the things they know about it reveal something distinctive about that country, or if they're manifestations of trends or underlying realities in other nations and thereby illuminate nothing about the particular country being examined.

We should, then, compare America's welfare state with other welfare states. Unfortunately for these purposes, the Office of Management and Budget confines its historical tables to spending by America's public sector. The framework we've built to analyze the American welfare state won't travel beyond our borders.

We can build an alternative framework for international comparisons by combining data from two sources. The first is the Organisation for Economic Co-operation and Development, the clearinghouse created in 1961 to help industrialized countries share economic data and policy assessments. Its annual *Factbook* offers a range of economic data on the 31 nations who belong to (and fund) OECD. The second is America's Bureau of Labor Statistics

(BLS), housed in the U.S. Department of Labor. Among its many publications, one annual report compares real, per capita GDP in 16 industrialized countries. (OECD publishes similar data in its *Factbook*, but in a form that is far clunkier due to the absence of GDP deflators that stretch across many years and readily yield income figures expressed in terms of a constant.)[11]

One *Factbook 2008* table compares "Public Social Expenditures" in 30 nations, year by year, from 1980 through 2003. Public Social Expenditures, as defined by OECD, are similar to OMB's Human Resources superfunction, but not identical. The category includes government outlays for "cash benefits, direct 'in-kind' provision of goods and services, and tax breaks with social purposes," such as those programs targeting "low-income households . . . the elderly, disabled, sick, unemployed, or young persons."[12]

There are three major differences from the Human Resources data we've used to this point. First, OECD's "welfare state" excludes expenditures on education. A different *Factbook* table covers those outlays, but only for the years 1995 and 2004, making it impossible to combine the data with the numbers in the Public Social Expenditures tables. Second, unlike Human Resources outlays, which are those made by the U.S. federal government, Public Social Expenditures include those made by central, state and local governments, though OECD allows that "spending by lower tiers of government . . . may be underestimated in some countries." Third, all measurements of Public Social Expenditures are expressed in just one way, as a percentage of GDP.

The OECD has incomplete data for some of the countries in its table on Public Social Expenditures. Other nations on its list aren't in the BLS report comparing per capita GDP. The overlap between the two tables yields 12 countries with which we can compare the U.S. Let's start by looking at Public Social Expenditures as a percentage of GDP at five-year intervals (Table 1.9).

TABLE 1.9   Public Social Expenditures, as a Percentage of GDP, in 13 OECD Nations

	1980	1985	1990	1995	2000	2003
Australia	10.9	13.0	14.1	17.1	17.9	17.9
Belgium	23.5	26.1	25.0	26.4	25.3	26.5
Canada	14.1	17.3	18.4	19.2	16.7	17.3
Denmark	25.2	24.2	25.5	28.9	25.8	27.6
France	20.8	25.8	25.3	28.3	27.6	28.7
Germany	23.0	23.6	22.5	26.6	26.3	27.3
Italy	18.0	20.8	19.9	19.8	23.2	24.2
Japan	10.3	11.2	11.2	13.9	16.1	17.7
Netherlands	24.1	24.2	24.4	22.8	19.3	20.7
Spain	15.5	17.8	20.0	21.5	20.4	20.3
Sweden	28.6	29.7	30.5	32.5	28.8	31.3
U.K.	16.6	19.6	17.2	20.4	19.1	20.6
U.S.A.	13.3	12.9	13.4	15.4	14.6	16.2

Next, let's look at per capita GDP in these nations (Table 1.10). (The BLS data for Germany in Table 1.10 are for West Germany

TABLE 1.10   Per Capita Gross Domestic Product, Measured by the U.S. Bureau of Labor Statistics and Expressed in 2005 U.S. Dollars, in 13 OECD Nations

	1980	1985	1990	1995	2000	2003
Australia	20,309	22,027	23,995	25,872	30,022	31,643
Belgium	18,529	19,399	22,336	26,810	30,296	30,929
Canada	23,164	25,162	27,056	27,853	32,562	33,671
Denmark	20,999	24,064	25,708	28,361	31,987	32,179
France	20,270	21,311	24,348	25,245	28,357	28,883
Germany	22,809	24,358	27,728	28,592	29,738	29,921
Italy	18,661	20,230	23,553	25,034	27,458	27,757
Japan	18,606	20,956	25,936	27,534	28,600	28,959
Netherlands	21,920	22,722	26,132	28,298	33,503	33,653
Spain	15,145	15,853	19,535	20,764	24,696	25,747
Sweden	20,708	22,578	24,916	25,045	29,364	30,651
U.K.	18,115	19,919	23,141	24,778	28,604	30,365
U.S.A.	25,613	28,682	32,125	34,045	39,277	40,006

from 1980 through 1995, and the reunified Germany in 2000 and 2003.)

Finally, we can combine the data from Table 1.9 and 1.10 to show per capita Public Social Expenditures in Table 1.11.

"Performance = Ability × Desire" says the poster the football coach tapes to the locker room wall. It's hokey, but that doesn't mean it's either untrue or unrelated to our inquiry. The size of any democratic nation's welfare state will be a product of the people's *ability* to pay for it, which is what real, per capita GDP is about, and their *willingness* to pay, which is what the percentage of GDP devoted to Public Social Expenditures gets at.

To speak at a high level of generality, the 13 nations we're examining here all show the tendency we observed when examining the historical OMB data on federal outlays for Human Resources in the U.S.: over the long term, both the ability and the willingness to pay for the welfare state increase. Every one of the 13 nations experienced economic growth over the 24 years under examination. The annual growth rates for their real, per capita GDP are shown in Table 1.12.

TABLE 1.11   Per Capita Public Social Expenditures, Expressed in 2005 U.S. Dollars, in 13 OECD Nations

	1980	1985	1990	1995	2000	2003
Australia	2,214	2,864	3,383	4,424	5,374	5,664
Belgium	4,354	5,063	5,584	7,078	7,665	8,196
Canada	3,266	4,353	4,978	5,348	5,438	5,825
Denmark	5,292	5,823	6,556	8,196	8,253	8,881
France	4,216	5,498	6,160	7,144	7,827	8,289
Germany	5,246	5,748	6,239	7,605	7,821	8,168
Italy	3,359	4,208	4,687	4,957	6,370	6,717
Japan	1,916	2,347	2,905	3,827	4,605	5,126
Netherlands	5,283	5,499	6,376	6,452	6,466	6,966
Spain	2,347	2,822	3,907	4,464	5,038	5,227
Sweden	5,922	6,706	7,599	8,140	8,457	9,594
U.K.	3,007	3,904	3,980	5,055	5,463	6,255
U.S.A.	3,407	3,700	4,305	5,243	5,734	6,481

It's reasonable to assume that Germany's economic growth rate would have been more in line with the other 12 countries' if it had not spent the final half of this 24-year period reintegrating the former East Germany into a larger, stronger national economy. Leaving that one exceptional case aside, the economic growth rates for the 13 countries are very tightly bunched.

Twelve of the 13 countries we're examining had a greater willingness to pay for the welfare state in 2003 than in 1980. Table 1.13 shows that there is a wider range in this variable than in the ability to pay for the welfare state, reflected in the per capita GDP data in Table 1.12. There is, however, discernible convergence in the data. The two countries with the lowest commitment to Public Social Expenditures in 1980, Japan and Australia, saw the most rapid increase in this variable. The four countries devoting the largest portion of their GDP to Public Social Expenditures in 1980—Sweden, Denmark, the Netherlands and Belgium—had the slowest growth rates, including a commitment of resources to Public Social Expenditures by the Netherlands that actually diminished, as a portion of GDP, by 14.1% between 1980 and 2003.

TABLE 1.12 Annual Growth Rate of Real, Per Capita Income, 1980–2003, According to BLS Data	
Spain	2.33%
U.K.	2.27%
Belgium	2.25%
U.S.A.	1.96%
Australia	1.95%
Japan	1.94%
Netherlands	1.88%
Denmark	1.87%
Italy	1.74%
Sweden	1.72%
Canada	1.64%
France	1.55%
Germany	1.19%

TABLE 1.13   Annual Growth Rate of Percentage
of GDP Devoted to Public Social Expenditures,
1980–2003, According to OECD Data

Japan	2.38%
Australia	2.18%
France	1.41%
Italy	1.30%
Spain	1.18%
U.K.	0.94%
Canada	0.89%
U.S.A.	0.86%
Germany	0.75%
Belgium	0.52%
Denmark	0.40%
Sweden	0.39%
Netherlands	−0.66%

Combine an increased ability to pay for something with an increased willingness to pay, and you'll get more of it. As we saw in Table 1.11, every one of the 13 countries devoted considerably more to Public Social Expenditures in 2003 than in 1980. Table 1.14 compares the growth rates of real per capita Public Social Expenditures.

Even in the Netherlands, where Public Social Expenditures grew most slowly, they were 31.9% higher in 2003 than in 1980. In Japan, at the other extreme, they were 167.5% higher. The U.S. is in the middle—six countries had faster rates of growth, and six had slower rates.

Lipset's admonition notwithstanding, it appears that when we're talking about the growth of the welfare state, those who know only one country know basically every country. The American trend from 1940 to 2007—steady growth of both the economy and the portion of the economy devoted to the welfare state—is evident in 12 other modern, prosperous democracies from 1980 to 2003. Leaving aside the Netherlands' slightly

TABLE 1.14   Annual Growth Rate of Real Per Capita
Public Social Expenditures, 1980–2003

Japan	4.37%
Australia	4.17%
Spain	3.54%
U.K.	3.24%
Italy	3.06%
France	2.98%
U.S.A.	2.84%
Belgium	2.79%
Canada	2.55%
Denmark	2.28%
Sweden	2.12%
Germany	1.94%
Netherlands	1.21%

diminished commitment to Public Social Expenditures, relative to GDP, the similarities among the 13 nations are far more striking than the differences.

What *is* distinctive about the United States is neither the fact nor the rate of the welfare state's growth, but the context. The U.S. has a significantly stronger economy than the other 12 industrialized nations, and a significantly weaker disposition to direct its economic output to public expenditures on social welfare. Table 1.15, using BLS data, shows the 2007 per capita GDP of the other 12 countries we've been examining, expressed in U.S. dollars as of 2005, along with the year that America's per capita GDP first exceeded that level.

Rather than saying that America is considerably more prosperous than the other industrialized nations, we could say that its economic development keeps it somewhere from one to two decades ahead of the others. In view of the small differences between recent rates of economic growth noted in Table 1.10, it will take dramatic economic changes before the gap separating the U.S. from the other countries is closed.

TABLE 1.15   Per Capita GDP in 2007, Expressed in U.S. 2005 Dollars, and the Year U.S. Per Capita GDP First Exceeded That Amount

Spain	28,079	1985
Italy	28,434	1985
France	30,724	1988
Japan	31,696	1989
Germany	32,228	1992
U.K.	33,191	1994
Belgium	33,607	1994
Australia	34,154	1996
Sweden	34,457	1996
Denmark	35,213	1997
Canada	36,243	1998
Netherlands	36,783	1998
U.S.A.	43,267	

As for the political commitment to the welfare state—or at least that portion of the welfare state that doesn't involve education—we saw in Table 1.9 that every other country cited devotes a larger percentage of its GDP to Public Social Expenditures than does the U.S. The only two countries that devoted a smaller portion of GDP to Public Social Expenditures at any point between 1980 and 2003 were Australia and Japan. Australia first caught up to the U.S. in 1985 and exceeded it in every year after 1989. Japan's Public Social Expenditures accounted for a larger share of its GDP than in America for the first time in 1998—14.9% to 14.8%—and exceeded it for each of the subsequent years measured by the OECD. At the other extreme, Sweden has consistently devoted more than twice as large a portion of its GDP to Public Social Expenditures as the U.S., while France, Germany and Denmark have devoted a bit less than twice the American percentage to that purpose.

The United States, with the greatest ability and the weakest desire to finance a welfare state, winds up in the middle of the pack in terms of the absolute value of the resources devoted to it. By 2003, as shown in Table 1.11, America's per capita Public Social Expenditures were greater than those in Japan, Spain, Australia, Canada and the United Kingdom, while lower than those in Italy, the Netherlands, Germany, Belgium, France, Denmark and Sweden. While Sweden devoted 31.3% of its GDP to Public Social Expenditures in 2003, the U.S. could have attained the same level of Public Social Expenditures—$9,594 per capita, measured in 2005 dollars—by devoting 24% of GDP to that purpose. Had it done so, its commitment to Public Social Expenditures as a percentage of GDP would not only have been lower than Sweden's, but also lower than that of France, Denmark, Germany, Belgium and Italy.

Conservatives will react with alarm to this suggestion, insisting that thoughts about how a dynamic economy makes a bigger welfare state possible gets the question backward. The reason America *has* a more prosperous economy than Sweden or France, they say, is that government here has less to say about how wealth is created and distributed than in Europe. America does not have a law, as France did, mandating that workweeks be no more than 35 hours long, enforced by government officials who drive through companies' parking lots looking for evidence of "antisocial industriousness."[13] For the decade ending in 2005, the average annual share of GDP collected in taxes by all levels of government in the U.S. was 28%, according to OECD data. In Sweden, Denmark and France it was 51%, 49% and 44%, respectively.[14]

The economic impact of marginal changes in welfare state spending is a question to which we'll return, although trying to settle it is beyond this book's scope and this author's expertise. For the moment, we'll note that the differences between America and the other countries tell us something about their different political cultures. Public Social Expenditures grew even under governments headed by Ronald Reagan and Margaret Thatcher, while the economies of even the most highly regulated and taxed countries have expanded. The poorest of the 13 countries, Spain, had a per capita GDP in 1980 that was, according to the BLS data, nearly twice as high as it had been in 1964. Per capita GDP in Spain was an additional 70% higher in 2003 than in 1980, and, in a reunified Germany, 31% higher than it had been in 1980 in West Germany. Besides Germany, the only nations that did not see per capita GDP increase by at least 50% from 1980 to 2003 were France (43%), Canada (45%), Sweden (48%) and Italy (49%).

Even the "basket cases," then, were pretty robust, contrary to the conservative belief that a big welfare state is necessarily ruinous. Robert Samuelson, for example, argues that Europe "is slowly going out of business" because its benevolent welfare states require "a strong economy, while the sources of all this benevolence—high taxes, stiff regulations—weaken the economy."[15] The nations with the strongest commitment to the welfare state do see slower growth, but not—or not yet, some conservatives would say—economic contraction.

At the same time, the data make it hard to accept liberals' frequent assurances that welfare state programs are better thought of as investments rather than spending. As such, the programs can "pay for themselves" and have the potential to pay for themselves "many times over." The 2008 Democratic platform, for example, used the words "invest" and "investment" compulsively. It called for investments in infrastructure, medical research, "women-owned small businesses," a "green energy sector," teachers' salaries, drop-out prevention programs, job training, space exploration, "financial literacy," playgrounds, mass transit, crime prevention, and "forests, grasslands and wetlands." As a nebulous catchall for international programs, the platform promised to "invest in our common humanity," a pledge the Obama administration will not find confining.[16]

This tendentious rhetorical tic does not alchemize reality. The welfare state may be a good thing, but it is not a free good. If its programs were really investments, as that term is ordinarily used and understood, Sweden would long ago have established itself as the world's most prosperous and dynamic economy.

We can plausibly conclude, based on the trends shown in the OECD data, that in none of the 13 democracies would voters reject, on principle, a hypothetical package deal that offered both American prosperity and a Scandinavian welfare state. No country or politician has yet figured out how to put this package together, however. Until somebody does, democratic nations are going to confront choices.

Based on their behavior in recent decades, Americans are disposed to a package that combines a relatively dynamic and prosperous economy with a thinner welfare state. It's difficult to imagine Americans exchanging that package for the Swedish one. America would have had to increase Public Social Expenditures by 48% in 2003 to match Sweden's per capita outlays. It also would have had to reduce its per capita GDP by 23% to equal Sweden's that year. America's reluctance to Swedenize, however, seems as strong as Sweden's reluctance to Americanize. If Sweden had reduced its per capita Public Social Expenditures in 2003 to the level of America's, it would have required cutting those outlays by nearly a third, taking Sweden's welfare state back to where it had been in 1985. It's hard to imagine the Swedish electorate acquiescing in that change, even if it guaranteed increasing per capita GDP to American levels.

THE SKY'S THE LIMIT?

We'll return to the significance of this aspect of American exceptionalism in the next chapter. First, we'll close this one by noting a dog-that-didn't-bark similarity among all 13 nations. The years 1980 to 2003 were a period of vigorous economic growth, one that began at a time when the citizens of industrial democracies were already the most prosperous people in human history.

What's notable is that all these democratic nations chose to regard growing prosperity over a quarter-century as an opportunity to expand the welfare state rather than an opportunity to reduce it. Public Social Expenditures grew, in absolute terms, in all 13 countries during these years, and grew relative to the size of the economy in 12 of them. No serious consideration—or at any rate, no consequential consideration—seems to have been given to the idea that greater prosperity had significantly increased the number of households who could provide for their medical care, education, economic security and retirement largely by relying on their own resources, thereby reducing the need and justification for the government to provide for these needs by transferring wealth from some people to others.

This subject of why prosperity never seems to curtail the welfare state is at the heart of our inquiry. We will return to a focus on the U.S. in the chapters after this one, but while we're still discussing wealthy nations as a group, we can make one more generalization: There are both supply-side and demand-side forces, in political terms, pressing big welfare states in wealthy societies to grow bigger as those societies grow wealthier. The supply-side forces are the politicians, writers and activists advancing the view that social justice and decency require a bigger welfare state. The demand-side forces are the ones that move voters in democracies to approve not only the steady increase in welfare state outlays— the easier part—but the corresponding increase in taxes and regulations.

As we return our focus to the U.S., we'll also concentrate on the political supply-side—the ideology of American liberalism as it pertains to a welfare state that grows indefinitely. We will conclude this chapter with a few observations about the voter psychology that shapes the demand-side forces expanding the welfare state. We'll begin by noting that the primary task of the welfare state is to alleviate poverty—but "poverty" is a relative term. Matt Bai of the *New York Times* wrote in 2007 that "the average income of an American taxpayer in 1929, using today's dollars, was about $16,000 a year; the entire middle class, in other words, was poor by modern standards."[17]

A wealthy society is not only better equipped to give public assistance to the needy than a poor society, but is more likely to regard standards of nutrition, housing, education, health care or economic security far below the norm as affronts to the conscience. The poor society, more familiar with such conditions than with their absence, is more likely to regard them as aspects of the human condition, rather than problems that can or should be solved. As a society grows richer, it not only acquires a greater ability to assist the poor, but it embraces a more expansive understanding of what it means to be poor, to be someone who needs and deserves public assistance.

It's not clear where, and how far, that trend can continue. We noted the OMB data for 1940 to 2007 showing real, per capita GDP in America increasing at the rate of 2.44% a year. (The BLS data for the U.S., covering 1960 to 2007, show a 2.19% annual increase.) At that rate, the average American household at the start of the 22nd century will have an income eight times as large as today's. Will such a nation have a welfare state that assists "poor people" whose incomes correspond to that of a household in the top fifth of America's income distribution today? The top tenth? Twentieth?

This is the logical conclusion of the argument that the "poverty line" should be expressed as some percentage—either 40% or 50% is the most commonly suggested benchmark—of median household income. In 2006 John Cassidy of the *New Yorker* recommended this approach. He noted a federal government survey had determined that 91% of the households classified as poor in 2001 owned color televisions, 74% had microwave ovens, 55% VCRs and 47% dishwashers. One reason to consider such people poor, says Cassidy, and continue or even increase the public assistance they receive, is that "they live in a society in which many families also possess DVD players, cell phones, desktop computers, broadband Internet connections, powerful game consoles, SUVs, health-club memberships, and vacation homes."[18]

If the economic trends of the past seven decades continue for the next seven and beyond, however, then it's only a matter of time before the vast majority of poor people own second and third homes equipped with broadband Internet access, and can drive their SUVs to get to them. An eight-fold increase in per capita GDP over a century means that a household with only 25% of the median income is likely to have twice as much purchasing power as the average family today. It's difficult to imagine how the question of alleviating their poverty will be addressed.

Much of what the welfare state does, however, is not to help people who are poor but to keep people who aren't from becoming poor. The motives of the increasingly prosperous citizens who vote for increasingly generous welfare states are numerous and complicated, rather than simple and uniformly disinterested. We can plausibly surmise that as a nation grows more prosperous, increasing numbers of its citizens find the prospect of a descent into poverty harder to imagine—in both senses of the term: It is more far-fetched but also more appalling. With so much farther to fall than their grandparents, their willingness to fund a high and reliable safety net increases.

The fact that the most ambitious welfare states in the OECD tables, such as Sweden's and Denmark's, have shown the slowest growth rates of Public Social Expenditures relative to GDP suggests that, over the long term, the growth of the welfare state is asymptotic rather than linear. If so, we will never see Caviar Stamps and Yachts for Tots programs for the future's underprivileged. At what point growing prosperity renders the liberal project of expanding the welfare state untenable, even ludicrous, is one question. Whether prosperity itself can indefinitely stand prosperity is another. It's difficult to imagine that a society so affluent that every baby is a trust-fund baby will possess for very long the "animal spirits" that express themselves in risk-taking, hard work, and ambitious or even audacious entrepreneurship.

In any case, the possibility that our great-grandchildren will be wrestling with the question of how much public assistance to give families that would be affluent today gives hope that they will look back on the 21st century as having been fundamentally peaceful and prosperous.

CHAPTER TWO

AMERICA'S WELFARE STATE IN THEORY

PROVIDING ITS RATIONALE

few writers, though no politicians, say explicitly what is usually intimated: the liberal
project seeks to do for America what social-
ists and social democrats have done for Europe. The *New Yorker's*
Hendrik Hertzberg scoffs at conservatives' alarm that America
might come to resemble "the gentle social democracies across the
Atlantic, where, in return for higher taxes and without any dim-
inution of civil liberty, people buy themselves excellent public
education, anxiety-free health care, and decent public transportation."[1] The economics journalist Robert Kuttner defines
"adequate social investment" as the U.S. devoting an additional
15 percent of its GDP to social programs. Based on the OECD
data we examined in the last chapter, that increment would give
America a welfare state that absorbed essentially the same portion of the nation's economic output as Sweden's. For as long
as America's markedly higher per capita GDP survived Kuttner's
agenda, the outlays on social programs would, in absolute terms,
be much larger in America than in Sweden.[2]

In 2003, Gerhard Schroeder, then chancellor of Germany,
insisted "a Europe formed by Social Democrats is more necessary today than ever before. Such a Europe is needed because
we Europeans, based upon our unique European model of
social participation and our embrace of the welfare state, have
something to offer to the whole world . . . an alternative of just
development and shared wealth."[3] Schroeder's formulation raises
questions about the political, almost anthropological, feasibility
of transplanting the social democratic model to America. The

don't-tread-on-me cussedness of the Americans is an impediment
to the liberal project, giving rise to Jonah Goldberg's suspicion
that "Sweden's government succeeds as much as it does because it
governs *Swedes*."[4]

Seymour Martin Lipset fleshed out the trans-Atlantic differences. Centuries of feudalism, during which governmental power
defined and secured reciprocal obligations between the classes,
prepared the way for Europe's welfare states. In the 19th and 20th
centuries, as the expanding rights of the working and middle
classes made greater incursions on the aristocrats' and established
churches' prerogatives, the tangible benefits of the revised social
contract were redirected to ordinary people.

America is different. Lipset quotes the political scientist
Walter Dean Burnham: "No feudalism, no socialism: with those
four words one can summarize the basic sociocultural realities that
underlie American electoral politics in the industrial era." European conservatives welcome government intervention to uphold
traditions and unify society. They look on American "conservatives," with their attachment to laissez-faire, as champions of
modern history's most convulsive force, capitalism.[5]

Lipset writes that, at the other end of the political spectrum,
"unlike Scandinavian social democracy, Fabian bureaucratic
socialism, and Soviet communism, American radicalism has been
permeated by suspicion, if not hostility, toward centralized power."
Deep misgivings about expanding the state's power characterized
the history of the American labor movement as well. These dispositions argue that the most distinctive strand of America's political DNA, wariness about the threat that centralized government
power poses to individuals' rights, is strong and durable:

> The Revolutionary Americans, having defeated a tyrannical
> king, feared the power of a unified, central state. They sought
> to avoid tyranny by checks and balances, dividing power

among different political bodies, all subject to a Bill of Rights limiting government authority. The antistatist, antiauthoritarian component of American ideology, derived from Jefferson's Declaration of Independence, remains an underlying source of the weakness of socialism in the United States.[6]

It remains, as well, the fundamental reason why America devotes a smaller portion of its GDP to the welfare state than any other modern democratic nation. The liberal project, expressed in terms of governance, is to expand the welfare state until the gulf that separates America's version from those in Europe disappears. The success of this project would not mean that the American welfare state would stop expanding, since the welfare states that American liberals want to emulate are all continuing to expand, both in absolute terms and relative to GDP. (That is to say, Sweden's social democrats have not declared victory and disbanded. Rather, they continue to insist that many grievous social ills could be alleviated if only the public sector weren't forced to scrape by with 50% of the country's GDP. The historical record predicts that the Swedish electorate will be receptive to such complaints.) It would mean, instead, that after the U.S. had ascended to a level of welfare state spending comparable to Europe's, further increases would also be on the scale taking place in Europe over the past quarter-century.

THE PROGRESSIVES' SECOND FOUNDING

This liberal policy project requires a companion political project—overcoming Americans' deep misgivings about having government, especially the central government, wielding broad power and imposing high taxes. These misgivings can be traced directly to America's political creed and experience. While Swedes and Frenchmen don't rejoice at the chance to pay taxes, or lionize government bureaucrats issuing and enforcing directives, Americans' aversion to expanding government is significantly greater than other peoples'.

This aversion is exceptional even now, after the American welfare state has grown for decades, but was still more pronounced when the project of creating an American welfare state was just beginning. The precursors of American liberals were the progressives. (During the 1980s, when "liberal" became a problematic political designation, some liberals reached back before the New Deal and described themselves as progressives.) The progressives' central concern, as they understood it, was to assuage Americans gripped by the Jeffersonian apprehension that the failure to keep government limited and local would be the first step on the road to tyranny.

Woodrow Wilson is the most important progressive. Over the quarter-century before his election to the presidency in 1912, he established himself as one of the nation's most prominent social scientists and one of progressivism's leading theoreticians. In his first book, *Congressional Government*, written in 1885, Wilson criticized the "blind worship" of the Constitution, for which the only antidote was "fearless criticism." The objective of supplanting worship with criticism was "to make self-government among us a straightforward thing of simple method, single, unstinted power, and clear responsibility. . . ."[7]

It is instructive to contrast Wilson's critique of the Constitution with the most famous defense of it, *The Federalist Papers*. The best-known passage in the latter appears in the 51st of its 85 essays, an explanation and defense of the separation of powers:

> Ambition must be made to counteract ambition. The interest of the man must be connected with the constitutional rights of the place. It may be a reflection on human nature, that such devices should be necessary to control the abuses of

government. But what is government itself, but the greatest of all reflections on human nature? If men were angels, no government would be necessary. If angels were to govern men, neither external nor internal controls on government would be necessary. In framing a government which is to be administered by men over men, the great difficulty lies in this: you must first enable the government to control the governed; and in the next place oblige it to control itself.[8]

Beginning his critique of the Constitution when it was not quite 100 years old, Wilson argued that the Constitution did not, in fact, strike a good balance between the government's need to control the governed and its need to be controlled by the governed. Even if the Madisonian equilibrium rendered American government sufficiently powerful and flexible to discharge its responsibilities in a small, 18th century agrarian society, it was woefully inadequate for fulfilling the governmental tasks required by a modern industrial nation that spanned a continent. Under these circumstances, the Constitution's famous architecture of separated powers, federalism, and checks and balances left American government excessively restrained but insufficiently powerful. The social and economic dynamism that had transformed Thomas Jefferson's America into John D. Rockefeller's was only accelerating, aggravating the disparity between the forces in America that required governing and the adequacy of the governmental powers to superintend them. "The government of a country so vast and various must be strong, prompt, wieldy and efficient," Wilson wrote in *Congressional Government*. However, "As at present constituted, the federal government lacks strength because its powers are divided, lacks promptness because its authorities are multiplied, lacks wieldiness because its processes are roundabout, lacks efficiency because its responsibility is indistinct and its action without competent direction."[9]

This disagreement over how fluidly and rapidly the governmental apparatus should be modified in response to changing historical circumstances is more fundamental than it first appears. The –ism of progressivism is the belief in progress. As the political scientist James Ceaser has written, "Whereas the nation's Founders embraced nature as a foundation and rejected History, the Progressives did just the opposite. They subscribed to [the] Philosophy of History, in which progress was taken to be not merely a hope or sustaining faith, but an objective fact." The progressives, according to Ceaser, "sought to replace, which meant virtually to efface or supplant, the original Founders." Their success, considerable but so far still partial, means that America has had two competing foundings—an 18th century one based on nature, and a 19th century one based on history.[10]

The first founders believed that in nature was to be found both the ultimate purposes of republican government, and the gravest dangers to it. The purposes were to secure humans' unalienable rights, the ones with which they are endowed by their Creator, in the famous words of the Declaration of Independence. In 1911 Wilson argued that "the rhetorical introduction of the Declaration of Independence is the least part of it. . . . If you want to understand the real Declaration of Independence, do not repeat the preface."[11]

By contrast, Calvin Coolidge, most progressives' idea of everything a president should not be, explained why he favored the original founding based on nature over the progressives' counterfounding based on history:

> About the Declaration [of Independence] there is a finality
> that is exceedingly restful. It is often asserted that the world
> has made a great deal of progress since 1776, that we have
> had new thoughts and new experiences which have given
> us a great advance over the people of that day, and that we

may therefore very well discard their conclusions for something more modern. But that reasoning can not be applied to this great charter. If all men are created equal, that is final. If they are endowed with inalienable rights, that is final. If governments derive their just powers from the consent of the governed, that is final. No advance, no progress can be made beyond these propositions. If anyone wishes to deny their truth or their soundness, the only direction in which he can proceed historically is not forward, but backward toward the time when there was no equality, no rights of the individual, no rule of the people.[12]

The chief danger to republican government, according to *Federalist* 10, was "faction," which it defined as "a number of citizens, whether amounting to a majority or a minority of the whole, who are united and actuated by some common impulse of passion, or of interest, adverse to the rights of other citizens, or to the permanent and aggregate interests of the community." The "latent causes of faction," *Federalist* 10 argues, are "sown in the nature of man," since human interests and opinions will always be at odds, and human reasoning always fallible.[13]

The modern undergraduate assigned *The Federalist Papers* usually makes the reasonable assumption that faction is dangerous because political fragmentation and contentiousness are to be avoided. The real point of *Federalist* 10 is counterintuitive: Republicanism is imperiled when society is not fragmented enough. *The* danger of faction is majority faction, which can employ all the mechanisms of democratic government to oppress whomever it wishes. Whenever a majority faction is united by an economic interest, sectional attachment or religious belief, it always consists of the same citizens. It will quickly become clear to those in the majority, as they win vote after vote on issue after issue, that democracy, as such, does not compel them to respect the rights of those in the minority, since the majority's constituents have little reason to fear they will ever find themselves *in* the minority. The citizens in the minority, with no realistic prospect of ever being in the majority, will just as quickly realize that the democratic process jeopardizes their rights, at the very least, and ultimately operates as the engine of their oppression. The bleak realization that they will *never* win an election gives the minority reason to seek power by undemocratic measures, not necessarily excluding violent ones.

The *Federalist Papers* express the hope that America might succeed in upholding majority rule, the essential principle of democracy, without succumbing to majority faction. An extended republic will have many factions, many interests, many sects, none of them large or durable enough to constitute a threatening majority. In such a republic the operation of self-interest will be moderating rather than radicalizing. Majorities will be transient coalitions of many small factions, respecting the rights of the minority not for high-minded reasons, but out of the awareness that the next coalition formed to address the next issue could leave a faction that belongs to today's majority in tomorrow's minority. This was defense in depth. The nation itself would be constituted to reduce the threat of majority faction, and then the government would be constituted—with federalism and the separation of powers—to reduce it further.

The second founding, according to Ceaser, was based on the progressives' philosophy of history, which drew on Hegel, Darwin and Auguste Comte without ever combining their ideas into a coherent and well-defined whole. The absence of theoretical precision did not, however, prevent the progressives from absolute confidence that although "the direction of History was inevitable, it was still helpful or necessary that matters be pushed along with the help of those who were conscious of its laws." In America, one century after the Constitution was ratified, that consciousness was possessed by social scientists, whose empowerment would bring about a "new era of governance, relying on the benign guidance of experts, beyond all partisanship."[14]

The progressives chafed against the ways the Constitution's "internal and external controls" divided and constrained government, thwarting the project of delivering single, unstinted power to disinterested experts. Ronald Pestritto's summary of Wilson's thinking explains why the progressives believed that the first founders' apprehensions about majority faction were excessive and misplaced:

> Wilson believed that the human condition improves as history marches forward, so protections built into government against the danger of such things as faction become less necessary and increasingly unjust. Ultimately, the problem of faction is solved not by permanently limited government but by history itself; history brings a unity of sentiment and fundamental will to the nation. Whereas *The Federalist* asserts that a diversity of interest will always underlie the extended republic, Wilson contended that history would overcome such particularism with an increasing unity of mind. So for him, the latent causes of faction are *not* sown in the nature of man, or if they are, historical progress will overcome this human nature.[15]

To make human nature the basis of a political philosophy or system of government guarantees big disagreements. Such a founding imbues arguments about what is natural and unnatural with the highest importance. Even "We hold these truths to be self-evident" introduces a hesitant subjectivity, one the authors of the Declaration evidently preferred to the more categorical formulation, "These truths *are* self-evident," or even "These propositions are true." Progressives regarded all the resulting arguments about nature as a waste of time, since the Darwinian revolution that came after the first American founding alerted us to the importance of studying change rather than discerning essences. As the historian Richard Hofstadter, an admirer of progressivism, wrote in 1948, "[No] man who is as well abreast of modern science as the [Founding] Fathers were of eighteenth-century science believes any longer in unchanging human nature."[16]

The progressives' belief that we should stop arguing about nature, because we can't envision those arguments being settled, and instead base our political life on history is a problematic one, however. While a founding based on nature may generate unresolvable differences of opinion, a founding based on history must generate unintelligible ones. It's hard to understand nature, but it's impossible to know the future. There is something hopelessly circular about the approach of those who appeal to the future to settle today's political arguments, since, as C.S. Lewis wrote, "what the future will be depends very largely on just those choices which they now invoke the future to help them make."[17]

The dubious authority asserted by those who claim they can see farther over the horizon than the rest of us is, among other things, a way to make their own political preferences cast a bigger shadow. The insights offered by the Party of the Future are, upon inspection, quite banal; the future always turns out to be a nicer neighborhood than the present, so everything we can do today to spruce things up will help usher in the future. As Richard Rorty argued, abandoning the whole enterprise of quarreling over human nature creates a new political environment where "it is not clear that any shift in scientific or philosophical opinion could hurt the sort of hope that characterizes modern liberal societies— the hope that life will eventually be freer, less cruel, more leisured, richer in goods and experiences, not just for our descendants but for everyone's descendants."[18] When you repudiate the founding based in nature, you're left with a politics based on faith in "the evolving standards of decency that mark the progress of a maturing society," as the Supreme Court said in 1958.[19]

Two problems, one intellectual and one political, impaired this reliance on the march of progress onward and upward. The intellectual one was that the serious doubts progressives raised about the founding based on nature could not be amalgamated to their willfully naïve faith in a future that grows perpetually nicer as it is populated by perpetually more decent and understanding people. There turned out to be no coherent argument for exempting the evolving standards of decency from the skepticism that had been trained on the laws of nature and nature's God. Once progressives accepted this reality, the idea of progress, once held to be objectively true, was downgraded to "no more than an opinion or object of faith," according to Ceaser. That realization left the new founding based on history exposed as a founding based on the transitory and idiosyncratic preferences of particular people who happened to be living in a particular time and place. Whether "mere personal expressions of commitment" to democracy and progress "would be enough to sustain liberalism over the long term," in Ceaser's words, was doubtful at best.[20]

The political problem is that the ideology of progress lends itself more convincingly to justifying governmental passivity than governmental activism. If a better future is our destiny, the need for political midwives to assist its birth is not urgent, and their involvement might turn out to be unnecessary or even counterproductive. This was the contention of the Social Darwinists, who thought that soft-hearted government interventions would only postpone the inevitable ascent of the fittest and descent of the least fit. In arguing against that position, the progressives bet heavily on the idea that the prescience of disinterested experts was indispensable to accelerating and smoothing the transition to the better future.

They did so, however, without acknowledging the dangers of giving unstinted power to experts who might turn out to be neither prescient nor disinterested. The progressives did not advocate that social scientists seize power in a coup. In a democracy, political leaders would play a crucial mediating role, helping the people to understand that the experts' insights about the future were nothing more than the people's own inchoate understanding of their next destination. "[No] reform may succeed for which the major thought of the nation is not prepared," Woodrow Wilson said in a lecture on leadership in 1889. Therefore, "the instructed few may not be safe leaders, except in so far as they have communicated their instruction to the many, except in so far as they have transmuted their thought into a common, a popular thought." Thus, said Wilson, leadership is "interpretation."[21] He reiterated this idea 23 years later as a candidate for president: "The business of every leader of government is to hear what the nation is saying and to know what the nation is enduring. It is not his business to judge *for* the nation, but to judge *through* the nation as its spokesman and voice."[22]

This Hegelian element of Wilson's thinking makes it easier to differentiate him from the Social Darwinists, but at the cost of making it harder to differentiate him from modern totalitarians. The 20th century saw unfathomable cruelties committed by political movements that seized control of national governments, then justified their brutalities by invoking their leader's transformational role as the voice of the people and the discerner and vessel of the nation's destiny. Jonah Goldberg called attention to the fact that liberalism's batting average on the question of totalitarianism was less than 1.000 in *Liberal Fascism*, which was denounced and ridiculed by the vast majority of critics who disagreed with the book's politics. One of them, Michael Tomasky, allowed that there have been "certain consanguinities between the far left and the far right," but insisted they have nothing to do with understanding liberalism:

> Anybody familiar with Liberalism 101 grasps that there is
> something deep within liberalism, from its earliest beginnings,
> that prevents it from degenerating into fascism, and that is its

explicit recognition that the state must serve both common purposes *and* individual liberty. . . . [Where] that collective urge crosses the line into coercion, well, that is where liberals—I mean liberals who know something about liberalism—get off the train, and do their noncoercive best to derail it.[23]

Tomasky's refutation of Goldberg is as adamant as it is unhelpful. He has nothing more to tell us about the "something deep within liberalism" that makes liberals play nice. Nor does Tomasky give us the coordinates of the line that divides permissible social reforms from impermissible curtailments of individuals' liberties.

NEW RIGHTS IN THE NEW DEAL

The bluster and defensiveness of Tomasky's response show the incompleteness of progressivism's victory over the American founding based on nature. Even into the 21st century, Americans retain a strong attachment to Lockean natural rights that can be endangered by an excessively strong, busy or undisciplined government. The progressive project was unable to persuade the American people to abandon, simply and confidently, their wariness about the threat unstinted government power posed to natural rights. Progressivism asked Americans, instead, to place their trust in giving visionary leaders and public-spirited experts all the governmental power that their efforts to hasten the arrival of a better future required. While that better future was destined, it was also a destiny that could be impeded or delayed by reactionary elements.

Progressivism scored additional victories over these elements due to the rhetorical innovations of Franklin Roosevelt. FDR, beginning in his campaign for the presidency in 1932, insistently framed the question of expanding the government in terms of upholding and updating the founding based on nature, rather than repudiating it. According to Sidney Milkis, "FDR's deft reinterpretation of the American constitutional tradition" gave "legitimacy to progressive principles by embedding them in the language of constitutionalism and interpreting them as an expansion rather than a subversion of the natural rights tradition." Significantly, FDR conveyed this orientation by enthusiastically embracing "liberalism" as the designation for the New Deal's philosophy, sending the term "progressivism," with its clearly implied critique of the American founding, into a long exile. To do so he wrested "liberalism" away from the defenders of limited government, who acceded unhappily to calling themselves "conservatives."[24]

FDR's innovations in the language of American politics were integral to his transformation of the substance of American government. Prior to the New Deal, the federal government "had been a remote authority with a limited range of activity," according to the political scientist V.O. Key. "It operated the postal system, improved rivers and harbors, maintained armed forces on a scale fearsome only to banana republics, and performed other functions of which the average citizen was hardly aware."[25] The New Deal succeeded in dramatically increasing the scope of the federal government by making a dramatically broader understanding of rights "the foundation of political dialogue in the United States," according to Milkis. "With the advent of the New Deal political order, an understanding of rights dedicated to limited government gradually gave way to a more expansive understanding of rights, requiring a relentless government identification of problems and the search for methods by which these problems might be solved."[26]

The political success of the New Deal was a victory not just of programs and arguments. The virtuoso performance of Franklin Roosevelt as a public figure was an indispensable element as well. According to the presidential scholar Richard Neustadt,

"Roosevelt, almost alone among our Presidents, had no conception of the office to live up to; he was it. His image of the office was himself-in-office."[27]

FDR introduced the term "new deal" in his acceptance speech to the 1932 Democratic convention. The fact of that speech was as resonant as its content. Prior to 1932, a presidential candidate would wait at home, far from the city holding the convention, for a delegation to inform him that the party had offered its nomination and then implore him to accept it. The ritual invoked the legend of Lucius Quinctius Cincinnatus, found plowing on his farm in 458 B.C. by a delegation from the Roman Senate that beseeched him to accept the office of dictator in order to repulse the armies threatening Rome. Cincinnatus accepted the office, defeated Rome's enemies, then gave up his dictatorship the day after the final battle and returned to his farm. George Washington, the "American Cincinnatus," had twice returned to Mount Vernon rather than use his eminence to perpetuate his own power and glory: first in 1783 after Yorktown, and then in 1797 after two terms as president.

FDR's appearance before them was "unprecedented and unusual," he told the Democratic delegates in 1932, but the crisis of the Depression required breaking many "absurd traditions." The absurdity FDR identified was the candidate pretending not to *know* he had been nominated until the delegation arrived on his front porch, an anachronism left over from the days before the telegraph, radio and telephone. In all the centuries prior to those technologies, encompassing the life of both Cincinnatus and Washington, information could travel only as fast as the humans who carried it in their heads or on paper.[28]

The more important absurdity, to which FDR referred obliquely, was the candidate pretending not to *care* about being nominated. The task of the delegates dispatched by the convention had been to prevail upon the nominee to forsake private life for high office by answering the call to duty for the good of party and country. There was indeed something ridiculous about a politician who had bargained furiously to secure a presidential nomination pretending to agonize over whether to accept it. Americans old enough to remember the 1952 presidential campaign constitute the dwindling cohort able to recall presidential nominees (Dwight Eisenhower and Adlai Stevenson) who took the trouble even to seem reluctant about running for president. All their successors have pursued it openly, avidly and, often, desperately.

However absurd, the tradition buried by FDR's actions and words in 1932 reflected fears about the dangers posed to individuals' rights by unstinted government power. The gravest concern was the emergence of a leader who would use his prestige the way Julius Caesar did, to amass more and more power, rather than elevate the good of the republic above his own, as Cincinnatus and Washington had done. FDR asked the Democratic delegates to let his appearance before them "be the symbol of my intention to be honest and to avoid all hypocrisy or sham." Hypocrisy about not desiring the presidency would no longer be a compliment the vice of ambition paid to the virtue of social reform. "Let it be from now on the task of our party to break foolish traditions," FDR said. "Let us now and here highly resolve to resume the country's interrupted march along the path of real progress, of real justice, of real equality for all our citizens, great and small."[29] The "foolish traditions" FDR intended to break included an excessively literal and narrow understanding of the founding. The resumption of America's interrupted march meant that the New Deal would be true to the spirit of the founding, which had been betrayed by the advocates of limited government who invoked Jefferson.

On September 23, 1932, FDR gave a speech at the Commonwealth Club in San Francisco, where he expanded on the meaning of progress, justice and equality. The speech is generally agreed to be "the New Deal manifesto," in Milkis's phrase.[30] The Commonwealth Club Address shows FDR adopting progressivism's understanding—and denigration—of the American founding based on nature. He speaks of government as a contract, but not a social contract among individuals to form a government in order to secure their natural rights. Rather, it is a contract where "rulers were accorded power, and the people consented to that power on consideration that they be accorded certain rights." There is nothing unalienable about such rights, since they weren't yours to begin with. Disagreeing with Coolidge, who had said in 1926 that the self-evident truths in the Declaration of Independence about unalienable rights were final, and that no advance could be made beyond them, FDR asserts, "The task of statesmanship has always been the re-definition of these rights in terms of a changing and growing social order."[31]

FDR concluded the Commonwealth Club Address by updating—in effect, redrafting—the American social contract, whose terms "are as old as the Republic, and as new as the new economic order." In it, the right to life means "a right to make a comfortable living." The right to property "means a right to be assured, to the fullest extent attainable, in the safety of his savings." Since "all other property rights must yield" to the safety of savings, the government may justifiably "restrict the operations of the speculator, the manipulator, even the financier."[32]

FDR's treatment of the final rights, to liberty and the pursuit of happiness, is especially interesting. He says that "the old 'rights of personal competency'—the right to read, to think, to speak, to choose and live a mode of life, must be respected at all hazards." This assertion seems to contradict FDR's argument that rights need to be redefined according to new circumstances, especially changing economic circumstances. By positing that some rights are less malleable than others, however, and by including in the honor roll of rights that must be respected at all hazards the nebulous right to choose and live a mode of life, FDR seeks to secure enormous leverage for the government. The "liberty to do anything which deprives others of those elemental rights," he asserts, "is outside the protection of any compact," which means it derives no protection from the contract between the rulers and the ruled. Rather, the business of the government is the "maintenance of a balance." There is little doubt whom FDR's balance will favor, since it is between those who exercise their elemental rights of personal competency in ways that harm no one else, and those who invoke an outdated understanding of the rights of property, not yet updated to reflect the new economic order. When the latter acts "the lone wolf, the unethical competitor, the reckless promoter" who "threatens to drag the [financial] industry back to a state of anarchy, the Government may properly be asked to apply restraint."[33]

Roosevelt spent his entire presidency reformulating and reemphasizing the central message that the New Deal was the adaptation of America's founding principles to the nation's new economic circumstances. As such, the New Deal's consequences could be dramatic, while its intentions were presented as benign and even conservative. At FDR's insistence, for example, the 1936 Democratic platform was based on the repeated use of the Declaration's iteration of self-evident truths.[34] Thus, the platform stated, "We hold this truth to be self-evident—that government in a modern civilization has certain inescapable obligations to its citizens, among which are: (1) Protection of the family and the home. (2) Establishment of a democracy of opportunity for all the people. (3) Aid to those overtaken by disaster." In praising the New Deal's discharge of the first obligation, the platform threw the same blanket over John Dillinger and the National Association of Manufacturers: "We have begun and shall continue the successful drive to rid our land of kidnappers and bandits. We shall continue to use the powers of government to end the activities of the malefactors of great wealth who defraud and exploit the people." Looking forward, it promised, "On the foundation of the Social Security Act we are determined to erect a structure of economic security for all our people, making sure that this benefit shall keep step with the ever-increasing capacity of America to provide a high standard of living for all its citizens."[35]

THE NEW DEAL AND THE NEW CONSTITUTION

FDR's landslide victory in the 1936 election demonstrated that voters were receptive not only to the New Deal's tangible benefits, but to the Democrats' reassurances about its continuing fidelity to America's founding principles. The 1936 Republican platform had argued, to little avail, that "America is in peril," because the people's liberty, opportunity and "their character as free citizens" are "today for the first time . . . threatened by government itself." To take one particular, the Republicans pledged "to resist all attempts to impair the authority of the Supreme Court of the United States, the final protector of the rights of our citizens against the arbitrary encroachments of the legislative and executive branches of government. There can be no individual liberty without an independent judiciary."[36]

This promise was a clear reference to the ways the Court had stymied the New Deal during FDR's first term, most famously by the unanimous decision in the 1935 *Schechter* case holding the National Industrial Recovery Act (NIRA) unconstitutional. The law, passed in 1933 during the "Hundred Days," had established the National Recovery Administration (NRA), under which over 700 industries had drawn up codes of fair competition, which ordinarily set minimum wages and maximum hours for workers, and maximum prices for the sale of goods. The president's signature gave a code the force of law. The NRA embodied the idea FDR had laid out in the Commonwealth Club address: The "responsible heads of finance and industry instead of acting each for himself, must work together to achieve the common end. They must, where necessary, sacrifice this or that private advantage; and in reciprocal self-denial must seek a general advantage." Later in the speech, he praised the idea of "private initiative, inspired by high responsibility, with such assistance and balance as Government can give."[37]

During the two years it operated, however, the NRA showed little evidence of responsibility or self-denial. Rather, according to David Kennedy, the "lamentably predictable results" were "codes that amounted to nothing less than the cartelization of huge sectors of American industry under the government's auspices." Furthermore, "NRA mushroomed into a bureaucratic colossus." A staff of 4,500 administered its codes, which ran to 13,000 pages and were interpreted in 11,000 administrative rulings. The relatively modest ambition of operating a hardware store required compliance with 19 different codes.[38]

More than a few New Dealers were relieved when the Supreme Court put the NRA out of its misery. By 1935, the agency had "few all-out defenders on Capitol Hill," according to Arthur Schlesinger. Even many who felt that the NRA was a bad program, however, reacted with alarm to the Court's assertion that NIRA was an unconstitutional law. *The New Republic* editorialized that "there is no point any longer in saying that the Constitution is infinitely flexible. . . . To have a socialist society we must have a new Constitution." At a press conference four days after the Court's ruling, FDR called the decision the most important since the Dred Scott ruling of 1857. "We have got to decide one way or the other," FDR said, "whether in some way we are going to . . . restore to the Federal Government the powers which exist in the National Governments of every other nation in the world." Then, giving headline writers across the country the front page for their next edition, he said, "We have been relegated to the horse-and-buggy definition of interstate commerce."[39]

The Court had indeed ruled in *Schechter* that the NIRA exceeded the authority of Congress to "regulate Commerce with foreign Nations, and among the several States, and with Indian Tribes," in the words of the Constitution. The Court had ruled that the NRA codes encompassed federal power over intrastate commerce, which was outside the constitutional authority to regulate interstate commerce. The fact that the Schechter Poultry Corporation bought some chickens in Philadelphia did not, the Court held, mean that a business licensed in New York, with all of its operations and customers in New York, was engaged in interstate commerce.[40]

There was a second argument the Court made against the constitutionality of NIRA. Article I, Section 1 of the Constitution states, "All legislative Powers herein granted shall be vested in a Congress of the United States, which shall consist of a Senate and House of Representatives." Once the Constitution assigns a particular power to a branch of government, the Court ruled in *Schechter*, that branch is forbidden from delegating the power to others. In a concurring opinion, Justice Benjamin Cardozo said that under NIRA, "anything that Congress may do within the limits of the commerce clause for the betterment of business may be done by the President upon the recommendation of a trade association by calling it a code. This is delegation running riot. No such plenitude of power is susceptible of transfer." In effect, Cardozo wrote, the NRA was "a roving commission to inquire into evils and upon discovery correct them." Furthermore, the evils are "not to be restricted to the elimination of business practices that would be characterized by general acceptance as oppressive or unfair." Rather, "It is to include whatever ordinances may be desirable or helpful for the well-being or prosperity of the industry affected."[41]

The idea that Congress *should* delegate a plenitude of its power to the executive branch was, in fact, a progressive aspiration carried forward into the New Deal. Wilson's goal of a government of unstinted power and clear responsibility was also the goal of the President's Committee on Administrative Management, usually known as the Brownlow Committee, which was convened by FDR in 1936 and which issued a report on strengthening and streamlining the executive branch in 1937. According to Luther Gulick, one of the three committee members, the adoption of its recommendations would reduce the typical law enacted by Congress to "a declaration of war, so that the essence of the program is in the gradual unfolding of the plan in actual administration."[42] At his press conference after the *Schechter* decision, FDR noted in passing that many laws passed in wartime delegated far more congressional authority than NIRA.[43]

Despite the anger of many of his supporters against the Supreme Court, FDR declined to make it an issue in the 1936 campaign. The 1936 Democratic platform limited its discussion of the question to the statement that the Democrats would seek clarifying amendments if it turned out that the Constitution did not give the federal and state governments adequate powers to address the nation's problems.[44] FDR's first big initiative after his re-election, however, was the attempt to bend the Supreme Court to his will. He proposed to "pack" the court by increasing the number of justices from nine to 15. The power to fill six new vacancies with pro-New Deal justices would guarantee the defeat of constitutional challenges to his policies.

Changing the number of justices was not prohibited by the Constitution; Congress had altered the size of the Court six times before settling on nine justices in 1869. The logic of an independent judiciary, however, was that excessive power and ambition in the executive jeopardized republican government and the liberties it secured. Despite the popularity of the New Deal, the Supreme Court's decisions against it had not altered the fact that the Court was, in David Kennedy's words, "one of the most respected and immutable American institutions . . . whose unshifting weight could be counted upon to steady the ship of state."[45]

FDR had told the Democratic convention in 1932 that he wanted to avoid all hypocrisy or sham. In 1937, however, rather than acknowledge his obvious desire for new justices who would outvote the sitting ones who disagreed with him, FDR claimed his real concern was that the federal judiciary required more and younger judges to cope with its growing docket of cases. This "transparently disingenuous" assertion, according to Kennedy, did "incalculable harm" to FDR's proposal.[46]

Further damage was done when opponents of the court-packing plan released a pointed letter from Chief Justice Charles Evan Hughes, arguing that a larger Supreme Court would have more difficulty, not less, in managing its workload. In the end, Congress never even voted on increasing the number of justices. Instead, FDR wound up filling six vacancies on the Supreme Court during his second term, ones created by ordinary retirements rather than by changing the number of justices.[47]

As every history of the 1930s relates, FDR's court-packing defeat turned out to be the cause of, or at least the prelude to, a much bigger victory. In 1937, during the political fight over the court-packing plan, the Supreme Court began upholding the constitutionality of the sort of New Deal legislation it had recently struck down. "Even before Roosevelt was able to staff the high bench with a majority of his own appointees," according to Kennedy, "he had wrought a momentous judicial transformation. He lost the battle to expand the Court, but won the war for a shift in constitutional doctrine."[48]

At the time of his death in 1945, seven of the nine Supreme Court justices were FDR appointees. During the eight years since the court-packing battle, the Court had dismantled every one of the constitutional impediments to government activism. In the six decades since FDR's death, these impediments have all stayed dismantled. In the words of the legal historian Bernard Schwartz, "To the post-1937 Supreme Court, the Congress, charged with all of the legislative powers granted by the Constitution, is entitled to its own choice among all rationally permissible opinions as to what the Constitution allows." In the spirit of this new understanding, a law professor, Peter Shane, recently argued that the "proper constitutional response" to concerns about Congress regulating any activity it chooses is, "So what?"[49]

Every idea about the Constitution that had limited the scope of governmental activity before 1937 was cast aside thereafter. The *Schechter* precedent against delegation of congressional authority has never been overturned. It has also never been re-applied. According to the political scientist Theodore Lowi, "Policy without law is what a broad delegation of power is. Policy without law is clearly constitutional according to present judicial practice."[50]

The doctrine of enumerated powers has also been discarded. It held that the powers enumerated in Article I, Section 8 of the Constitution—to collect taxes, borrow money, declare war, maintain a navy, etc.—were limiting. The final clause of Section 8 says that Congress shall have the power to "make all laws which shall be necessary and proper for carrying into execution the foregoing powers, and all other powers vested by this constitution in the government of the United States, or in any department or officer thereof." Any "broad reading" of this clause that "expands the ends Congress may pursue," according to the legal scholar Richard Epstein, "makes pointless the entire system of enumerated powers of which the Necessary and Proper Clause is the last." Nonetheless, the Court since 1937 has, with rare, minor and evanescent exceptions, made clear that it is happy to see "a Constitution with few and enumerated powers" yield to "one that gives the national government full sway over all human activities."[51]

The post-1937 Court has also repudiated two other constraints on the government. According to Epstein:

> The first of these concerned the structure of American feder-
> alism, in which a national government of enumerated powers
> had a few defined tasks, with all else, including the regulation
> of economic activity, left largely to the states. The second had
> to do with the protection of individual liberty . . . chiefly the
> liberty of entering into voluntary contracts with whomever
> one pleased, and only with such people.[52]

Federalism was hollowed out by Court rulings that all commerce is interstate commerce and that, indeed, all human endeavors
are interstate commerce. In 1942, the Court upheld a Department of Agriculture fine against Roscoe Filburn for harvesting 461
bushels of wheat on his farm, exceeding the allotment the Department had set for him of 223 bushels. The fine was imposed despite
the fact that Filburn fed the 238 illicit bushels to his own livestock.
The Court's decision rested on the belief "that feeding one's own
grain to one's own cows counted as a form of commerce among
the several states," according to Epstein, "because of its effect on
overall supply and price."[53] That is, Filburn engaged in interstate
commerce by declining to engage in interstate commerce. The
wheat he fed to his cows was wheat he didn't have to purchase
in the markets for agricultural commodities, markets the government was trying to stabilize and regulate. Widespread emulation
of his Thoreauean disengagement from the national economy
would stymie the government's plans. The case made clear, in the
words of the political scientist Robert McCloskey, "that Congress
could reach just about any commercial subject it might want to
reach and could do just about anything it was likely to want to
do to that subject, whether for economic, humanitarian, or other
purposes."[54]

As for the liberty of contract, Epstein argues that the best policy,
and the best construction of the Constitution, would recognize
that the government has every reason to regulate against harms

imposed on third parties, but little justification for imposing its judgment about what arrangements are best on parties who have reached different contractual terms for the exchange of goods and services, including hired labor. Such an argument runs counter to *West Coast Hotel Co. v. Parrish* in 1937, which upheld the constitutionality of a state law mandating minimum wages for female employees. In doing so, it impaired both the liberty and the interests of the minimum wage law's ostensible beneficiaries, according to Epstein. Starting from the certainty that a law establishing a minimum wage only for women would be rejected immediately today as a violation of equal protection, he argues:

> That suspicion about who is protected should not end even if the coverage of the statute is extended to men. . . . The "protection" of all low-paid workers may benefit other higher paid workers, often union workers, in competition with firms that use cheaper labor. Or the minimum wage laws may benefit rival firms that have a heavier dependence on capital. The intuition in the equal protection sex discrimination case—that legislation benefits strangers to the contract and not the ostensible protected parties—is correct. It is also subject to generalization. The minimum wage laws continue to do mischief to the poor and dispossessed, as well as to the overall productivity of society at large. Both liberty and utility are hurt by the same legislation.[55]

THE LIVING CONSTITUTION

According to William Leuchtenburg, "In 1937 the Supreme Court began a revolution in jurisprudence that ended, apparently forever, the reign of laissez-faire and legitimated the arrival of the Leviathan State."[56] Laissez-faire had a dwindling fan club after eight years of the Depression, but that did not mean Americans were eager to embrace Leviathan. To this day, liberals find it necessary to insist that a government entrusted with all the powers of European social democracies will be gentle and do nothing to reduce civil liberties.

This defensiveness reflects conservatives' ability to speak to Americans' unallayed fears when they warn, as Gerald Ford once did, that a government big enough to give you everything you want is a government big enough to take away everything you have.[57] New Dealers tried to respond to these fears with reassurances that were heftier and more tangible than vague promises that "something deep within liberalism" would keep it from violating individuals' liberties.

One of these reassurances was the idea of a "living Constitution." New Dealers realized there was something unnerving about their contention that the Constitution, long thought to have imposed strict limits on the ends the federal government could pursue and the means it could employ, was in fact an authorization for the government to pursue virtually any goal it wanted through any mechanism it chose. The interpretation of a Constitution of enumerated powers meant to secure inalienable rights had been a matter of applying timeless principles to changing circumstances. A living Constitution denied the existence of timeless principles; its fundamental principles changed as the nation's economic and social circumstances changed. This notion was fully congruent with the rhetorical thrust of the Roosevelt presidency: The New Deal meant the continuous updating of the 18th century founding, not its repudiation. A living Constitution was one that kept faith with both America's heritage and its destiny.[58]

The assurances that the New Deal represented continuity rather than a breach with the founding were too abstract to be completely reassuring. The heritage to which the New Deal is faithful is the redefinition of rights in terms of a changing order, as FDR said at the Commonwealth Club in 1932. He called it a commitment to "wider freedom" and "an American way of life" in his 1936 acceptance speech.[59] To characterize the stewardship of the nation's political patrimony in that fashion doesn't exclude much. The commitment to promote progress is even less restrictive, given the impossibility of knowing the future.

One way to strengthen the claim about the benignity of the government's newly discovered capacities to address any problem it chose by any means it preferred was provided in *United States v. Carolene Products Company*.[60] In a famous footnote to that 1938 decision, Justice Harlan Stone sketched out a way for the Court to "hedge its bets," in Epstein's phrase, by applying different levels of scrutiny to different kinds of government activities.[61] In subsequent decisions, the Court embraced Stone's categories and made them a key element of modern constitutional jurisprudence. As a result, governmental policies affecting economic activity have to satisfy the lowest level of judicial scrutiny: the demonstration that the law or regulation is rationally related to a legitimate state interest. To state the point negatively, the Court would rule against an economic regulation only if "it is of such a character as to preclude the assumption that it rests upon some rational basis within the knowledge and experience of the legislators."[62] Once the courts determine that a government policy has to satisfy no higher standard, they invariably conclude that it has indeed satisfied the rational relation test. Other sorts of governmental activities, however, can be subjected to "strict scrutiny," which requires the government to demonstrate that its activities are in the pursuit of a compelling state interest, and the means selected is necessary for advancing that interest. Strict scrutiny is triggered by government actions that might harm "discrete and insular minorities," or ones that compromise fundamental rights.[63]

Inventing tiers of judicial scrutiny allowed the living Constitution to further the liberal agenda during the New Deal, and beyond. The rational relation test, applied to both federal and state governments, has meant that legislatures and the agencies to which they delegate power can expect judicial acquiescence to almost anything they do that comes under the broad heading of economic regulation. The thrust of the New Deal was that such broad powers would be applied only to "malefactors of great wealth" and "economic royalists," as FDR sometimes described the rich and powerful. (The notion that the Schechter Poultry Company and Roscoe Filburn were among those oligarchs was more than a bit of a stretch, however.)

The strict scrutiny test was meant to reassure the rest of us, who weren't captains of industry or Wall Street financiers, that the Court and the Constitution were still protecting *our* rights. The other branches of government couldn't justify violating them simply by saying it seemed like a good idea at the time. The different tiers of judicial scrutiny meant the Constitution was not just living, but protean. It would yield up, to practitioners of the "happy endings" approach to constitutional interpretation, a sufficient rationale for the government to do anything for you, if liberal reformers considered it desirable, or to you, if they considered it necessary. As James Ceaser has explained, the rational relation test promoted liberal judicial restraint in the 1930s in response to decisions like *Schechter*, while strict scrutiny promoted liberal judicial activism later on.[64] In 1969, for example, the Court's strict scrutiny of the Constitution revealed a fundamental right to travel, one that a state violated by requiring new residents to wait one year before receiving welfare benefits.[65] Four years later the Court scrutinized the Bill of Rights and its penumbras until it determined that the fundamental right to privacy is "broad enough to encompass a woman's decision whether or not to terminate her pregnancy," thereby invalidating laws in force at the time in every one of the 50 states as excessively restrictive.[66] In doing so, the justices displayed a fierce indifference to what the legal theorist

Alexander Bickel described laconically as the countermajoritarian difficulty.[67]

THE SECOND BILL OF RIGHTS

The living Constitution attained its apotheosis in Pres. Roosevelt's 1944 State of the Union address. That speech saw the culmination of FDR's effort, begun at the Commonwealth Club 11-and-a-half years earlier, to amalgamate the New Deal to the American founding. For good measure, he amalgamated it as firmly to the consuming national effort to achieve victory in World War II. Describing the Teheran conference he had attended in October 1943, FDR told Congress that "the one supreme objective" he discussed there with Churchill, Chiang Kai-shek and Stalin "can be summed up in one word: Security." He explained that security did not mean merely the security from cross-border aggression that is the obvious concern of a wartime meeting of the leaders of allied nations, but "also economic security, social security, moral security."[68]

Though Roosevelt devoted most of the speech to laying out the policies needed for waging and winning the war, the relatively brief section at the end on domestic policy after the war is the part still remembered. In it, he discussed the duty to "begin to lay the plans and determine the strategy for the winning of a lasting peace and the establishment of an American standard of living higher than ever before known," even while the war was being fought. A lasting peace, and a high and comprehensively shared standard of living, were not two goals, but one, since "unless there is security here at home there cannot be lasting peace in the world." This may sound like a bromide, but the speech shows FDR unmistakably advancing the idea that the nation that had elected him to the presidency was a threat to become an international aggressor, indistinguishable from the nations America was fighting, if his domestic policy agenda was thwarted. The progres-

sive reforms undertaken by Pres. Wilson were abandoned after
World War I, and a similar triumph of "rightist reaction" could
have far more dire consequences after World War II: If "history
were to repeat itself and we were to return to the so-called 'nor-
malcy' of the 1920's—then it is certain that even though we shall
have conquered our enemies on the battlefields abroad, we shall
have yielded to the spirit of Fascism here at home." Having characterized his opponents as fascists, FDR immediately added to the
demagoguery, denying that those who questioned his domestic
agenda deserved any respect as a loyal opposition:

> Our fighting men abroad—and their families at home—
> expect such a program and have the right to insist upon it.
> It is to their demands that this Government should pay heed
> rather than to the whining demands of selfish pressure groups
> who seek to feather their nests while young Americans are
> dying.[69]

The agenda for which soldiers were bleeding and against
which fascists and subversives were scheming was the Second
Bill of Rights. FDR's presentation of it is exactly in line with the
New Deal rhetoric he had used since the Commonwealth Club
Address: The American founding pointed the way, but modern
circumstances require the addition of new principles to the ones
bequeathed to us by Jefferson, Madison and Hamilton.

> This Republic had its beginning, and grew to its present
> strength, under the protection of certain inalienable politi-
> cal rights—among them the right of freedom of speech, free
> press, free worship, trial by jury, freedom from unreasonable
> searches and seizures. They were our rights to life and liberty.
>   As our Nation has grown in size and stature, however—
> as our industrial economy expanded—these political rights

proved inadequate to assure us equality in the pursuit of happiness.[70]

FDR's editing of the Declaration's principles to make the assurance of equality in the pursuit of happiness one of the nation's central commitments is particularly striking, and an echo of the 1936 Democratic platform's call for a "democracy of opportunity."

"Necessitous men are not free men," FDR continued, using a phrase he had employed on many previous occasions. Political liberty is no longer self-sustaining; its preservation in the aftermath of industrialization requires economic security. "People who are hungry and out of a job are the stuff of which dictatorships are made." Invoking the Declaration and Constitution in one brushstroke, FDR said, "In our day these economic truths have become accepted as self-evident. We have accepted, so to speak, a second Bill of Rights under which a new basis of security and prosperity can be established for all—regardless of station or race or creed."[71]

FDR offers a list of the rights to economic security that is extensive, but he is careful to stipulate that it is not exhaustive; after the war the government must seek to realize "these and similar rights." The rights he does name are:

- The right to a useful and remunerative job in the industries, or shops or farms or mines of the nation;
- The right to earn enough to provide adequate food and clothing and recreation;
- The right of every farmer to raise and sell his products at a return which will give him and his family a decent living;
- The right of every business man, large and small, to trade in an atmosphere of freedom from unfair competition and domination by monopolies at home or abroad;
- The right of every family to a decent home;

- The right to adequate medical care and the opportunity to achieve and enjoy good health;
- The right to adequate protection from the economic fears of old age and sickness and accident and unemployment;
- The right to a good education.[72]

It's difficult to see how FDR's list should or even could be expanded, because it's hard to come up with candidates for the list of economic rights that FDR failed to mention. "All of these rights spell security," Roosevelt said, and their implementation after the war will move the nation forward to "new goals of human happiness and well-being."[73] If the eight rights he did specify turned out to be politically and economically feasible, Americans would never have to worry about being out of work, or stuck in a lousy job that doesn't provide for their day-to-day necessities. It doesn't appear, given the way FDR presents the rights, that the jobs to which people are entitled need to be remunerative enough to pay for bigger, long-term needs of housing, medical care and education; these economic rights are free-standing, not needs like food and clothing that people are supposed to be able to cover out of their paychecks. Similarly, the right to economic security for the aged, disabled or unemployed also crowds out the need to provide for such contingencies through savings or insurance.

Finally, for those who want to be self-employed rather than employed by others, FDR strongly hints that every enterprise has a right to succeed, or at least to operate indefinitely. He doesn't spell this out, of course. Rather, farmers have a right to expect a return sufficient for a decent living, while entrepreneurs have a right to be exempt from unfair competition. By the time the vague terms "decent" and "unfair" are defined in a political process accommodating to interest groups, however, it's unlikely that any business failure will ever be blamed on forces *within* any farmer's or entrepreneur's control.

Someone who set out to feel economically insecure in a society where all those rights had been proffered and guaranteed would really have to work at it. As we saw in Chapter One, however, there's overwhelming evidence that most people in modern, prosperous democracies are determined to meet this challenge of feeling precarious while living in ever more prosperous and solicitous welfare states. Those countries, such as France and Sweden, that have most avidly embraced the idea that economic security is an entitlement, are ones where the correlation of political forces constantly pushes the government to guarantee ever more economic security.

Modern politics and economics keep moving the goal posts for the welfare state. The politicians who favor the welfare state have encouraged and even insisted that their own efforts be Sisyphean. In 1887, for example, the Fabian socialist Sidney Webb asserted, "There will never come a moment when we can say '*now* Socialism is established.'"[74] In his 1936 "Rendezvous with Destiny" acceptance speech at the Democratic convention, FDR said, "Liberty requires [an] opportunity to make a living—a living decent according to the standard of the time, a living which gives man not only enough to live by, but something to live for."[75] It was an idea reformulated by Wilson Wyatt, the first national chairman of the Americans for Democratic Action, in a speech at the ADA's first national convention:

> [We reject] the view that government's only responsibility
> is to prevent people from starving or freezing to death. We
> believe it is the job of government to function to lift the level
> of human existence. It is the job of government to widen the
> chance for development of individual personalities. It is not
> enough for society to guarantee the physical survival of its
> inhabitants; it must also nourish the dignity of an individual
> human being.[76]

Given such expansive understandings of the government's obligations to its citizens, it's no surprise that FDR insisted on—and liberals have availed themselves of—the right to discover new rights. One of the influences on the Second Bill of Rights was the report submitted to FDR in 1943 by the National Public Resources Board, an entity he had created for the purpose of mapping a postwar domestic policy agenda. The report called for recognizing rights to various requirements for well-being, including "rest, recreation, and adventure, the opportunity to enjoy life and take part in advancing civilization."[77] In a similar vein, the Universal Declaration of Human Rights, adopted by the United Nations in 1948, proclaims rights to "rest and leisure, including reasonable limitation of working hours and periodic holidays with pay," to "participate freely in the cultural life of the community," and "to enjoy the arts and to share in scientific advancement and its benefits."[78]

The content of the Second Bill of Rights—and of rights to minimum levels of economic welfare, social dignity and the ability to choose a mode of life—remains murky. We'll examine this problem in the next chapter but summarize it in this one by saying that the harder question is not about what welfare rights include, but what they exclude. Once the enterprise of positing that people have a right to a decent life is launched, on what basis can we tell people who repeatedly demand additions to the honor roll that some things are indeed conducive to a decent life but, at the same time, are not rights?

The other question worth noting here is the formal standing of rights to the prerequisites for a decent life. Some New Dealers were open to the idea that welfare rights, and the Second Bill of Rights in particular, should be added to the "First" Bill of Rights by amending the Constitution, or even by holding a new constitutional convention. FDR decided against this approach, telling Congress in his 1944 address that implementing the new bill

of rights was "definitely" its responsibility. If it didn't meet that
responsibility, he signaled his determination to galvanize popular
pressure to change the legislators' minds, or the legislature's personnel. Milkis argues that FDR's rejection of formally adopting
the Second Bill of Rights was not due to any aversion to clut-
tering the Constitution, or qualification of his support for those
new rights, but to a desire to protect and maximize administrative
discretion in effecting economic security.[79]

FDR must have expected serving out the fourth presidential
term he sought and won later in 1944, and may have hoped that
the embrace of the Second Bill of Rights, as a political fact and a
series of policy commitments, would effectively make all his successors New Dealers, too. FDR died 15 months after delivering
his Second Bill of Rights speech, however, and the Second Bill
itself did not decisively shape American politics after 1944. The
legal scholar Cass Sunstein, in a book praising the Second Bill
of Rights, calls FDR's 1944 speech "the greatest of the twentieth
century." His reason for writing the book, however, is that by
the start of the 21st century, FDR's speech had become "widely
unknown." The problem is not simply historical forgetfulness,
but political resistance. "The country seems in the past decades
to have lost sight of the very ideas that paved the way toward a
second bill."[80]

By the 1960s, many jurists and legal scholars had grown tired of
waiting for Congress and popular pressure to secure the economic
rights proclaimed by FDR. They decided that the Constitution,
if examined with sufficient determination and ingenuity, would
be found to already contain the guarantees FDR declined to put
there. According to Sunstein, the Supreme Court was "moving
toward ruling that the Constitution requires government to provide a decent minimum for all." Richard Nixon's narrow victory
over Hubert Humphrey in the 1968 presidential election, however, meant that the four Supreme Court justices appointed by

the 37th president (Burger, Blackmun, Powell, and Rehnquist) were all opponents of this project. Humphrey, "in all likelihood," would have filled those vacancies with "justices who understood the Constitution to protect social and economic rights." Instead, the Burger Court repudiated every step in the direction of welfare rights taken by the Warren Court, and "by 1975 the whole idea of minimum welfare guarantees had become implausible."[81]

What elections have rendered implausible, however, can be rendered plausible again by subsequent elections. Sunstein's book, an extended exercise in tergiversation, strongly suggests that the liberal jurists and constitutional scholars have come to regard the judicial enactment of the Second Bill of Rights as an undertaking about which it is best to maintain a discreet silence, not one that was in any fundamental way misconceived. Sunstein insisted to one reviewer that his "bottom line" was opposition to the judicial discovery of welfare rights. In the service of emphasizing this bottom line, Sunstein's book provides detailed and approving accounts of how the Warren Court, various state supreme courts, and high courts in Syria, Bulgaria, Russia, Peru, Paraguay, Singapore, Nigeria, South Africa, and Papua New Guinea have improved the lives of the people under their jurisdiction by interpreting constitutions to guarantee welfare rights. From his treatment, it is safe to conclude that neither the Second Bill of Rights nor the determination to discover it within the Constitution's penumbras and emanations is a spent force, politically or intellectually.[82]

CHAPTER THREE

LIBERALISM'S CONTINUING INABILITY TO MAKE SENSE

The New Deal changed America's Constitution from one where the powers of government were enumerated into one where they were innumerable. There has been no going back. A government whose province extends as far as the eye can see will always try to see a little bit farther. The political scientist James Q. Wilson explained how Big Government breeds Bigger Government:

> Once politics was about only a few things; today, it is about nearly everything. . . . Once the "legitimacy barrier" has fallen, political conflict takes a very different form. New programs need not await the advent of a crisis or an extraordinary majority, because no program is any longer "new"—it is seen, rather, as an extension, a modification, or an enlargement of something the government is already doing. . . . Since there is virtually nothing the government has not tried to do, there is little it cannot be asked to do.[1]

Despite this decisive political victory, liberals remain frustrated, believing—chronically, it seems—that the welfare state America should have is always much bigger than the one it does have. What's more surprising, in view of Franklin Roosevelt's exertions to explain the New Deal philosophy, and the consistency of the themes he laid out throughout the 12 years when he was the nation's dominant public figure, is that liberals are not only uncertain about what, exactly, their principles are, but disagree over whether they even need principles. In January 2005 *The American Prospect* ran this notice on its website:

> **We're Taking Suggestions: What *Does* Liberalism Stand For?**
> We all know the basic outline of conservatism's eleva-
> tor pitch: "We believe in freedom and liberty, and we're for
> low taxes, less government, traditional values, and a strong
> national defense." But what is liberalism's? We at the *Prospect*
> have, among us, attended or sat on about eleventy hundred
> panels since the [2004] election at which someone invariably
> says something like the following: "We know what conserva-
> tives stand for. But what do we stand for?"
> No one in Washington seems to know. So we turn to you.
> Give us liberalism's elevator pitch.
> We want you to submit a single sentence of no more than
> 30 words. . . .[2]

The year after running this appeal, *The American Prospect* published an article by Michael Tomasky, its editor at the time, addressing the same question—what is the overarching liberal idea that makes sense of all its individual goals? Democrats have "a more than respectable roster of policy proposals," he said, but lack "a philosophy, a big idea that unites their proposals and con-verts them from a hodgepodge of narrow and specific fixes into a vision for society." He calls this "*the* crucial ingredient of politics, the factor that helps unite a party (always a coalition of warring interests), create majorities, and force the sort of paradigm shifts that happened in 1932 and 1980."[3]

The *Prospect's* rendition of conservatism's elevator pitch is mis-taken in one respect: It overlooks conservatives' big disagreements about big ideas. Libertarians, neo-conservatives and traditionalists each have their own take on what conservatism stands for, world-views that are not only distinct but irreconcilable. Conservatism can't be the sum total of these agendas, as the *Prospect* implies, because the goals they pursue sometimes conflict—libertarians and traditionalists taking opposite views on gay rights or legalizing marijuana, for example.

Conservatives argue so much about big ideas because they're convinced that big ideas matter. "For conservatives, it is clear that the attention they devote to their theoretical principles is meant as much more than a gesture to good breeding. Conservatives consider these principles to be directly related to the political world and to how it should be governed," according to James Ceaser.[4]

POLITICS ON A CASE-BY-CASE BASIS

It's harder to make sense of liberals' intramural fights because they haven't settled the question of whether they even need big ideas. Kenneth Baer and Andrei Cherny, the editors of the quarterly *Democracy*, side with Tomasky. They want to revive liberalism by "grappling with essential questions about how the world works and how it should work."[5] *The New Republic's* Jonathan Chait, however, scoffs at big ideas because, for liberals, "everything works on a case-by-case basis." The question of what liberalism stands for won't be answered, and shouldn't even be asked, because "you cannot, and should not, formulate sweeping dogmas when you're operating on a case-by-case basis."[6] America's most prominent leftist philosopher, the late Richard Rorty, rejected big ideas, too. "The idea that liberal societies are bound together by philosophical belief systems seems to me ludicrous," he wrote. "Philosophy is not that important for politics."[7]

The big-idea liberalism of Tomasky, Baer and Cherny reaches back to FDR's tireless efforts to reformulate the American founding and, before the New Deal, to Woodrow Wilson and the progressives, who tried to supplant the old founding based on nature with a new one based on history. The case-by-case liberalism of Chait and Rorty can also lay claim to the New Deal legacy, however. In an address at Oglethorpe University in May 1932, Franklin Roosevelt said, "The country needs and, unless I mistake its temper, the country demands bold, persistent experimentation. It is common sense to take a method and try it: If it fails, admit it frankly and try another. But above all, try something."[8] This is exactly the point Chait makes when he claims that liberalism is "less of an ideology than the absence of one." The resulting "incoherence is simply the natural byproduct of a philosophy rooted in experimentation and the rejection of ideological certainty."[9]

The New Deal turned out to be as unscripted as FDR promised. In 1940 Alvin Hansen, one of Roosevelt's most influential economic advisors, gave a speech to a group in Cincinnati. After his prepared remarks an audience member asked, "In your opinion, is the basic principle of the New Deal economically sound?" Hansen replied, "I really do not know what the basic principle of the New Deal is. I know from my experience in the government that there are as many conflicting opinions among the people in Washington as we have in the country at large." Another New Dealer, Raymond Moley, found the theme connecting FDR's policies as elusive as Hansen did. In memoirs written after his bitter departure from the Roosevelt administration, Moley said, "To look upon these programs as the result of a unified plan was to believe that the accumulation of stuffed snakes, baseball pictures, school flags, old tennis shoes, carpenter's tools, geometry books, and chemistry sets in a boy's bedroom could have been put there by an interior decorator."[10]

Constant tactical improvisation in the service of a disposition rather than a strategy was, according to some experts' retrospective views, the essence of the New Deal and of liberalism generally. "At the heart of the New Deal there was not a philosophy but a temperament," according to Richard Hofstadter. The economist Robert Lekachman made, and applauded, the same point:

"Liberalism is even more an attitude than it is a program. Liberals are critical of injustice, suspicious of vested interests, friendly to change, hopeful of peaceful improvement and convinced that reasoned argument ultimately overcomes selfish opposition."[11]

Were there two New Deals, a coherent one explained by the Second Bill of Rights and the rhetorical path FDR paved to it throughout his presidency, and also a random assortment of bold experiments? No, says the political scientist Charles Kesler. He argues that FDR made it clear, in the Oglethorpe speech and later, that he favored persistent experiments in the *methods* used by government, but sought "consistency and continuity," in Roosevelt's words, in the *objectives* government pursued.[12]

This explanation reflects FDR's own view of the matter but leaves open the question of how New Dealers like Hanson and Moley, or a sympathetic historian like Hofstadter, could have been so distracted by the New Deal's programmatic bustle that they lost sight of the distinction between means and ends. The best answer to that puzzle is that while the ends pursued by the New Deal were consistent, they were also defined *very* broadly, as when FDR said that the Second Bill of Rights would lead to economic security, and the attainment of new levels of human happiness and well-being. The only goals such a framework excludes are those pursued by an openly tyrannical regime. By the same token, a vast array of government programs could be plausibly defended as methods to deliver security and happiness to all.

"The day of enlightened administration has come," Roosevelt declared in the Commonwealth Club Address.[13] Sidney Milkis argues persuasively that FDR was as determined to "thoroughly reconstruct the institutions and practices of constitutional government" as he was to dramatically expand the government's role in providing economic security. Indeed, the New Deal proceeded in the belief that "programmatic rights, such as Social Security and collective bargaining, would not amount to anything unless new institutional arrangements were established that would reorganize the institutions and redistribute the powers of government." The ultimate goal of these reorganizations was to maximize the political space needed by enlightened administrators to pursue the experiments that would deliver economic security to all. The way to do this was to expand the people's reverence for the goals of the American founding until the circle also encompassed the New Deal's goals, treating them as political objectives to be exalted with Jefferson's and Madison's, equally above and equally beyond partisan politics. Roosevelt's "political genius," according to Milkis, was "to comprehend how the New Deal could transform American political culture without seeming to do so." The intended, and largely achieved, result of this transformation was "an administrative constitution that would protect reforms and reformers from future contests of opinion."[14]

It's not surprising that FDR's efforts to remove the need for liberals to explain themselves have left them unable to do so when they want to, and divided over the question of whether specifying what they stand for discharges a political obligation or is a waste of time and a gift to liberalism's enemies. ("Any debate that takes place at the level of ideological generality . . . inherently favors the right," according to Chait.)[15] One of the implications of proclaiming a "New Deal" is that new bets are going to be made. FDR made a big one, with high rewards and high risks. He intended for the Second Bill of Rights to become "constitutive commitments," in Cass Sunstein's phrase, "a set of public commitments by and for the citizenry, very much like the Declaration of Independence," or "a catalog defining our most basic principles." Had he succeeded, liberals would have had no reason to worry about whether they could or should explain what they stand for. Americans would be matter-of-factly but decisively opposed to reconsidering the Second Bill of Rights, as they would to reopening the question of whether a monarchy might be, after all, preferable to a republic.[16]

In fact, says Sunstein, "Roosevelt's triumph is only partial." The Second Bill of Rights is "not implemented" and "largely unknown." Americans have "lost sight of it." Throughout his book on the Second Bill, Sunstein makes it clear that the incompleteness of this triumph is in no way due to any defects in Roosevelt's ideas, or how he explained and acted on them. Rather, "the public commitment [to FDR's vision] is often partial and ambivalent, even grudging," because "the United States seems to have embraced a confused and pernicious form of individualism," owing to "the influence of powerful private groups." Conservatism and conservatives, in other words.[17]

This tendentious explanation cannot account for why a political project as wise and noble as FDR's would ever be put at a political disadvantage by an ideology as half-baked and insidious as conservatism. Rather than accept the stipulation that the problems of liberalism can be cured by more liberalism, we need to explore why liberalism has been only partially successful, both politically and intellectually. The political success of liberalism is that people are generally very receptive to the tangible benefits the welfare state delivers, and have largely forgotten their qualms about the propriety of the government dispensing such benefits. That political success is only partial, however, because Americans remain leery of the financial costs and high taxes a big welfare state requires, and apprehensive about the size and strength of a government powerful enough to confer so many benefits on so many people. The New Deal was a partial success intellectually because many key terms of the "deal" were never defined clearly and have remained, in the 65 years following FDR's death, nebulous to the point of uselessness.

These two problems, the political and the intellectual, are related. The misgivings people have about the implications of the vigorous and unstinted pursuit of the liberal project are related to the haziness of the project. It's impossible to say what ends liberals will pursue; more precisely, it's impossible to draw up a list of the goals they *won't* pursue, out of a belief that providing certain human needs and allaying some discontents lies beyond the scope of what a government may legitimately address or feasibly undertake. It's also impossible to say which means liberalism will employ; more precisely, it's impossible to say which ones it will foreswear to avoid violating individuals' rights or exceeding government's proper sphere.

There is an additional problem that follows from the first two: Liberalism's political and intellectual problems are related but not identical or neatly synchronized. Solving the intellectual problem doesn't necessarily solve the political one, and could even aggravate it. Clarifying liberalism to the point that its principles are widely understood, its limits specified or its lack of limits candidly acknowledged, might not make liberalism more popular, and could make it less so.

THE FACULTY LOUNGE

Predictably, the contradictory imperatives facing liberal theoreticians—be clear, but be cautious—have generated enormous confusion. In response, liberals have created two species of big ideas. The first, though genuinely bold, are esoteric; the second are designed for public consumption by engaged intellectuals who are so reluctant to say anything controversial that they wind up saying nothing that can be parsed or used.

The first sort of big ideas are produced in the academy and, crucially, *for* the academy. Books like *Strong Democracy*, *Liberal Equality* or *Spheres of Justice* by, respectively, Benjamin Barber, Amy Gutmann and Michael Walzer are written by theoreticians for theoreticians. Their arguments are not formulated, either by the authors or the authors' admirers, for broad public consumption. The preeminent effort to theorize a liberal agenda, *A Theory of Justice* by John Rawls, has been the subject of countless dissertations and symposia since its publication in 1971. People who call themselves Rawlsians, however, are always candidates for the faculty senate, not the U.S. Senate.

These books are difficult—hard to read, understand, summarize and popularize. That problem explains only a small part of the fact that they've left so few footprints on the world of contested elections and political advocacy. The people working at liberal magazines and think tanks are no less intellectually nimble than their conservative counterparts, who are constantly mining the books of Leo Strauss, Eric Voegelin, Russell Kirk and Friedrich von Hayek for policy advice—not to mention the attention they devote to even deader white males like Aristotle, Burke, Tocqueville or Madison.

The real problem is that the big ideas of campus liberalism are too *politically* difficult to translate into the vernacular. The conclusions that win assent in the faculty lounge would all require a *much* bigger welfare state—not only bigger than any that Americans have ever seen, but bigger than those that any country has ever seen. Liberal politicians and activists have no reason to object to this goal as a goal—if liberalism doesn't stand for a much bigger welfare state then it doesn't stand for anything at all.

But they do object to it as a tactic. It would be a colossal blunder for an American liberal to blurt out that what he really wants is to see Sweden's Social Democrats 20 GDP percentage points and then raise them 10. A country that gave the Socialist presidential candidate 2% of the vote in 1932, when more than one-fifth of the workforce was unemployed, must be brought along *very* carefully to embrace a dramatically larger welfare state. The political strategy is not only to build the welfare state brick by brick, but to sell it one brick at a time. As Arthur Schlesinger wrote in 1947, "There seems no inherent obstacle to the gradual advance of socialism in the United States through a series of New

Deals."[18] Tenured theoreticians' arguments are camouflaged by footnotes, bibliographies and appendices; liberal politicians and writers, who must confront public opinion in order to shape it, are determined to keep them hidden from view.

That being the case, we need to consider the possibility that the causes of liberalism's incoherence include deliberate political strategy as well as intellectual dereliction. We'll do so by returning to the question of welfare-state rights, examining how this idea has fared in the decades since FDR unveiled the Second Bill of Rights. Then we'll look at two other ways of rationalizing the welfare state, communitarianism and adhocracy.

RIGHTS
The Right to the Means to a Good Life

In November 2006, *The American Prospect* offered an answer to the what-does-liberalism-stand-for question it had posed in 2005. It ran an article by Bruce Ackerman and Todd Gitlin, "We Answer to the Name of Liberals," co-signed by 44 liberal intellectuals, including Tomasky; the sociologist Christopher Jencks; Robert Reich, Bill Clinton's first secretary of labor; and Arthur Schlesinger. "We reaffirm the great principle of liberalism: that every citizen is entitled by right to the elementary means to a good life," the article proclaimed. These elementary means include "rights to housing, affordable health care, equal opportunity for employment, and fair wages, as well as physical security and a sustainable environment for ourselves and future generations."[19]

The assertion of rights to the means to a good life contained different particulars from FDR's Second Bill of Rights, but the substantive differences are small, and the spirit of the two enterprises is identical. That such a reaffirmation, along with the one to which Cass Sunstein devoted an entire book, was needed suggests that the great principle of liberalism has not worn particularly well over the decades since FDR's speech. The right to the means to a good life creates political problems for which liberalism has not offered a convincing solution.

Liberalism's protean understanding of rights complicates and ultimately dooms the idea of a principled refusal to elevate any benefit that we would like people to enjoy to the status of an inviolable right. This is not just a hypothetical slippery slope. The historian Robert H. Wiebe examined how rightsization played out long after FDR codified it:

> During the 1980s, concepts of rights expanded far faster than the law allowed. . . . Among their most enthusiastic publicists, rights changed as needs changed. The essence of democracy one philosopher [C.B. Macpherson] declared, was "not only 'one man, one vote' but also 'one man, one equal effective right to live as fully humanly as he may wish.'" A legal theorist [Roberto Unger] identified rights with "the infinite quality of the personality . . . to transcend the limited imaginative and social worlds that it constructs." Translating grand propositions such as these into a bill of particulars had an almost arbitrary quality about it, as if the same person might well compile a different list on another day. "What I'm talking about now," Elaine Jones of the NAACP said in an interview, "is basic human rights, which include the right to a safe environment, health care, the right to participate in the electoral process fairly, to have employment, the right to some significant opportunity in training and education."[20]

A Matter of Right

Liberalism, according to this rendition, stands for the belief that every genuine need corresponds to a right to have that need addressed. Additionally, and even more happily, it holds out the hope that sufficient examination of any want will eventually reveal that it, too, is a kind of need, the satisfaction of which will further expand the catalog of rights. At first glance, the political advantages of this position are overwhelming. How could voters not be grateful for liberals' assurances that any day might be Christmas, when they'll wake up to find a shiny new entitlement under the tree?

Liberals, however, have a reason for hesitantly proclaiming the right to well-being—their awareness that discovering an endless list of new rights has significant political dangers as well as advantages. The problem is twofold. First, many citizens refuse to understand the issue in terms of "society" providing jobs, health care, housing, education, rest, recreation and adventure. They insist on noticing that for the government to recognize these rights it must impose taxes and regulations to confer all the benefits it has promised. Not everyone can come out ahead as a result of these compulsory transfers, and many voters will fear ending up as conscripted benefactors rather than fortunate beneficiaries.

Secondly, awarding the status of rights to an endless list of means to well-being says something unsettling to these already nervous voters. If these rights really *are* rights, then they're going to trump every competing political consideration. The meaning of such rights is that those people who, through their own efforts and resources, cannot—or at any rate do not—secure adequate jobs, health care, housing, education, rest, recreation and adventure are entitled to the "surplus" wealth of those who already enjoy such benefits. This claim is stronger than the latter's right to keep what they, selfishly or naively, thought of as "theirs." (The one item that never gets included on any list of rights to the means to well-being is the right to keep some inviolable portion of private wealth or income, regardless of the lofty purposes social reformers wish to make of it.)

This dilemma—how to make the right to well-being sound like a blessing without simultaneously making it sound like a threat—has led liberals to hedge their rhetorical bets. They often speak of providing government benefits as "a matter of right," a phrase that invites everyone to hear whatever they need to hear.[21] It would be merely tautological, on the one hand, for the government to deliver benefits as a matter of right because they *are* rights. Alternatively, if the government is giving out economic benefits as if they *were* rights, the formulation is a polite way of saying— they're not. The needy and the less needy are each encouraged to believe that they have the decisive claim on the less-needy's wealth. One of them must be wrong, unless what liberalism really stands for is jettisoning the law of non-contradiction. The Ackerman-Gitlin formulation seems less equivocal than the "matter of right" one, although being "entitled by right" to economic benefits retains some ambiguity: Does it mean "as a matter of right" or "in recognition of the right"?

The unqualified assertion of rights to well-being doesn't have this problem. It does, though, have the theoretical problem of being unable to explain the source of those rights, or on what basis a person convinced he really, really needs something for a good life can be told decisively that, sorry, the right to it simply does not exist. The corresponding political problem is that rights-based claims will proliferate endlessly, an ominous prospect for voters who fear they are the ones against whom these expansive and expensive claims will be made.

Rights and Goals

The implications of rights to material or even psychological well-being are problematic in another way. Once liberalism has fashioned a mechanism capable of turning any policy goal into a right, there is no way to keep it from running the assembly line in the other direction and turning any right into one more policy goal.

In 1994 the federal department of Housing and Urban Development was forced to rein in some of its investigators after weeks of terrible publicity and angry criticism. In New York City; Berkeley, California; Seattle and several other places, HUD's enforcement of the Fair Housing Act had become remarkably aggressive. Enacted in 1968 to prohibit discriminating against home buyers or renters on the basis of race, the law was enlarged by Congress in 1988 to outlaw discrimination against the handicapped, defined as a person with a "physical or mental impairment," but not including someone engaged in the "current illegal use of or addiction to a controlled substance." That distinction meant that the category of persons protected from housing discrimination included the mentally ill; alcoholics, since they do not use a controlled, illegal substance; and former drug users or recovering drug addicts, a group whose distinction from active drug users is often subtle and ephemeral.[22]

As interpreted and enforced by HUD under Pres. Clinton, Secretary Henry Cisneros, and Assistant Secretary Roberta Achtenberg, the working definition of "discrimination" became equally capacious. Citizens who opposed plans for halfway houses and assisted living facilities in their neighborhoods found themselves accused of violating the housing rights of the disabled. Their political opposition threatened to visit illegal "coercion, intimidation and interference" on the mentally ill, according to the non-profit organizations that wanted to build the facilities. These advocates charged that "organized opposition to homeless shelters, drug treatment centers, and residences for the mentally ill violates the rights of the disabled."[23]

Asst. Sec. Achtenberg later argued that when housing advocacy groups made their complaints to HUD, the department's investigators had a legal obligation to investigate the political opponents of the facilities. The zeal of some of the investigations seems to have been animated by something far more adversarial than a mere sense of professional duty, however. In New York, three residents, opposed to plans for a new residence for the mentally ill in a neighborhood that already had several homeless shelters and drug rehabilitation centers, formed the Irving Place Community Coalition to lobby against it. Community Access, the non-profit that wanted to establish the residence, filed a complaint with HUD. In the course of the department's investigation, its staff members "demanded that [the three residents] turn over their personal diaries, petitions and phone messages, and threatened them with $50,000 fines," according to *The New York Times*. After the investigation of the Coalition began, "The whole group disappeared," according to one of its leaders. "People said: 'I wrote to the Governor. Can I be investigated?' It really frightened people, and they never came back to another meeting." In Berkeley, a similar group opposed a similar facility, and "HUD investigators demanded every article, flier and letter to the editor that [its leaders] had written—as well as the minutes from every public meeting at which any of the three spoke."[24]

Achtenberg later complained about the "high level of irresponsible conduct on the part of the media," which made it look "as if somehow HUD was on some kind of mission to intimidate people who oppose group homes being placed in their neighborhood." The opposition, however, included not just *Wall Street Journal* editorialists, but the Democratic congresswoman whose district includes Irving Place, who said that using the Fair Housing Act to "silence opposition" was "going beyond the limit." Even the director of Community Access, the agency that had complained about the Irving Place Coalition "said he was 'surprised by the level of intrusion' by HUD, adding that his agency 'didn't mean to bring innocent citizens into the spotlight and have their personal lives investigated.'"[25]

Achtenberg herself took the position that the HUD investigations had been indefensible, telling a friendly interviewer in 1995 that the actions that had been investigated were all "protected political activity," and she had put "a binding policy in place" to prevent such investigations from recurring once she learned about them. She had taken a more equivocal position in a *Washington Post* op-ed at the height of the controversy in August 1994, however. She wrote, "Where the efforts of neighbors or others *appear primarily directed* toward achieving a governmental decision—such as denial of a zoning variance—their behavior will *most likely* be considered protected free speech, no matter what their motives may be." (Emphasis added.) More generally, according to Achtenberg, "In every case of this nature, HUD walks a tightrope between free speech and fair housing. We are ever mindful of the need to maintain the proper balance between these rights."[26]

Democracy and the Welfare State

The aggressive tactics of the HUD investigators reflect something deeper than a casual disdain for the Constitution. It is the odd theoretical tension between modern liberalism and democracy. Odd, because liberals always insist they are on the side of the little guy. As Harry Truman said in his 1948 acceptance speech, "the Democratic Party is the people's party," while the Republican Party "favors the privileged few and not the common everyday man."[27] Mario Cuomo paid his party the same compliment at their convention 36 years later: The difference between Democrats and Republicans is that Republicans believe that "some of the old, some of the young, some of the weak [must be] left behind by the side of the trail. . . . Their policies divide the nation—into the lucky and the left-out, into the royalty and the rabble." Democrats, however, "believe that we can make it all the way with the whole family intact."[28]

This solicitude for the ordinary American, however, often results in a lofty disregard for the prosaic mechanisms connecting that American to the government and giving him the means to resist or redirect it. This attitude goes back to the Progressives, whose impatience with Madison's balky Constitution occasionally gave rise to surprisingly illiberal sentiments. Herbert Croly was the author of one of the most important books of the Progressive era, *The Promise of American Life*, written in 1909, five years before he became one of the founding editors of *The New Republic*. In 1927 Croly wrote, "whatever the dangers of fascism, it has at any rate substituted movement for stagnation, purposive behavior for drifting, and visions of [a] great future for collective pettiness and discouragement."[29]

Liberals rarely wander *that* far off message. John Dewey's one memorable phrase—"the cure for the ailments of democracy is more democracy"—sounds far more benign. As his biographer Alan Ryan points out, however, Dewey understood democracy to encompass not merely "a political system in which governments elected by majority vote made such decisions as they could." It was, rather, "a society permeated by a certain kind of character, by a mutual regard of all citizens for all other citizens, and by an ambition to make society both a greater unity and one that reflected the full diversity of its members' talents and aptitudes."[30]

Things get sticky because this imperative to pursue *more* democracy, in the expansive sense Ryan describes, turns out to be entirely compatible with curtailing or even discarding *mere* democracy. As Dewey wrote in 1937, "Universal suffrage, recurring elections, responsibility of those who are in political power to the voters, and the other factors of democratic government are means that have been found expedient for realizing democracy as the truly human way of living. They are not a final end and a final value. They are to be judged on the basis of their contribution to [that] end."[31]

According to Robert Wiebe, such "heavy emphasis on results" attenuates the democratic process. He criticizes more recent liberal theoreticians: "After the philosopher Amy Gutmann inserts in her model of the just constitution 'universal welfare rights and a relatively equal distribution of income,' among other entitlements, governments are largely administrative, and elections ritual." The paradox is that making an extensive welfare state a prerequisite for democracy has the effect of delegitimizing democratic deliberation *about* the welfare state. Voices and votes against it become subversive and undemocratic; democracy's ability to make a difference contracts as the list of democracy's prerequisites expands.[32]

The effort to rule full consideration of this central domestic policy question out of bounds is neither recent nor tangential to liberalism. Sidney Milkis says, "New Dealers did not view the welfare state as a partisan issue. The reform program of the 1930s was defined as a 'constitutional' matter, which required eliminating partisanship about the national government's obligation to provide economic security for the American people."[33] One of the foundations of Arthur Schlesinger's cold-war liberalism was his belief that by containing the Soviet Union, "we have a good chance to test the possibilities of a peaceful transition into a not undemocratic socialism." Schlesinger was circumspect enough to avoid elaborating the distinction between democratic socialism and socialism that was merely "not undemocratic."[34]

What Affirmative Action Says About the "Rightsization" of Liberalism

This balancing of old, boring rights imagined by the naïve to be inalienable with the sort of new and interesting rights to which the New Deal opened the door is an endless process. Its ability to produce results as surprising as the federal harassment of citizens for organizing against a new homeless shelter in their neighbor-hood is perennial. In 1972, for example, the Equal Employment Opportunity Commission ruled that it was racially discrimina-tory for employers to fire employees who had been convicted of serious crimes. A "substantially disproportionate percentage of persons convicted of 'serious crimes' are minority group persons," it contended. Besides, some "serious" crimes are less serious than others. Thus, non-discriminatory employment practices cannot encompass "automatic discharge for any 'serious' crime." Rather, the employer must demonstrate that dismissal of a convicted criminal was undertaken after considering factors such as employ-ment history and the "job-relatedness of the conviction." Firing an embezzler from a job as a teller probably leaves a bank unex-posed to charges of discriminatory practices, as would a fireworks factory's decision not to employ an arsonist. Whether the bank could fire the arsonist, or the factory the embezzler, is far less certain.[35]

Similarly, the country was surprised to learn in 1989 that the federal Department of Labor had, for nearly a decade, pressured state employment services to "race-norm" the results of job skills tests before referring test takers to private employers. "Some forty states using the [General Aptitude Test Battery] had done as Labor counseled," according to Terry Eastland, "with the number of tests being normed climbing into the millions every year." Race-norming entailed reporting how test takers had scored *rela-tive to others in the same racial group*, but not their test scores in absolute terms or relative to all other test takers. "Thus a black, a Hispanic and a white achieving the same raw score of 300 (in one example based on the Labor Department's conversion score table) were given the race-normed scores of 83, 67 and 45, respectively." The test itself was not biased, according to the National Academy of Sciences, but its racially disparate results were unacceptable to Labor. As was true of HUD's rough tactics against neighborhood groups, race-norming was condemned and abandoned shortly after its existence and extensive use became publicly known.[36]

Generally speaking, affirmative action has been controversial for a long time, but not in a way that has had much overlap with arguments about the welfare state. Close scrutiny, however, will reveal that the two liberal policies rest on the same New Deal foundation.

We can trace how civil rights based in nature gave way to ones based on history in the arc of three presidential speeches. Pres. Kennedy gave the first, a televised address from the Oval Office on June 11, 1963, after he had ordered the National Guard to guarantee the entrance of two black students to the University of Alabama. He made it clear that fraternity and, above all, equality were the antidotes required to end racism. Kennedy closed the speech by invoking the "color-blind Constitution," the term Justice John Harlan used in his famous dissent from *Plessy v. Ferguson*, the 1896 Supreme Court decision that upheld the constitutionality of "separate but equal" public facilities. Kennedy spoke of the nation's founding principle, "that all men are created equal, and that the rights of every man are diminished when the rights of one man are threatened." And he expressed his intention to ask Congress "to make a commitment . . . to the proposition that race has no place in American life or law."[37]

The bill Kennedy advocated was signed into law by his successor as the Civil Rights Act of 1964. Though JFK didn't live to see its enactment, his legacy played an important role in the political campaign on behalf of the bill. Just five days after Dallas, Pres. Johnson told a joint session of Congress, "[N]o memorial oration or eulogy could more eloquently honor President Kennedy's memory than the earliest possible passage of the civil rights bill for which he fought so long." The bill's advocates consistently echoed Kennedy's emphasis on the ideal of a color-blind Constitution. When opponents of the bill expressed the fear that Title

VII, its section prohibiting discrimination by employers, would engender workplace barriers to whites, Sen. Hubert Humphrey replied, "Title VII prohibits discrimination. In effect, it says that race, religion and national origin are not to be used as the basis for hiring and firing." According to a defense of Title VII published by the Leadership Council on Civil Rights, "[P]referential treatment of Negroes or any minority group would violate this section. Its whole point is that all workers should be treated equally."[38]

The second speech, delivered only two years after Kennedy's and one year after the Civil Rights Act was signed into law, was the first clear sign that the color-blind principle had served its purpose and liberals would now begin to qualify it. Pres. Johnson gave the commencement address at historically black Howard University on June 4, 1965. In it, he announced "the next and the more profound stage of the battle for civil rights," in which we seek "not just equality as a right and a theory but equality as a fact and equality as a result." Johnson devoted most of that speech to extolling how Great Society programs, enacted and envisioned, would go beyond the theory to the fact of equality by finding and fixing the "root causes" of poverty.[39]

It quickly became clear, however, that securing equality as a result would mean not just going beyond but curtailing equality as a right, notwithstanding liberals' repeated and insistent pledges before 1965 that color-blindness was an inviolable principle. The report of the White House Conference on Equal Employment Opportunity, held in August 1965, stressed that the "conferees were eager to move beyond the letter of the law to a sympathetic discussion of those affirmative actions required to make the legal requirement of equal opportunity an operating reality."[40]

The Equal Employment Opportunity Commission, the federal regulatory agency created by the Civil Rights Act of 1964, immediately set out to demonstrate that the most expeditious way to move beyond the letter of the law is to ignore it. An early

EEOC memorandum said, "Under the literal language of Title VII . . . an employer is not required to redress an imbalance in his work force which is the result of past discrimination." Rather than wait for Congress to amend the law, the Commission forged ahead with its own "affirmative theory of nondiscrimination," under which "Negroes are recruited, hired, transferred, and promoted in line with their ability and numbers." The "anti-preferential hiring provisions [of Title VII] are a big zero, a nothing, a nullity. They don't mean anything at all to us," one EEOC staffer said.[41]

In the 1970s the EEOC, and the civil rights movement generally, got the courts to embrace its efforts to interpret away the inconvenient provisions of civil rights legislation. In *United Steelworkers of America v. Weber*, one of their triumphs, the Supreme Court ruled in 1979 that what mattered was not the letter but the spirit and intention of the Civil Rights Act, which, according to Justice Brennan's majority opinion, was to address "the plight of the Negro in our economy," and to open "opportunities for Negroes in occupations which have been traditionally closed to them." Thus, the law afforded no relief to Brian Weber, a white worker at Kaiser Aluminum, who was kept out of a training program to improve employees' skills and prospects after his employer and union decided to inoculate themselves against EEOC litigation by requiring that 50% of the program trainees be black.[42]

In 1995 Pres. Clinton gave the third speech, one defending affirmative action against its critics, who were growing in number and determination. This was his "mend it, don't end it" speech. Clinton's argument did, however, allude to the prospect of ending affirmative action. Any particular affirmative action program, whether in employment, education or public contracting, "must be retired" as soon as it has succeeded, he said. And affirmative action, in general, "should not go on forever" and "should be retired when its job is done."[43]

The fact is, however, that in the absence of a clear definition of what it means for affirmative action's job to be done, it will *never* be retired, except through the political victories of its opponents. We see here liberalism's defining shortcoming in action. Even as liberals cannot say how big the welfare state should be, only that it should always be bigger than it is at the moment, they cannot say how long affirmative action should go on, just that its rightful conclusion should not take place today, or tomorrow, or soon, but only at some unspecified date far, far beyond the horizon.

In its 2003 decision upholding the University of Michigan Law School's affirmative action program, the Supreme Court said, "We expect that 25 years from now, the use of racial preferences will no longer be necessary. . . ."[44] Since this ruling came 25 years after the Court first asserted (in its *Bakke* decision of 1978) that affirmative action in college admissions could be squared with equality before the law, it would take heroic optimism to circle 2028 on the calendar in anticipation that affirmative action's defenders will declare victory and go home. Indeed, the "unanimous opinion" of a panel convened in 2008 by the American Educational Research Association was that there is "no chance in hell" to phase out affirmative action by 2028.[45]

Even as he promised to retire affirmative action when its work was done, Pres. Clinton characterized that work in a way that makes its completion a virtual impossibility. One of the "standards of fairness" to which he vowed to make all affirmative action programs conform was, "No quotas in theory or practice." In doing so, Clinton availed himself of a straw-man argument on behalf of affirmative action, distinguishing heavy-handed and indiscriminate quotas from affirmative action programs that are, in words the Supreme Court used to praise the University of Michigan Law School's admissions policies, "flexible," "individualized" and "holistic." Extending that logic, Catherine Horn of the University of Houston told the American Educational Research Association conference that the way for colleges to resolve any tensions between their desires for highly selective entering classes and demographically correct ones is through the "reconceptualization of merit."[46]

No matter how many procedures or management seminar buzzwords get wrapped around an affirmative action program, however, the fact remains that its *raison d'être* is to "rectify" statistical "disparities" among various demographic subcategories. Pres. Clinton, for example, disputed the claims of those who say "that even good affirmative action programs are no longer needed" by citing statistical evidence of "the persistence of the kind of bigotry that can affect the way we think even if we're not conscious of it, in hiring and promotion and business and educational decisions." As an example he cited a study showing that white males "make up 43 percent of our work force, but hold 95 percent" of "senior management positions" in our "nation's largest companies."

The disparity-free America that finally retires its affirmative action programs may be described in both mathematical and political terms. In numbers, that America will be a place where every occupation, every slice of the income distribution—every category, in general, that suggests a more or less favorable station in which to spend one's life—will be an exact demographic miniature of the society as a whole. If white males are 43% of the work force, they should be 43% of corporate big shots—no more, no less. Similarly, the percentage of Puerto Rican orthodontists should equal the percentage of Puerto Ricans in the population, so that a Puerto Rican is as likely as anyone else to be an orthodontist, and an orthodontist is as likely as anyone else to be a Puerto Rican.

In words, the goal is that America, whose history came to be seen by liberals during and after the 1960s as a chronicle of the victimization of the weak by the strong, should reconstitute itself as the society that would have come into being if there had never been slavery, racism, sexism, homophobia, ageism, bigotry or discrimination. America will, finally, be a just society when every advantage and disadvantage that can be traced to its historical sins has been eradicated. In 1978, for example, the four most liberal Supreme Court justices who voted in favor of affirmative action in the *Bakke* decision said they were simply trying to put "minority [medical school] applicants in the position they would have been in if not for the evil of racial discrimination." As the Hoover Institution economist Thomas Sowell has argued, "the idea of restoring groups to where they would have been— and *what* they would have been" if past discrimination had never taken place, "presupposes a range of knowledge that no one has ever possessed."

> What would the average Englishman be like today "but for" the Norman conquest? What would the average Japanese be like "but for" the enforced isolation of Japan for two-and-a-half centuries under the Tokugawa shoguns? What would the Middle East be like "but for" the emergence of Islam? In any other context besides preferential-policy issues, the presumption of knowing the answers to such questions would be regarded as ridiculous, even as intellectual speculation, much less as a basis for serious legal action.[47]

The planted axiom is that there is no difference in the economic, educational or occupational profile of the nation's various sub-populations that is not ultimately attributable to bigotry. The way for defenders of affirmative action to refute this objection as a *reductio ad absurdum* argument is to lay out the non-absurd limits affirmative action must observe. They never do. They are careful to say that affirmative action's purpose is to "reduce" intolerable disparities, rather than "eliminate" them, but they are also careful never to describe the point short of their elimination at which the work of reducing disparities is supposed to stop. The plight of the "under-represented" needs to be addressed by curtailing the advantages of the "over-repre-sented," but affirmative action's advocates never make clear what it means to complete this task, other than creating a society in which every group is represented—period—exactly and propor-tionally in every walk of life.

As a result, the mending of affirmative action is as nebulous as the ending of it. Affirmative action "should be changed now to take care of those things that are wrong," said Pres. Clinton, but determining which things those are is very hard. At *some* point the Brian Webers of the world, whites who see their career opportuni-ties curtailed by programs that advance the spirit and intent of the civil rights laws, will receive protection from affirmative action policies that go too far. But that point, like the temporal conclu-sion of affirmative action, is far off and hard to specify. "It is not necessary in these cases," the Court said in *Weber*, "to define the line of demarcation between permissible and impermissible affir-mative action plans; it suffices to hold that the challenged Kaiser-USWA plan falls on the permissible side of the line."[48]

A government of laws, not men, needs to justify its actions with arguments more compelling and respectful to the governed than such "because we say so" pronouncements. It's impossible to see how an affirmative action plan can be called permissible in the absence of criteria defining what would make one impermissible. If the Court doesn't know—or won't say—where the demarcation line is, the holding that a particular plan falls on one side of it is an assertion, not a conclusion.

Perhaps sensing the difficulties with this position, the majority opinion goes on to suggest the general vicinity of the line of demarcation, saying that "the [Kaiser-USWA] plan does not unnecessarily trammel the interests of white employees, nei-ther requiring the discharge of white workers and their replace-ment with new black hirees, nor creating an absolute bar to the advancement of white employees since half of those trained in the program will be white." In other words, Brian Weber still has a job and still has some chance for promotion, just a smaller chance than he would if he were black or if his employer had color-blind personnel policies. The only relief the Court can offer him is that he should stop complaining and take comfort from the justices' determination that while his interests were trammeled, they were done so *necessarily*.[49]

The astonishingly quick and complete transformation of the Civil Rights Act of 1964, from a law requiring all citizens be treated equally to a policy requiring that they be treated unequally, is one of the most audacious bait-and-switch operations in American political history. Specifying what affirmative action says about liberalism would require knowing to what extent the liberals who did the baiting before 1965 anticipated or intended the switching that came after. In the absence of confessions delivered under the influence of truth serum, it can be noted only that there is a thunderous lack of evidence for the null hypothesis, which would hold that the post-1965 repudiation of color-blindness was an event logically and causally unrelated to the pre-1965 advocacy of that principle. Such evidence would consist of expressions of shock and dismay over the emergence of affirmative action by liberals who spoke fervently on behalf of the color-blind principle before 1965. Some liberals *were* irreconcilable on the question, but sooner or later they were all assimilated into the neo-conservative ranks, as it became clear that heterogeneity of opinion about affirmative action would not be tolerated by and for liberals in good standing. Sen. Joseph Lieberman, for example, apologized abjectly for his past criticism of affirmative action as soon as Al Gore selected him to be his running mate in 2000.[50]

As for the rest, they kept their misgivings, if any, to themselves. During the Senate debate on the Civil Rights Act, Sen. Humphrey dramatically promised to "start eating the [bill's] pages one after another" if its opponents could find "any language" requiring quotas. Immediately after the bill's passage, civil rights champions began, energetically and successfully, to tease out this forbidden meaning. But Humphrey never dined on any of the law's provisions.[51]

The protean quality that allowed liberals to pivot so quickly from embracing to repudiating color-blindness derives from the right to well-being. Rights, which aren't grounded in nature but determined by the evolving flow of history, can be whatever we need them to be. It would be nice to tell Brian Weber that treating him differently because of the color of his skin is intolerable—we remember vaguely having once said something in favor of a color-blind Constitution—but the government has a lot of important things it's trying to do, there are always going to be complications, and people need to be patient and realistic. The ideal of a government that exists to secure rights and guarantee equal justice under the law gives way to a government that brokers an endless series of accommodations with an endless array of interest groups. Seen in this light, affirmative action is not some mutation of the liberal principle but the perfect expression of it.

Welfare Rights

As noted, the political theories of John Rawls have had little discernible impact on off-campus liberalism. One exception is Matthew Yglesias, a journalist who has married Clintonian rhetoric to Rawlsian postulates. Insofar as those whose native intelligence and talents are unlikely to carry them very far in the world are "willing to work hard, contribute to society as best they can, and abide by the rules of the game, they deserve a *fair share* of society's wealth—the highest standard of living we can manage to arrange for them." In other words, it's wrong for people to lead "crappy lives" just because they got low scores on the Scholastic Aptitude Test.[52]

This modification of Rawls suggests why there are so few Rawlsians in American politics. Unlike Yglesias, Rawls treats the dispositions to work hard and play by the rules as innate qualities that get apportioned unequally in the great lottery of life. People who happen to lack those dispositions deserve the highest possible standard of living, no less so than people who happen to lack keen intelligence, winning personalities or good looks. A person who devotes his life to counting blades of grass opts for a colossally pointless life, but Rawls insists that a just society must give the highest priority to making sure that the grass counter, too, should live as agreeably as possible.[53]

The political problem is not that Rawls was saying something that most liberals rejected. It is that he made explicit a sentiment most liberals had learned from harsh experience to keep to themselves. "You can't force somebody to work if they [sic] don't want to work," Sen. George McGovern said in 1972, nicely compressing several chapters of *A Theory of Justice* into one sentence. (McGovern's point had been made with greater animation at a Senate hearing in 1970 by Beulah Sanders, vice chairman of the National Welfare Rights Organization. She testified, "You can't force me to work! You'd better give me something better than I'm getting on welfare." Another woman told the senators that she would rather see her children dead than for them to endure the humiliation of being forced to take a job or enroll in a training program as a condition for receiving welfare benefits.) Thus, said McGovern, "I would just provide that every person in this country is given a certain minimum income. If he wants to work in addition to that, he keeps what he earns." McGovern's "demogrant" proposal, which codified these impulses into a guaranteed income plan, proved so controversial and murky that McGovern abandoned it by the time he won the Democratic nomination.[54]

Bill Clinton was the coordinator for the McGovern campaign in Texas where the Democratic nominee wound up getting

33% of the vote, only slightly worse than the 37.5% he received nationwide. When he ran for president himself 20 years later, Clinton's incessant talk about helping Americans who work hard and play by the rules was clearly designed to inoculate his campaign from lingering suspicions that the Democrats still believed in a McGovernite, no-questions-asked welfare policy. Clinton's even more explicit promise during the 1992 campaign to "end welfare as we know it" was fulfilled, far more sweepingly than he intended, when the Republican Congress presented him with a bill in 1996 that replaced the Aid to Families with Dependent Children program, under which those in financial need were entitled to welfare benefits, with the Temporary Assistance to Needy Families (TANF) program.

The key word was "temporary"—the federal government would continue to assist the poor through grants to the states, but the law imposed a lifetime limit of 60 months of welfare benefits for any recipient. The benefits were, furthermore, conditional on taking jobs or participating in training programs. Pres. Clinton vetoed two versions of the bill in 1996, but signed a marginally less stringent version into law less than three months before the general election. Clinton was denounced, often hysterically, for ceding so much ground to the Republicans. *The Nation* predicted the abolition of AFDC would bring "massive and deadly poverty, sickness, and all manner of violence. People will die, businesses will close, infant mortality will soar, everyone who can will move. Working- and middle-class communities all over America will become scary, violent wastelands."[55]

This revulsion against parsimony was reflected in a 1998 *New York Times* article on Idaho. Noting that the state's restrictive policies had reduced its welfare rolls by 77% over the preceding four years, the article quoted a researcher who called Idaho "the worst place in the nation to be poor." The criterion implied by that resonant phrase is that each jurisdiction within the United States should compete to be the best place in the nation to be poor, even as the country strives to be the best place in the world to be poor.[56]

The historians Fred Siegel and Vincent Cannato have shown that John Lindsay devoted his two terms as New York's mayor (1965 to 1973) to winning that competition. During Lindsay's first six years in Gracie Mansion, the number of New Yorkers receiving welfare doubled to 1,165,000. This increase was a matter of policy and ideology much more than a result of circumstance. The highest priority of Lindsay's first social services commissioner was to increase the number of people receiving welfare. His policies reflected the ascendance of a doctrine Siegel calls "dependent individualism," which simultaneously guaranteed an absolute right "to the lifestyle of one's choice (regardless of the social cost) with an equally fundamental right to be supported at state expense."[57] The prominent sociologist Christopher Jencks made the case for this worldview in a 1965 article criticizing the controversial "Moynihan Report":

> If [poor black families] are matriarchal by choice (i.e., if lower-class men, women, and children truly prefer a family consisting of a mother, children, and a series of transient males) then it is hardly the federal government's proper business to try to alter this choice. Instead, the government ought to invent ways of providing such families with the same physical and psychic necessities of life available to other kinds of families.[58]

Ten years after the demise of AFDC, the worst thing *The Nation* could find to say about its replacement was that "we know very little about the fate of those moved off welfare," an epistemological problem that would have been obviated by the descent into barbarism the magazine had predicted.[59] Whatever welfare reform says about liberals' clairvoyance, it sharpens the question about what they stand for. A significant minority within the liberal camp acquiesced to the abolition of AFDC in 1996, and most liberals subsequently accepted the idea that welfare reform worked out pretty well. This concession seems to suggest the possibility of a limiting principle in liberalism. "Welfare should be a second chance, not a way of life," Clinton often said, both as a presidential candidate and after his election.[60]

It is difficult, however, to tease out what exactly is limiting or principled about this limiting principle. Yglesias is blunt: "[F]rom the beginning the promise to 'end welfare as we know it' was primarily a *political* gambit," one which has been "tremendously successful" because "it vastly improved the overall prospects for progressive politics in America." The biggest problem with AFDC was that it was "massively unpopular," according to Yglesias, and the public's disapproval of that program "hobbled" the "whole idea of the activist state." Happily, "[E]liminating [AFDC] has *vastly* increased the public's willingness to contemplate new programs and initiatives and it accomplished that without being nearly as harmful to the poor as opponents predicted it would be at the time."[61]

The New Republic's editors concurred. Because of the 1996 law, "welfare-bashing has lost its political resonance. . . . [and] welfare reform has expanded the constituency for activist government. Democrats now have more political room to fight Republican austerity—and to propose, in its place, a stronger safety net." Rather than indicating where liberals want to establish the limits of the welfare state, the abolition of AFDC was a tactical retreat designed to further the strategic goal of pushing those boundaries outward, ever outward.[62]

COMMUNITARIANISM
The Common Good

Michael Tomasky lent his signature and the pages of *The American Prospect* to the Ackerman-Gitlin article that called the right to the means to well-being the great principle of liberalism. Under his own byline, however, Tomasky not only came up with a different description of liberalism's big idea, but one that cannot be harmonized with the great principle of welfare rights stretching back to FDR's famous speech in 1944.

According to Tomasky, "Democrats need to become the party of the common good," by attempting "to enlist citizens in large projects to which everyone contributes and from which everyone benefits." Liberalism needs this orientation because liberals since the 1960s have been "united in only two beliefs, and they demand that American citizens believe in only two things: diversity and rights." The "rightsization" of liberalism that was married to the insistence on diversity in the 1960s compromised liberalism's political appeal. An exaggerated concern for the rights of welfare recipients and criminals, according to Tomasky, made liberalism vulnerable when conservatives appealed to the common sense of the common citizen. He complains that conservatives' arguments against welfare cheats and coddled criminals were "manipulative," but concedes they weren't "entirely untrue."[63]

Tomasky is not the first political thinker to be beguiled by the concept of the common good, and then encounter difficulty in trying to make it clear. His problem is the usual one—he wants the common good to be enveloping without being restricting. "Liberal governance is about demanding of citizens that they balance self-interest with common interest," he says. Fair enough, but on what *basis* are we supposed to pursue this balance? How will we know whether or not we're getting it right?[64]

Tomasky clearly believes that liberalism, and America, suffer because centrifugal forces have become far stronger than centripetal ones, but his call for correcting this imbalance is hortatory rather than clarifying. "[W]e're all in this . . . together," Tomasky writes, so "we have to pull together, make some sacrifices, and, just sometimes, look beyond our own interests to solve our problems and create the future." One suspects that Tomasky is more interested in the cohesion of the liberal coalition than

the coherence of his argument when he does cite a clear particular: the PATCO strike of 1981. The sinners against the common
good were *not*, however, the air-traffic controllers who broke the
law, threatened the transportation system with chaos, and put
thousands of travelers at risk in order to extract higher salaries.
Tomasky is apparently satisfied that these actions were all consistent with the liberal imperative for citizens "to look beyond
their own self-interest and work for a greater common interest."
Rather, and predictably, the villains were Pres. Reagan for firing
the strikers, and the "TV loudmouths" who "aped" his "line"
about the strike's illegality.[65]

Togetherness

Tomasky's position—selfishness is bad, except when it's good—
partakes of the larger confusions of communitarianism, whose
salience within liberal thinking has grown during the past two
decades. Communitarians recoil from the prospect of "a society of
unencumbered individuals who press claims of individual rights
without limit," according to James Ceaser's definition. They view
the politics built by and for such individuals as artificially derived
from abstract theorizing about natural rights, rather than formulated for "genuine human beings—human beings as they should
be—who are formed inside of particular communities in their
mutual interactions."[66]

Elizabeth Anderson, a philosophy professor at the University
of Michigan, suggested the surprising destinations to which communitarianism can carry liberalism when she likened Social Security to "the Amish practice of community barn-raising."

> When a young farmer starts out on his own farm, he does not
> build his barn all by himself, nor does he pay others to help
> him build it. Instead, he enlists his community to build it

without pay. This is no offense against self-sufficiency: he will reciprocate when other members of the community need their barns raised."

Inside the Amish community, cohesion and reciprocity accomplish the work that calculations of self-interest do in the raw world of capitalism outside it. In the larger, looser society, welfare state programs are the equivalent corrective to rugged individualism. "In a democracy, government is nothing more than citizens acting together, through state officials functioning as their agents. It's no different in principle from the barn-raising system. It's just on a vastly larger scale that, due to its size, requires an intermediary administrative apparatus."[67]

The difference between a barn-raising and the Social Security Administration is *not* just a matter of scale, however. The former could only take place in a small, tightly ordered community. The sanctions against community members who shirk their duties or disobey the rules acquire all their practical and moral force from the strict religious beliefs that bind the Amish together.

The problem is that liberalism—secular, skeptical and adamant about giving people the means and latitude to cultivate their distinctive talents and outlooks—typically abhors this kind of togetherness as narrow-minded and oppressive. After the 1980 Republican convention, *The Nation* published an article by the novelist E.L. Doctorow deriding Ronald Reagan's upbringing in such small downstate Illinois towns as "Galesburg, Monmouth and Dixon—just the sorts of places responsible for one of the raging themes of American literature, the soul-murdering complacency of our provinces. . . . The best and brightest fled all our Galesburgs and Dixons, if they could, but the candidate was not among them."[68]

Two months after it published Tomasky's essay on the common good, *The American Prospect* published several shorter critiques of it, two of which zeroed in on this problem of trying to have it both ways on the question of social solidarity. According to Amy Sullivan of *The Washington Monthly*, "It's hard to insist that how I behave in the economic sphere has implications for others, but when it comes to the social sphere, I can behave however I want and no one else should care. The idea of social communitarianism seems to tie liberals up in knots." Jedediah Purdy, a law professor at Duke, wrote, "Decades of real progress in tolerance and openness have made the country a much better one, but have also made us more nearly a country of strangers. I will take that combination in a heartbeat over a country of racial oppression, sexual inequality, and cultural conformity. But taking it means taking its costs. The equality of tolerance is not that far from indifference and very far from the equality of opportunity. . . . Whether we can have both is, at the very best, an open question."[69]

This liberal contradiction is older than Tomasky's article on the common good, older even than the emergence of communitarianism as a viewpoint with a name. In an essay written in 1965, the political philosopher Joseph Cropsey described how the conflict between individual expression and social cohesion inheres in liberalism: "Liberalism wishes simultaneously for the cultivation of men's idiosyncratic freedom and their coalescence into social community united by the intimate bonds of their natural brotherhood under the skin." The key word is "wishes." Real human beings, who are noble far less reliably than they are vain, self-interested and small-minded, are the sort of creatures unlikely to create or sustain this utopia. Liberalism's gorgeous mosaic of utterly diverse but utterly compatible individuals "may permit or require the cultivation and expression of all idiosyncratic differences," according to Cropsey, "but it could not tolerate differences of an invidious character. At least two classes of differences are invidious: differences of opinion as to good and bad, right and wrong, or just and unjust; and differences of interest. Whether a liberal society would be in fact a free society, and if not, whether the oppressions would conduce to the highest good, are grave questions unknown to liberalism."[70]

Spiritual Unemployment

It is easy to forget, in our age of ironic detachment, how earnestly liberals once labored to supplant Americans' private preoccupations with a greater concern for public affairs. A 1949 *New Republic* article calling for a national housing program said that "every town, metropolitan area and rural region in this country should have an energetic citizens' housing and planning organization, representing a cross-section of popular interests and professional knowledge, intimately acquainted with the operations of local agencies." Today's expectation, based on the trajectory of hundreds of regulatory bodies over the past century, is that the control of any such agency would quickly pass from the hands of high-minded experts and citizens, for whom it would take up too many evenings, and become an instrument dominated by interested parties, such as realtors and developers.[71]

During its ascendancy, however, liberalism held that self-interest would be transformed into an enhanced concern for the public good, which would express itself through greater political support for welfare state programs. Arthur Schlesinger, for example, ascribed the displacement of Eisenhower-era conservatism by New Frontier liberalism to the decline of narrow self-interest. Citing no evidence or examples, he asserted, "Farmers dislike the excesses of the farm program. Workers begin to wonder whether higher wages are the answer to everything. Businessmen know that everything else in society cannot be sacrificed to their own profits."[72]

The alchemy that changes self-interest into a commitment to social reform can even guide the character formation of the young.

In 1960 a can't-be-parodied article in *The New Republic* claimed that juvenile delinquency could be prevented by generous welfare programs, whose existence "might provide the youth of this country with living institutions which would represent a buffer against the prevailing values of the marketplace. If children could grow up believing that it is considered socially legitimate for them seriously to work toward group ends rather than individual ones (while not, thereby, losing 'individuality'), much of the competitiveness which now seems to promote cases of delinquency might be reduced."[73] The Jets and Sharks will lay down their switchblades once they come together in admiration of the Tennessee Valley Authority.

An America filled with people who work toward group ends without surrendering—while, in fact, cultivating—their individuality is the liberal vision of a society that replaces self-interest with self-expression. Self-interest is isolating and antisocial; FDR called for "the collaboration of all of us to provide, at the least, security for all of us. Those words 'freedom' and 'opportunity' do not mean a license to climb upwards by pushing other people down."[74] Self-expression, however, is socially benign and individually fulfilling. Saved from economic precariousness by a generous welfare state, individuals can develop and affirm their unique individual natures, infinitely diverse yet perfectly harmonious.

By the time John Kenneth Galbraith's *The Affluent Society* was published in 1958, some liberals had come to worry that the New Deal had worked too well. They were concerned that prosperity was a political problem for liberalism, and a psychological menace for Americans. The much-anticipated resumption of the Depression after 1945 never happened. Instead, the economy embarked on a long boom. When liberals got over their surprise, they took credit for Keynesian policies that, in their view, had relegated sharp economic downturns to the dustbin of history. Their corresponding fear was that the voters would see liberalism as an ideology that had served its purpose and had nothing more to say or contribute.

The broader social problem was that the alleviation of poverty, whether from government programs or the advance of capitalism, had liberated people to pursue private goals, which, though not necessarily antisocial, were apt to be *a*social in ways liberals did not approve of. Echoing *The Affluent Society*, *The Nation* editorialized in 1965, "The affluent tend to be mindless, shut off from reality, lost in a surfeit of silly possessions and sillier pursuits."[75] Galbraith himself was fond of the adage that we should comfort the afflicted and afflict the comfortable, "especially when they are comfortably, contentedly, even happily wrong."[76] The implication of that "especially" is that when the comfortable are *not* smug, or not even wrong, they still deserve to be afflicted just for the transgression of being comfortable.

In 1957, Arthur Schlesinger tried to solve both these problems, to give liberalism something to be about in a time of prosperity and to give economically secure citizens a reason to welcome its new reforms. He wrote that the New Deal's establishment of the welfare state and Keynesian management of the economy heralded the completion of the work of "quantitative liberalism." Its logical and necessary successor should be "qualitative liberalism," which would "oppose the drift into the homogenized society. It must fight spiritual unemployment as [quantitative liberalism] once fought economic unemployment. It must concern itself with the quality of popular culture and the character of lives to be lived in our abundant society."[77]

The fact that liberals once thought they could define, much less alleviate, "spiritual unemployment," confirms Amy Sullivan's warning that communitarianism ties liberalism in knots. Richard Pells, in an intellectual history of the post-war era, describes how liberal intellectuals professed "admiration for any signs of marginality, eccentricity [or] self-expression."[78] In *A Theory of*

Justice, Rawls tried to codify this disposition, arguing "democracy in judging each other's aims is the foundation of self-respect in a well-ordered society."[79] "Different strokes for different folks" is a meager philosophy, but what there is of it makes sense.

Liberals have rarely been content to let the matter rest there, however, feeling themselves entitled and obligated to judge their fellow citizens' aims and preferences, often harshly. The era that saw the discovery of spiritual unemployment was a time when social critics lined up to decry the "crisis" of conformity—in language so shrill and similar that they seemed, collectively, to be demonstrating their thesis.[80] It was not enough for an architecture critic to denounce the new suburbs; it was also necessary to castigate their inhabitants, people "eminently satisfied with the established ugliness. They do not even know it's ugly." This condescension was both inherent in and ruinous to the efforts of qualitative liberalism to address the "problems" of newly affluent people who were, in Alan Ehrenhalt's words, "somehow miserable without knowing it."[81]

FDR's Second Bill of Rights was hugely ambitious, but there were hints that it was a mission whose successful completion could be intelligibly described. An "American standard of living higher than any ever known before" was necessary, but not sufficient. It was also imperative that the affluence be all-encompassing, at least to the point that no one was left so far out of the prosperity as to lack the necessities of life: "We cannot be content, no matter how high that general standard of living may be, if some fraction of our people—whether it be one-third or one-fifth or one-tenth—is ill-fed, ill-clothed, ill-housed, and insecure." Implicitly, once even the tiniest fraction of our people—one-thousandth or one-millionth—are economically secure, we finally *can* be content.[82]

The War on Poverty was Lyndon Johnson's effort to continue and complete the task Roosevelt had placed before the nation. It's often forgotten that the Great Society was much bigger than the War on Poverty. The Great Society aimed to alleviate the suffering of those who were not affluent, but also the spiritual hollowness of those who were well-fed, well-clothed and well-housed. According to Johnson, the Great Society's aspiration was to "build a richer life of mind and spirit," a society not "condemned to a soulless wealth," but one where "man turned the exploits of his genius to the full enrichment of his life."

> The Great Society is a place where every child can find knowledge to enrich his mind and to enlarge his talents. It is a place where leisure is a welcome chance to build and reflect, not a feared cause of boredom and restlessness. It is a place where the city of man serves not only the needs of the body and the demands of commerce but the desire for beauty and the hunger for community.[83]

It was never clear, to put it gently, what the government was supposed to *do* about all this. LBJ insisted he did not envision a "massive program in Washington." Instead, he promised to assemble working groups of experts from around the world "to prepare a series of White House conferences and meetings" that would "begin to set our course toward the Great Society," whose realization will "require us to create new concepts of cooperation, a creative federalism, between the National Capital and the leaders of local communities."[84]

Very little of this elaborate planning ever happened and very little ever came of what did take place. The problem was not administrative follow-through or lack of political will. It was that no amount of money or determination could have wrested something tangible from fatuities about panels of experts figuring out how creative federalism would rescue a society condemned to soulless wealth. The ill-housed and ill-fed did not have to be persuaded that they needed help. The government employees who showed up promising a richer life of mind and spirit were certain to have a much tougher time talking their way past the front door.

A few Great Society cultural initiatives did emerge, such as the National Endowment for the Arts and the Corporation for Public Broadcasting. While they had their share of failures and successes, it's doubtful that even their most enthusiastic supporters believe there was a level of funding at which they could have banished Americans' boredom, restlessness and hunger for community. In the wake of the false start of Johnson's vague, grandiose venture, "the search for a richer life that LBJ identified with the Great Society is under way everywhere but in government," according to Jedediah Purdy, "in yoga and Pilates studios, churches and living rooms, pharmaceutical labs and psychotherapy clinics . . . the hundreds of thousands of places where billions of dollars and hours go into the unending search for meaning and satisfaction." Much of this national quest for self-discovery has been inane and solipsistic, and some of it has been harmful, but it would be as hard today to find liberals as conservatives who think the project would have turned out fine if only there had been more White House conferences issuing more reports written by experts.[85]

Affirmative Action and Callous Compassion

Returning to the question of affirmative action can help us understand communitarianism by examining compassion. It is not only the moral quality that liberals regard most highly, and which they believe demonstrates liberalism's moral superiority to conservatism most decisively. It is, they believe, a politically centripetal force that is morally admirable. Conservatives believe society is held together by enlightened self-interest, which leads to the formation and preservation of a social contract. Liberals doubt the decency and feasibility of this scheme to turn private vice into public virtue. They prefer to rely on the social cohesion created by the working of an elemental human sentiment.[86]

Convinced that moderation in advertising their compassion is no virtue, liberals act out the belief that mawkishness in the pursuit of political advantage is no vice. At the conclusion of his speech accepting the vice-presidential nomination at the 1992 Democratic convention, Al Gore described in harrowing detail the automobile accident that nearly killed his son, then compared it to "our democracy . . . lying there, in the gutter, waiting for us to give it a second breath of life." Conservatives realize that even such bathetic excess does not erase the edge liberals have established as the compassionate vanguard, and try to compensate for it. George W. Bush ran for president in 2000 as a "compassionate conservative," 12 years after George H.W. Bush ran for president by assuring the people, "I want a kinder, gentler nation."[87]

It's obviously uncomfortable for compassionate liberals to focus on the way affirmative action thwarts the aspirations of the country's Brian Webers. Liberalism likes to concentrate on giving things to people, while limiting the discussion about the corresponding enterprise of taking things away. Justice Brennan slowed the car down to look out the window at Brian Weber as briefly as possible, before satisfying himself that Weber's injuries weren't life-threatening and driving on.

Thomas Sowell has argued that the problem is deeper. Affirmative action, in his view, is a zero-sum game *at best*, but most of the time works as a negative-sum game. The sacrifices imposed on the Brian Webers by affirmative action are not equaled by the benefits delivered to society at large or even to the programs' beneficiaries. Sowell cites, as an example, a study showing black freshmen at the Massachusetts Institute of Technology receiving scores on the math portion of the college aptitude tests that were, on average, in the top 10 percent of all college freshmen—but also in the bottom 10 percent of all *MIT* freshmen. The "beneficiaries" of MIT's affirmative action program are students capable of being stars at the majority of America's colleges—but who are induced to enroll in one of the handful of institutions where they're likely to fail. "There is neither glory nor money to be had from flunking out of MIT," Sowell writes. "But you can have a fulfilling professional career after graduating from Texas Tech or Cal State Pomona."[88]

Sowell's argument that affirmative action results in the pervasive mismatching of students and colleges has been buttressed by the research of Richard Sander of UCLA Law School. He determined that black law students "are nearly two-and-a-half times more likely than whites not to graduate from law school, are four times more likely to fail the bar on their first attempt, and are six times more likely to fail after multiple attempts." Furthermore, "the black-white gap in graduation and bar passage is more than twice as large as can be explained by controlling" for law school admissions test scores and undergraduate grades. Sander, too, concludes that affirmative action hurts the people it purports to help by guaranteeing that many students will be admitted to institutions where they are unlikely to succeed, and says that "we must face the fact that the legal education system is currently doing something that seriously harms blacks."[89]

The reaction to Sander by affirmative action's defenders, however, reflects the conviction that facing unpleasant facts is always a last resort. Strident denunciations are the *lingua franca* of modern campus discourse. "We shouldn't have to take these racist attacks," said one protester, a UCLA law student, at a public address by Sander. Sander tried to respond to more substantive critics, who challenged how well his multiple regressions hung together, by seeking data from the California Bar Association on bar exam results. One of the critics of his research immediately argued against the disclosure of the data, because it "risks stigmatizing African-American attorneys." The Society of American Law Teachers threatened to sue the bar association if it complied with Sander's request.[90]

It's difficult to believe that such defenders of affirmative action will ever be presented with *any* facts or arguments that give them pause. Something bigger than the refusal to discuss a possible mistake is at work here. Compassion turns out to be an unreliable and surprisingly hard-hearted foundation on which to base an ideology.

Consider the famous line from Pres. Roosevelt's "Rendezvous with Destiny" speech to the 1936 Democratic convention: "[D]ivine justice weighs the sins of the cold-blooded and the sins of the warm-hearted on different scales. Better the occasional faults of a government that lives in a spirit of charity than the consistent omissions of a government frozen in the ice of its own indifference."[91]

FDR's argument raises two questions, one about its application, the other about the underlying principle. Concerning the first, FDR slips in the assumption that the faults of a government that lives in a spirit of charity will be only occasional. But where does that leave us when these "occasional" missteps become too frequent to be dismissed as anomalies? Where does that leave us when public housing projects routinely become vertical slums? When welfare dependency becomes an intergenerational way of life? When an emphasis on rehabilitation and "root causes" leads to soaring crime rates? When affirmative action harms its intended beneficiaries? When busing schoolchildren proves to be racially incendiary? When, despite ever increasing expenditures, urban public education is routinely delivered in school-free drug zones?

Every one of these policies was conceived and carried out in "the spirit of charity." When so much charity generates so much misery, it's fair to ask whether the "sins of the warm-hearted" deserve to be weighed on the lenient scale FDR chose for them.

It's a category mistake to expect the workings of the institutions of government to be infused with the virtues of warmth and generosity we prize in individuals. FDR told the Democrats in 1936, "We seek not merely to make government a mechanical implement, but to give it the vibrant personal character that is the very embodiment of human charity."[92] When governments, which exist to render justice, are instead required to behave like indulgent rich uncles, they wind up doing a bad job at dispensing both justice and mercy.

Etymologically, "compassion" means to suffer together. "Together," however, is different from "identically." Compassion is not the same as selflessness, and not really the opposite of selfishness. Rather, it provides a basis for helping other people that is materially disinterested but emotionally self-regarding. As Rousseau wrote in *Emile*, "[W]hen the strength of an expansive soul makes me identify myself with my fellow, and I feel that I am, so to speak, in him, it is in order not to suffer that I do not want him to suffer. I am interested in him for love of myself. . . ." Or, as Jean Bethke Elshtain has said, "Pity is about how deeply I can feel. And in order to feel this way, to experience the rush of my own pious reaction, I need victims the way an addict needs drugs."[93]

At the level of moral psychology, the difficulty arises when I can alleviate my suffering, which is brought on by the evidence of your suffering, despite the continuation of your suffering, despite the collateral damage my response inflicts on bystanders, and even despite the creation of new and worse problems for you. Because of compassion we suffer together. I help you in order that I might feel better. But once I *do* feel better, compassion has done its work—and provides no basis for me to concern myself with all the messy implications of whatever I've done for (or to) you.

Does affirmative action place minority students in colleges where they're likely to fail while depriving other applicants of the chance to attend the most challenging schools where they are capable of succeeding? Does rent control drive up the cost of housing, depriving property owners of the same opportunity to profit as any other investor while driving down the quality and quantity of the housing stock? Do minimum wage laws reduce the number of entry-level jobs, making it harder to escape from poverty? Because compassion, by its nature, subordinates doing good to feeling good, these are questions the warm-hearted rarely pursue.

It is also, by its nature, perfectly suited to liberal politics because it has no interest in making distinctions or defining boundaries. Compassion, according to Mickey Kaus, "provides no basis to tell us when our abstract compassionate impulses should stop," which results in "the indiscriminate dispensing of cash in a sort of all-purpose socialized United Way campaign." To govern is to choose, Pres. Kennedy once said, but because compassion is an emotional response rather than a moral principle, it defeats every attempt to make wise choices about which sufferers do and don't deserve governmentally dispensed solace.[94]

The sentiment of compassion undermines not only rational deliberation but, as Elshtain suggests, the effort not to become jaded. Routinizing compassion, as in the helping professions or state-sponsored bureaucracies meant to be "the very embodiment of human charity," leads to the hollowing out of our sympathetic instincts. Compassion "defies institutionalization," according to the political scientist Clifford Orwin: "He who undertakes for a wage to be compassionate for 40 hours a week will soon be so for no hours a week." This paradox does not mean that, after the wells of compassion have run dry, the callous social worker will register as a Republican and urge his clients to go forward into the world in a spirit of rugged individualism. The welfare state's wards and wardens may no longer suffer together, after compassion has played out, but since they share an interest in perpetuating and enlarging the welfare state's budget they can prosper together by acting in concert to expand its benefits and oppose their contraction.[95]

Communitarianism and the Welfare State

The enduring desire to find a communitarian foundation for the welfare state, of which Tomasky's article is the most recent effort, confronts two insoluble problems, one having to do with the nature of communitarianism, the other with the nature of the welfare state. The first problem is that communities can't have insides without having outsides—indeed, what it means to be inside rests heavily on stipulating what's outside and insisting on the maintenance of that distinction. By contrast, a community to which everyone does or can belong is one to which no one really belongs; its inside-ness is devalued to the point of triviality.

Communitarians cherish inside-ness but recoil from any preoccupation with outside-ness, which they believe is never really free from the taint of bigotry, chauvinism, ethno-centrism or xenophobia. Robert Putnam, for example, became famous as the author of *Bowling Alone*, the elegiac study of fading social cohesion in America. His subsequent research found that growing ethnic and cultural diversity "challenge social solidarity and inhibit social capital," at least in the short- to medium-run. "Thus," he writes, "the central challenge for modern, diversifying societies is to create a new, broader sense of 'we.'"[96] "Central challenge" is an optimistic description of an undertaking that sounds so much like squaring the circle: It's impossible to see how the sense of "we" can become broader and more encompassing without simultaneously becoming more attenuated. As Cropsey wrote, "if it is narrower, it is also more human, surely more civil, to love what is near and similar, as such, than what is remote and strange, as such."[97]

The second problem is that liberals have had much more political success selling the welfare state as a way to enhance individual welfare rather than as a vehicle to promote the common good. Consequently, they have devoted most of their efforts to promoting the items on their shelves that people really want. Then, having heard such arguments from liberals, Americans have come to understand the welfare state in terms of the individual benefits it bestows rather than the communal ties it strengthens.

A *New Republic* essay reacting to Tomasky's argument quoted Guy Molyneux, a pollster who works with labor unions, on the very limited prospects for advancing liberalism by advocating the common good:

> We have found that the most powerful way to talk about Social Security benefits is to frame it in terms of a contribution people make through their payroll taxes . . . I've contributed to this same system all my working years. Having done that, the government owes me back. . . . Honestly—and I say this as someone whose own politics are of the social democratic variety—I wish the generational compact, the social solidarity language were as powerful. But they [sic] aren't, they simply aren't. . . . [The first idea] brings it much more to you—what you have a right to, as opposed to this sense of obligation to one another.[98]

Communitarianism is easily sold by emphasizing how individuals benefit from being part of a caring and generous community, by telling people that the welfare state can keep adding items to the "what you have a right to" list. It's the nebulous and potentially burdensome "sense of obligation to one another" where things get difficult. "The inconvenient fact," says Purdy, "is that Americans are more willing to spend money to support people they see as

like themselves than to support strangers. . . ." Since the crucial
and really hard part of the liberal project is to make Americans
willing to spend more and more money to support more and more
people, the challenge is to promote or if necessary synthesize communal feelings among people inclined to regard one another as
strangers.[99]

Robert Kuttner, the founding editor of *The American Prospect*, thinks there's a way out of this dilemma:

> In a democratic polity that also happens to be a highly un-
> equal market economy, there is immense civic value to treat-
> ing middle-class and poor people alike. A common social
> security program, or medical care program, or public school
> program, helps to create the kind of cohesion that Europe's
> social democrats like to call "social solidarity"—a sense that
> basic humanity and citizenship in the political community
> require equal treatment in at least some areas of economic
> life.[100]

The hope that we will overcome our estrangement from one
another through cherishing the togetherness created by receiving
benefit checks from the same social welfare agency is a textbook
case of the "granfalloon," Kurt Vonnegut's term for "a proud
and meaningless association of human beings." "Hands Across
America" was an inane but harmless exercise in granfalloonery. In
May 1986 more than 5 million Americans held hands in an (unsuc-
cessful) attempt to form a human chain from lower Manhattan
to Long Beach, California. Kuttner's argument for anchoring the
welfare state in social solidarity is a variant on the Hands Across
America model; instead of holding the hand of the person next to
us, we help ourselves to the contents of his wallet.[101]

Liberalism needs to induce people to make sacrifices for the
common good, but is chronically unable to find language to per-

suade them to do so. One result, as we'll see in the next chapter, is that the whole inconvenient question of paying for the welfare state is pushed offstage, so that its benefits can be discussed as if they fell from the sky. Another is that a handful of rhetorical tropes that summon people to make sacrifices are asked to bear a heavier load than they were built for. William James expressed the hope in 1906 for a "moral equivalent of war" that would direct such martial virtues as "unstinted exertion" and "universal responsibility" to non-martial goals of social improvement. Jimmy Carter appropriated the phrase in 1977 to galvanize America to overcome the energy crisis. The political theorist William Galston, writing in response to Tomasky's article on the common good, said that liberals who try to elicit sacrifice on this basis "search in vain; there is no moral equivalent of war."[102]

ADHOCRACY
In Lieu of Ideas, Instincts

The problems, intellectual and political, with welfare rights and communitarianism explain the desire of liberals like Chait simply to dispense with big ideas. Indeed, these theories are not really alternatives to his case-by-case approach, because both of them turn out to be adhocracy on stilts. Case-by-case liberalism admits, and even insists on, the incompatibility of liberalism and intellectual rigor. "The recipe for retaining liberty is not doing anything in one fine logical sweep, but muddling through," according to *The Vital Center*, the influential book written by Arthur M. Schlesinger, Jr. in 1949, when liberalism was politically strong and intellectually unchallenged.[103]

The proponents of big ideas believe they cannot galvanize the electorate and bend history without promising something loftier than the intention to mess around. The problem is that any idea big—and rigorous—enough to say something important will eventually have to say something objectionable. What liberals stand for will reveal what they stand against, and each of the things they stand against will have its partisans, all of whom have votes to cast.

Ad hoc liberalism, by taking America's practicality as a given, doesn't run this risk. It approaches the crucial but mundane business of securing majorities in the belief that the U.S. isn't France, where large numbers of votes can be won by elegant syllogisms or soaring manifestos. Case-by-case liberals seek to create a virtuous cycle between policies that win favor with voters and electoral victories that return liberals to power, where they can fashion more programs to attract more votes. "Pragmatism is the magic word to describe what liberals want, but do not want to argue for," according to James Ceaser.[104]

Fittingly, liberals chose pragmatism for pragmatic reasons. Some liberals found John Dewey instructive, but they never relied on him the way socialists relied on Marx. Trying something and, if it doesn't work, trying something else is a "philosophy" political activists probably would have figured out without studying any sacred texts.

Adhocracy's elevator pitch is, "You've got a problem? We've got a program." That's not only a small idea, but one that can be subdivided into even smaller ideas as often as political necessity dictates. A big idea has to be broadcast. As Noam Scheiber of *The New Republic* wrote in response to Tomasky's article, it's impossible for liberals to invoke the common good whenever it's convenient and ignore it when it's not. National health insurance, for example, can't be mandated by the common good if abortion remains solely a question of inviolable privacy rights. But the latter position, clearly, is not open for discussion among liberals. At a forum hosted by the liberal Center for American Progress in 2006, Rachel Laser, an abortion rights activist, said that 1.3 million abortions in America each year is too many. She reports that when the moderator asked how many people in the room felt the same way, "It was only me and maybe one other who raised our hands."[105]

Ad hoc liberalism, however, lends itself to narrowcasting. If you fashion enough programs to solve enough problems, you can amass an electoral majority of people aggrieved by the problems and gratified by the programs. Critics who complain about the big picture—the cost of all these initiatives, or the legitimacy of the government intervening in so many places—are at a disadvantage once people get accustomed to receiving benefits from the government programs addressing their particular problems. Such voters can be counted on to punish any "mean-spirited" politicians who threaten to "take away" what's "theirs."

Everything Is Good to Do

Desiring a world where a growing list of discontents are alleviated by a growing roster of government programs is not, however, a sufficient basis for making the difficult political choices required to bring that world closer. Chait asks, "Should government provide everybody's education? Yes. Should government manufacture everybody's blue jeans? No. And so on."[106] And so on . . . what? Where? "And so on" suggests continuation in a direction. But if there are *only* political particulars, there is no direction, and nothing to be said about how liberalism relates one policy to another or settles conflicts between competing goals.

This determination to govern on the basis of I'll-know-the-right-answer-when-I-see-it asks the governed to make an exceptionally big bet on the sensibilities of the governors. Liberalism, in this understanding, doesn't have a theory, and violates its nature by trying to formulate one. It will have to acquire all its meaning in practice: "Liberalism" will be nothing more than the accumulation of policy choices that "sound about right" to the sort of

bright, decent, well-intentioned people who share a certain disposition. There is, ultimately, no way to explain this disposition
to people who don't understand it, or commend it to people who
don't share it.

Ad hoc liberalism is better suited to avoiding than addressing
hard choices. The liberalism that makes it up as it goes along will
always have room for one more program to address one more
problem. As we have seen, this lack of a limiting principle is the
defining characteristic of liberalism. Its philosophy amounts to
the belief, "Everything is good to do." When everything is good
to do, everything gets done, or at least tried.[107]

Chait says that "liberals never claim that increasing the size
of government is an end in itself. Liberals only support larger
government if they have some reason to believe that it will lead
to material improvement in people's lives." The corollary of this
position demonstrates its uselessness: liberals oppose larger government whenever they have *no* reason to believe it will lead to
material improvement in people's lives. Not even the most stu-
pidly conceived and ineptly administered government program,
however, has failed to help somebody, somehow, somewhere. A
test that no program ever fails isn't much of a test.[108]

There will be, in other words, countless ways to satisfy Chait's
lenient criterion for justifying the growth of government: "Some
reason to believe" could be almost any reason to believe. The John-
Kerry-for-president website, for example, described "79 separate
initiatives that would create new programs or step up spending
on current programs."[109] Liberals are much better at compiling
than culling their to-do list. There is no basis in liberalism for
saying the government lacks the capacity, wisdom or legitimate
authority to solve any problem, or even that some "problems" are
really aspects of the human condition that we might ameliorate
but can never eliminate.

In the 78 years since FDR promised to try one method, and "if it fails, admit it frankly and try another," there is not one clear instance of a welfare state program that liberals by consensus came to regard as a failure, to be frankly admitted and abandoned. Liberals *have* seen programs like the National Recovery Administration or Aid to Families with Dependent Children eliminated as a result of political victories by their opponents. There is no credible case, however, that had the Supreme Court not put NRA out of its misery in 1935, or the Republican Congress done the same to AFDC in 1996, the weight of liberal opinion would have demanded, or even permitted, any changes bigger than perpetual adjustments to fundamentally flawed endeavors. All such programs grow individually and proliferate collectively because every one of them is working well enough, according to the inscrutable but infinitely generous liberal scoring system, to merit continuation and expansion.

The programs that succeed are the ones that deserve to continue. The ones that don't succeed are the ones where the recipients of transfer payments, goods, services or other economic advantages scornfully refuse the benefits proffered by the welfare state. Every program, in other words, is a success and deserves to continue. Naturally, the thing to do with successful programs is not merely to continue them but expand them. Instead of acting as a check on the natural tendencies of government programs to go on and on and get bigger and bigger, liberal adhocracy turbocharges them.

The unchecked forces are logical, political and bureaucratic. Any program that helps some people but not all people is going to have eligibility standards. Those standards are an attempt to define a group or condition, one that resists quantification. Drawing bright lines through cloudy realities means that people who are very similar are going to be treated very differently. At the margin of the standards there will always be people whose circumstances are only slightly better than those receiving benefits but who get nothing from the government. The impulse of the people who created the program in the first place, in order to serve needy people, is to make the standards less restrictive so that the people nearly as needy as the current recipients get help, too—and, after a decent interval, to include the people located just outside the new cutoff point, and so on.

Elected officials are going to be more than amenable to this expansionary process. The unbeatable formula of concentrating benefits while dispersing costs means that the political risks of expanding a program are small, while the risks of reducing it are grave. Voting for endless incremental additions to the welfare state is a happy instance where the right thing to do is also the expedient thing, Robert Kuttner advises, because it "creates a reliable constituency for the Democratic Party."[110]

Frequently, however, these decisions about who gets government help and who doesn't need not await formal, legislated changes in the rules. Administrative agencies interact with people applying for and receiving government benefits every day, and the cumulative effect of these encounters is always to expand the roster and definition of the eligible. Charles Murray gives one example, the disability insurance program that was added to Social Security in 1956. (It's the "D" in OASDI: Old Age, Survivors and Disability Insurance.) Congress liberalized the program's eligibility rules in 1960 and revised them without really expanding them in 1965. After the 1960 changes, the number of Americans receiving benefits from the program was 687,000, rising to 1,739,000 in 1965 and 2,655,000 in 1970. By 1975 the number of beneficiaries reached 4,352,000. During those 15 years, Murray notes, the official definition of a disability did not change, medical advances to help people overcome disabilities made important strides, and the number of people covered by the program increased by 30%. The number of recipients, how-ever, increased by 533%.[III]

There was a time when most of the welfare state's civil ser-vants had the souls of bill collectors; now, most have the souls of social workers. The gatekeepers have become gate-openers, whose professional duty is to make sure that deserving people get the benefits they're entitled to, rather than to prevent undeserving people from getting benefits they're not entitled to. The ideology of the welfare state has created an ethos, one that acts on clients as well as staff, encouraging people to secure all the benefits they "have coming to them" out of a sense of entitlement, rather than to be inhibited by a sense of shame.

The Economic Costs of Adhocracy

Unlike socialists, liberals who emphasize their indifference to political theories see their task as correcting capitalism's flaws rather than hastening the advent of history's next system. It is not necessary, however, to be a Marxist or to have any other doc-trinal animus against capitalism in order to come up with a set of policies that cripple its operations. The adhocracy Chait praises is fully adequate to that task. "Above all, try something," may be the least bad approach to averting a shipwreck, such as the one FDR faced in 1932. That does not make it, in general, a sound principle of seamanship.

The 62nd Federalist Paper anticipated the "calamitous" effects from "mutable" policies begotten by governing, year-in and year-out, by means of bold, persistent experimentation: "It will be of little avail to the people, that the laws are made by men of their own choice, if the laws be so voluminous that they cannot be read, or so incoherent that they cannot be understood; if they be repealed or revised before they are promulgated, or undergo such incessant changes that no man, who knows what the law is to-day, can guess what it will be tomorrow." The impact of adhocracy on what we today call capital formation is especially devastating:

> What prudent merchant will hazard his fortunes in any new branch of commerce when he knows not but that his plans may be rendered unlawful before they can be executed? What farmer or manufacturer will lay himself out for the encouragement given to any particular cultivation or establishment, when he can have no assurance that his preparatory labors and advances will not render him a victim to an inconstant government? In a word, no great improvement or laudable enterprise can go forward which requires the auspices of a steady system of national policy.[112]

The Political Costs of Adhocracy

We must note, finally, the tension between liberalism's partiality for the common man and its preference for governing on a case-by-case basis. Bold, persistent experimentation doesn't work as well in politics as in the laboratory, where the mice can't vote, form pressure groups or hire lobbyists. Complicated, constantly changing laws and regulations are more easily bent to favor strong claimants, who have savvy and clout on their side, than strong claims, artlessly put forward by those who simply need help.

The perverse but inevitable result is that the government agency, created to help the little guy, stays in business long enough to confer advantages on the big shots. It, too, was foreseen in Federalist #62:

> Another effect of public instability is the unreasonable advantage it gives to the sagacious, the enterprising, and the moneyed few over the industrious and uninformed mass of the people. Every new regulation concerning commerce or

revenue, or in any way affecting the value of the different species of property, presents a new harvest to those who watch the change, and can trace its consequences; a harvest, reared not by themselves, but by the toils and cares of the great body of their fellow-citizens. This is a state of things in which it may be said with some truth that laws are made for the *few*, not for the *many*.[113]

In 1981 the Democrats in Congress "opposed" Pres. Reagan's spending and tax cuts by offering more favorable terms to as many interest groups as possible. The Democrats, Michael Kinsley wrote contemptuously in *The New Republic*, "found enough money, against Reagan's wishes, to continue, and even expand, the subsidized loan program of the Farmers Home Administration." Nor were they "deaf to the hungry sobs of large exporters like Boeing. Reagan wanted to limit Export-Import Bank loans to $4.4 billion, but the House found another $600 million in its heart." No rhetorical volleys against the Republicans and the greedy rich will disguise the awkward fact that a Democratic party conducting itself this way is, according to Kinsley, "a dwindling collection of special interest groups whose interests are less and less those of either the general populus [sic] or the tired and poor."[114]

CHAPTER FOUR

LIBERALISM'S CONTINUING INABILITY TO MAKE PAYROLL

Oh, yeah. There's one other thing. The welfare state needs to be *paid for*.

It's true that the clear, comprehensive and rigorous account of the welfare state's premises, objectives and limits has yet to be delivered to a nation that has seen the New Deal's 75th anniversary come and go. Time spent asking liberals to be clear could be put to better use urging pygmies to be tall. The magnitude and duration of liberalism's theoretical defects make it difficult to avoid concluding that incoherence is woven into the liberal genome, not some solvable problem liberals have been too busy to address. The steady advance of the welfare state in the absence of this tidy theory suggests, however, that it would be flattering democracy to assume that unexplained or even inexplicable clusters of public policies cannot survive unless all their syllogisms have been carefully wrought and securely fastened.

If politics were a graduate seminar, that would be the extent of the difficulties. The need for the welfare state's advocates to secure a large and steady funding stream for it compounds their problems, however. Any welfare state is constrained by the government's inability to disburse money, benefits and services in excess of the resources it can secure through taxation, borrowing and regulation. In a democracy, these latter actions are all vulnerable to repudiation by the voters, many of whom will be rendered less prosperous by taxes and borrowing, or less free by regulations. Thus, the economic imperative to pay for the welfare state is, ultimately, a political imperative as well, since the sacrifices required by the welfare state need to be justified to the voters in a convincing way.

It is here that the failure to explain the welfare state becomes a political problem, rather than just an intellectual one. Liberals have operated in the belief, largely vindicated, that the welfare state's benefits will speak for themselves. One week before the 1964 election Lyndon Johnson gave a "little preview" of the Great Society at a campaign rally. Its realization would mean "nobody in this country is poor," that the aged would enjoy not just "full social security," but lives with "meaning, purpose and pleasure." The Great Society will be the time "when we have a job for everyone who is willing to work, and he is going to be paid a decent wage," and when "every slum is gone from every city in America." By contrast, Barry Goldwater, whom Johnson never mentioned by name, had "voted no, no, no," whenever Congress considered any "program of common responsibility for anything, from national defense to education, [to] social security."[1]

In other words, the welfare state's benefits are . . . beneficial. Liberals want the government to give things to you and do things for you. Conservatives don't, either out of a mean-spirited indifference to people's needs, or because the verandas of their country clubs afford no view of the precarious lives endured by some of their fellow citizens, or because they're more concerned about upholding antique dogmas about free markets and limited, constitutional government than alleviating real suffering.

It's easy to understand liberals' hope that a welfare state that speaks for itself will also pay for itself. That is, they hold the enormous value of the welfare state's benefits to be self-evident. As a result, the voters who enthusiastically accept those benefits and welcome their perpetual continuation and indefinite expansion will be more than sufficiently amenable to whatever taxes, borrowing or regulations the government needs to render them. With such a strong wind at their backs, it should be sufficient for liberals merely to remind people to pay for the welfare state, rather than persuade them to do so. The resulting argument could be admirably simple and candid: The welfare state we're building will make our country a better place to live. The sacrifices it requires are ones we all should make, not joyously, perhaps, but with satisfaction and confidence that they are a just and necessary price for improving our society.

What's striking is that this confident argument is not only *not* the template for rhetoric justifying the welfare state's costs, but the frame for this crucial question that liberals employ least often. Apparently, the welfare state can sell itself, but only up to a point. Its benefits are sufficiently appealing that liberals can point to them and effectively refute conservative politicians who say "no, no, no." They are not, however, so attractive that they will guarantee easy political victories for liberal politicians who try to sell a dramatic expansion of those benefits by calling for "more, more, more." The question of paying for the welfare state cannot be moved offstage, and voters cannot be induced to ignore it while liberals shine the spotlight, instead, on all the humane and uplifting things a much bigger welfare state would provide.

The liberal response to the question of paying for the welfare state has been a protracted exercise in intellectual dishonesty, borne of a conviction that the question doesn't need to be answered if it can be made to go away. Liberals have, generally, been happy to tell people what they want to hear: It's possible to have a big welfare state without worrying all that much about the costs. The programs will pay for themselves. Or, an affluent society can pay for them out of the petty cash drawer. Or, the taxes required for a much bigger welfare state are ones that will be borne largely by the very rich and big corporations. None of these propositions can withstand even gentle interrogation, however, making it difficult to know whether the liberals who put them forward are remarkably cynical or remarkably feckless. In either case, whatever political advantages are secured by telling people what they want to hear about paying for the welfare state, the already murky argument for the welfare state becomes even more incoherent.

MONOPOLY MONEY

We can see one example of wanting the cost question to go away when liberals draw solace from public opinion surveys that suggest broad support for their agenda. According to Michael Tomasky, "majorities of the public tend to agree with Democrats on the issues. . . . On health care, the environment, investment [i.e., government spending], education, just about everything except national defense, majorities lean toward the Democratic position."[2]

The anomaly is that people seem more liberal when answering questionnaires than when casting ballots. Tomasky contends that conservatives overcome their unpopular stands on the issues by being "scurrilous liars" who are "organized and good . . . at what they do." High-minded liberals, meanwhile, get clobbered because they "want to believe the best about the world . . . to believe that they actually can win a campaign on the issues."[3]

Aside from self-congratulation, the problem with this thesis is that it takes public opinion survey data at face value, treating all the election day departures from that baseline as baffling and distressing incongruities. It overlooks the fact that polls elicit opinions that are often made up on the spot and have very shallow roots. A ten-minute telephone survey on health or education policy will be the longest conversation that many of the respondents will have on that topic in their entire lives.

Furthermore, people nice enough not to hang up when a pollster calls, a subset significantly smaller than the total, are apt to care about presenting respectable selves to the stranger on the other end of the line. To avoid sounding apathetic or ignorant, many will give opinions they don't have about issues they haven't thought or even heard about. And, to avoid sounding callous, they will choose to say that they're in favor—make that *strongly* in favor—of more spending for Head Start or job training.

Finally and crucially, it's easy to favor increased government spending for anything a pollster mentions because the citizen responding to the survey is handing out Monopoly money. Spending more on X never means spending less on Y, and it never means raising anyone's taxes. Liberals like the results of polls about domestic issues because the artificial laboratory of the public opinion survey corresponds to their ideal framework for making public policy. Everything really is good to do when there are no choices to make. The government can be treated like somebody's rich uncle, who needs constant prodding in order to become constantly more generous.

When, however, the costs of the liberal agenda are put before the voters in a contested election, it's no longer a matter of demonstrating to the nice young lady from Gallup that you are an informed citizen and decent person, but of facing hard questions about allocating real resources. Some programs have stronger claims to be worth the money, some have weaker claims, and some should be zeroed out. Debating the merits of each welfare state program is likely to be difficult and contentious, especially since the costs are real, not conjectural.[4]

There's a story about a Catholic priest who takes up an Anglican friend's request to spend a couple days reading the Book of Common Prayer, then reports back, "You left in all the pretty parts and took out all the hard parts." Liberalism works that way, too, because it lends itself to a discussion of the pretty parts of governance—doing and building and giving—but not to the hard part of extracting the wealth presupposed by the pretty parts. Not for nothing did Milton Friedman find it necessary to insist "There is no such thing as a free lunch."

THE AFFLUENT SOCIETY

One way to make the welfare state's costs go away is to walk by them and look the other direction. In the wake of John Kenneth Galbraith's *The Affluent Society*, liberals embraced the happy conclusion that in the second half of the 20th century the American economy had entered an era of permanent and permanently growing prosperity. The endless cornucopia would render scarcity itself obsolete. The only limit on what the government could do would be the limit on our ability to come up with things for it to do. As a 1964 *New Republic* article put it:

> In an age of affluence we no longer ought to fear making value-judgments rather than cost-judgments. If ballet is worth having, as we earlier decided public libraries were worth having, go ahead and provide for ballet, even though there is not sufficient "demand" to make it "economic." This attitude can obviously be extended from ballet to beautifying the countryside, and in a dozen other different directions. With all this wealth we can afford to try.[5]

Many did. Pat Brown, a politician "never ashamed to call himself a liberal" according to the journalist Peter Schrag, was the Democratic governor of California from 1959 to 1967. When an aide warned him that his spending plans for infrastructure and education were on a collision course, Brown replied, "We'll find enough money to do both. We'll build the water project and we'll build new universities and new state colleges and new community colleges and elementary schools, too. We've got plenty of money and we have to do it."[6]

It's an approach that can work—but only as long as you really have got plenty of money. The government won't have plenty of money, though, if it turns out that the Affluent Society hasn't transcended scarcity or even permanently relegated recessions to the past. Nor will government be able to do everything its leaders want if taxpayers insist on limits that officials would prefer not to think about. Californians did so in 1978, capping property taxes with the passage of Proposition 13. Voters, both in California and other states, approved additional limits on taxes in the ensuing years.

By the time they were all on the books, the determination for the government to do this, that and the other thing, too, had been reined in. To govern was, once more, to choose. In their book on the California tax revolt, David Sears and Jack Citrin say that Prop. 13 "transformed California's dominant political style."

> Austerity and self-reliance replaced planning and social reform as symbols of legitimacy. Politicians increasingly came to speak the language of trade-offs and constraints rather than growth and progress. In the pre-Proposition 13 era, policy-makers could think first of what programs they wanted to expand and feel comfortable that revenues would be available. After 1978, the dominant mood forced officials to revise spending priorities to fit fixed revenues. New programs had to be "marketed," not merely announced, since they took money away from ongoing activities or necessitated raising fees or taxes.[7]

The tetchy tone of this analysis is revealing. Sears and Citrin lament the passing of the era when politicians could simply announce new programs, free from worries about where the money to pay for them would come from. Like a slacker who resents the real-world imperative to get a job and provide for himself, there is something adolescent about complaints that we can't have all the new government programs we want simply because we want them, and shouldn't have to think about disagreeable subjects like higher taxes or lower spending on other programs.

A grown-up liberalism would engage, rather than disdain, the governance questions inherent in building a welfare state. What should the government do to promote individuals' economic security, and what shouldn't it do? What criteria distinguish the people who should be the recipients of social welfare benefits from those who shouldn't? Since the resources for the welfare state won't fall from the sky, what are the most candid and cogent ways to make people understand how the benefits from its programs justify the taxes and regulations they'll require? And, as a corollary of addressing that question in good faith, what distinguishes those welfare state initiatives, existing or proposed, whose benefits do *not* justify increased taxes and regulations?

Liberals have devoted *much* more time and energy to avoiding these questions than to grappling with them. One conspicuous example of refusing to treat serious questions seriously is the assertion that the costs of a bigger welfare state, however large, are slight compared to the consequences of failing to expand it. "This country cannot *not* afford the [elimination of poverty]," *The New Republic* editorialized in 1969.[8]

Liberalism harmed itself by relying on such unfalsifiable contentions that a bigger welfare state couldn't conceivably be anything but an improvement. The tax revolt was the voters' way of saying the nation can't afford to do all the things liberals keep insisting it can't afford not to do. And the liberal reply was scathing. *The New Republic* said the message from the Californians who passed Prop. 13 was, "Launch the lifeboat—I'm aboard. Everybody else can swim to shore." According to *The Nation*, Prop. 13 passed because of "the ugliest kind of *ressentiment* and barely concealed racism," reflecting "an America one thought blessedly gone, a country of raw economic greed. . . ."[9]

Liberals are in a weak position to complain that the voters resort to sweeping, indiscriminate measures to curtail government spending. Since liberalism itself offers no criteria to distinguish between more and less deserving programs, it's churlish to abuse the voters for coming up with the wrong answer, when they have received so little guidance from liberals about how to find the right one. Instead, liberalism presents voters with just two stark alternatives. They can either agree with liberals that everything is good to do, or face being denigrated as greedy bigots for refusing to give the welfare state a blank check.

THE EUROPEAN IDEAL

American liberals look enviously across the Atlantic. In Europe, the mere suggestion of curtailing welfare-state benefits by the occasional center-right coalition government is enough to trigger general strikes and protests in the streets. The American Left, by contrast, has to worry about tax revolts.

The transformation liberals hope and work for requires that Americans ultimately come to adopt the European mindset, where voters insist on ample welfare-state benefits and acquiesce in the taxes to pay for them, rather than insist on lower taxes and acquiesce in the relatively meager safety net they can afford. Jonathan Cohn contends in a *New Republic* article that Denmark boasts "not only one of the world's most expansive welfare states, but also one of its most robust economies." The "broadest lesson" he wants Americans to take from the Danes is that "it is entirely possible to have a large welfare state, with generous benefits, without choking the economy." The key to Denmark's success, according to Cohn, is that high taxes don't hurt . . . if you do the right things with the money. The Danes tolerate an income tax system with a top bracket of 63% because "they feel like they're getting something for the money: good public services."[10]

A year after Cohn's essay appeared, however, an article in the *International Herald Tribune* raised serious doubts about the sustainability of Denmark's social contract. The 63% tax bracket, it pointed out, is not only much higher than America's top bracket since Pres. Reagan's legislative triumphs in 1981, it also applies to a far larger percentage of the total taxpaying population, kicking in when incomes rise above 360,000 kroner, the equivalent of $70,000. The good public services bought by these taxes have not been enticing enough to prevent a steady increase in the number of tax exiles leaving Denmark, the primary reason the Danish economy faces a worsening shortage of skilled labor. One Danish bank, for example, has given up trying to keep teams of employees together in Copenhagen. The only way to hire and retain the people it wanted was to situate them in Britain, Switzerland and Singapore, where income taxes are significantly lower. "The high tax rate is the No. 1 problem we have," says the bank's CEO. "It's that simple."[11]

Nowhere in the rhetoric of American liberals can we find an unequivocal assertion that the welfare states of Europe are too big. At most, there is an occasional suggestion that the right answer is somewhere between the American and European extremes . . . and probably much closer to the latter. According to Cohn, "While high taxes in Europe have sometimes choked economies there, there is an enormous middle ground between the United States, where taxes are 25 percent of gross domestic product, and Sweden, where taxes are 50 percent of gross domestic product. (Besides, Sweden's economy has actually been performing pretty well lately.)"[12] The arguments for expanding the American welfare state are always specific and urgent, while the occasional acknowledgment that Europe's welfare states might be a little too big are grudging and vague.

THE POST-SOCIALIST LEFT

There can never be more than 100% of anything, including a nation's gross domestic product. Europe's social democrats have built welfare states that are somewhere between one-tenth and one-fifth of an economy closer than America's welfare state to this absolute limit. There is a lower, less precisely defined ceiling. The numerous and expensive things social democrats and liberals want the government to do require prosperous economies. It would be a cruel joke if the government of Liberia, where the per capita GDP is less than $1,000, informed the citizenry that it would henceforth recognize their rights to employment, housing, health care, education, rest, recreation and adventure.

For most of the 20th century, many intelligent people were convinced that prosperity required discarding capitalism in favor of state ownership of the means of production, or at least a centrally planned economy. As late as 1975 two Democratic senators, Adlai Stevenson III and Henry Jackson, were advocating that the federal government respond to the energy crisis by getting into the oil business—in a big way. Stevenson called for the creation of a National Energy Supply Corp., which would "gradually get into the full range of oil and natural gas exploration, development and production," according to *Time* magazine. The publicly owned and operated company would serve as both a competitor to existing, privately owned oil companies, and a "yardstick" by which the public could "realistically gauge" their "prices, profits and overall performance."[13]

Jackson's idea was even more ambitious. He proposed the creation of a National Energy Production Board, charged with the responsibility "to organize and speed up exploration and production efforts by all U.S. oil enterprises." Jackson envisioned "an energy superagency that would establish priorities, let huge contracts and even set up new companies for specific jobs." It's worth noting that both Stevenson and Jackson were considered liberals in good standing, rather than politicians at the left edge of the Democratic coalition. That is to say, neither would have been regarded in 1975 the way Rep. Dennis Kucinich or Sen. Bernard Sanders is today.[14]

The two decades after Stevenson and Jackson's proposals saw the fall of the Berlin Wall and the Soviet Union, and the slower but still utter collapse of the intellectual respectability of socialism. "The socialist economic project, consisting fundamentally of national planning and extensive public ownership, has been thoroughly discredited as a means of economic growth," Paul Starr advised fellow liberals in *The American Prospect* in 1991. "It is now indisputable that communism impoverished the people who lived under it, and it is not clear how or why a more democratically planned socialist economy would do much better—or that such a system is feasible at all." Even in western Europe, "the idea of a planned national economy has been abandoned or planning of limited scope has accommodated the basic contours of capitalism. Although European social democrats have Marxist grandparents on their family tree, they have largely outgrown not just Marxism, but socialism itself. . . ."[15] In Brian Morton's novel, *Starting Out in the Evening*, published in 1998 and set in New York, a character tells his girlfriend that he still considers himself a socialist. When she presses him to explain that commitment, he says, "A socialist is someone who sits around pondering the question of whether it can possibly mean anything anymore to call yourself a socialist."[16]

The post-socialist Left is never going to sign up for the Chamber of Commerce idea that capitalism is the best system imaginable. Liberals and social democrats, however, have had to more or less sullenly admit that it is the best system available. In 1998 Richard Rorty voiced the hope that "cumulative piecemeal reforms . . . might someday produce a presently unimaginable nonmarket economy." He derided, however, those leftists content to "just wait for capitalism to collapse, rather than figuring out what, in the absence of markets, will set prices and regulate distribution. The voting public, the public which must be won over if the Left is to emerge from the academy into the public square, sensibly wants to know the details. It wants to know how things are going to work after markets have been put behind us."[17]

Rorty's hope has been the Left's hope ever since it became impossible to admire the Soviet Union: There must be *some* alternative to capitalism other than control of the economy by government bureaucrats. Starr thinks it's a hope that should be accorded a decent burial, urging liberals "to give up on the idea of a grand synthesis or a third way, if by that is meant some system midway between capitalism and socialism or an alternative altogether 'beyond' them."[18] According to *A Nation of Rebels*, by Joseph Heath and Andrew Potter, who also regard themselves as men of the Left, this third way has remained so elusive because it is a logical impossibility:

> The amount of intellectual energy that has been dedicated to the task of searching for an alternative to the market in the past century is staggering. And yet no matter how you run the numbers, the answer always comes out the same. There are essentially two ways of organizing a modern economy: either a system of centralized, bureaucratic production (such as was found in the former Soviet Union), or else a decentralized system, in which producers coordinate their efforts through market exchange. . . . Central planning works fine for

the military, or some other organization where members are willing to accept a standardized allotment of clothing, food rations or housing and to be assigned specific jobs to perform. But in a society where individuals hope to pick and choose among a range of lifestyle opportunities, there is no getting around the need for a market.[19]

Prices set in markets convey information. They convey information about "demand"—how widely and avidly each of the various goods and services being offered is desired. And they convey information about "supply"—how difficult or disagreeable it is to bring each of these goods and services to the market. These are not fixed, metaphysical properties that inhere in the individual goods or services, but attributes about scarcity, tastes and the state of technology, all of which are in permanent flux. That flux is reflected in constantly changing prices.

The attempt to organize a society by disregarding or suppressing the knowledge embodied in those prices guarantees that economic activity will be systematically misinformed, and that the economy will be less productive and dynamic than it might have been. Cass Sunstein applauds the key insight of Friedrich Hayek, a conservative hero—"no planner could possibly obtain the 'dispersed bits' of information held by individual members of society." As a consequence, "the knowledge of individuals, taken as a whole, is far greater than that of any commission or board, however diligent and expert. The magic of the system of prices and of economic markets is that they incorporate a great deal of diffuse knowledge."[20]

THE HAPPY DISCOVERY OF AGGREGATE DEMAND

The socialist dream of organizing an economy around the purpose of advancing social welfare, as it is governmentally determined and meted out, seems destined to remain an abstraction irrelevant to the world's political and economic needs. One strange result of the collapse of socialism, and the absence of any other credible way to avoid relying on markets, is that the welfare state is heavily dependent on the health of capitalism. The government cannot disburse wealth that never gets created, and creating the wealth required for modern, prosperous societies without the knowledge conveyed by prices set in markets appears to be impossible.

The problem, then, is to modify a market-based economy, and extract wealth from it, without impairing capitalism's ability to go on creating wealth. Operating at a time when capitalism was widely considered to have impaired and discredited itself, the New Deal was not hemmed in by this problem. In *The End of Reform* Alan Brinkley tells, with some wistfulness, the story of how the ascendance of Keynesianism in the late 1930s led to the eclipse of the earlier New Deal belief that "the nation's greatest problems were rooted in the structure of modern industrial capitalism and that it was the mission of government to deal somehow with the flaws in that structure." Freda Kirchwey, for example, writing in *The Nation* in 1940, said "collective control" was "necessary to keep the industrial machine going." The New Deal, therefore, needed to be "enormously extended. Collective control over our natural resources, the railroads and other major monopolies must be accepted as obvious first steps in the direction of industrial planning." (In keeping with our general observation about liberalism, rhetoric about "first steps" is commonplace; discussions about "final steps" that complete the project are nowhere to be found.)[21]

Brinkley says that by the end of World War II, however, liberals had come to understand their agenda "less as a commitment to restructure the economy than as an effort to stabilize it and help it grow. They were no longer much concerned about controlling or punishing 'plutocrats' and 'economic royalists,' an impulse central to New Deal rhetoric in the mid-1930s. Instead, they spoke of their commitment to providing a healthy environment in which the corporate world could flourish and in which the economy could sustain 'full employment.'" Brinkley makes clear that a large part of the political ascendance of Keynesianism involved filling a vacuum: Despite years of vigorous improvisation, the New Dealers, determined to "deal somehow" with the structural defects of capitalism, never settled on a single assessment of those defects nor sorted out the annoying but crucial "somehow" of dealing with them.[22]

The widespread expectation at the end of World War II was that the return of millions of servicemen to the civilian workforce would trigger a new Depression. Liberals who had been laying the groundwork for the next New Deal that would respond to this downturn, were initially flummoxed by an economy that soared rather than plunged. They quickly recalibrated their message, taking credit for the surprising postwar boom by ascribing it to the enlightened use of Keynesian levers to tame the business cycle. This was a plausible contention, up to a point, but overlooked the unprecedented economic advantages America enjoyed after being spared the devastation the war inflicted on other industrialized nations. By the late 1940s the United States, with seven percent of global population, produced 43 percent of the world's electricity, 57 percent of the steel and 80 percent of the automobiles.[23] Arthur Schlesinger was insistent enough about giving liberalism credit for the surprising prosperity that he could sneer at the ingrates who elected Dwight Eisenhower over Adlai Stevenson in 1952: "Having been enabled by Democratic administrations to live like Republicans, the new suburbanites ended up voting like Republicans."[24]

The lack of a plan and the loss of the will to restructure capitalism hardly rendered liberalism reluctant to expand government. Influenced by *The Affluent Society*, many liberals argued that a permanently growing economy would yield the government a permanently growing "fiscal dividend," which would easily accommodate a permanently growing welfare state. And not just accommodate, but require. The happy discovery of liberals who had enrolled in Keynesianism 101 was that ever-increasing government spending was crucial to the management of aggregate demand, which was, in turn, crucial to the continuation of prosperity.

In 1961, for example, *The New Republic* argued:

> The way to achieve the best of all economic worlds (rapid growth, full employment, stable prices, favorable balance of payments, more investment, no recessions, better living standards) is to spend as much government money as possible, and make sure that the amount the government spends rises rapidly each year. . . . [A] very high level of government spending, *no matter where the money goes*, assures a very high level of demand. And a high level of demand is the open sesame to everything else.[25]

One of the reasons for launching the War on Poverty, according to Daniel Patrick Moynihan, was that in 1965 Pres. Johnson's advisors believed the possibility of a recession required a new federal venture to inject buying power into the economy.[26]

Spending as much money as possible was, in fact, faithful to only one-half of Keynesian theory. Macro-economic policy was supposed to be counter-cyclical. Spending furiously was a good idea when the economy was going into a recession, but exactly the wrong remedy when a boom was threatening to cause inflation. The other, expansionary phase of the business cycle needed to be moderated by a combination of higher taxes and lower government spending. This fasting-and-penance part of the Keynesian faith, however, was never as popular with the voting public as the

Mardi Gras part and, not coincidentally, has never had any champions among liberal politicians and writers.

The liberal dogma about government spending that emerged from and synthesized these disparate considerations has a distinct heads-I-win-tails-you-lose quality. When the economy is weak, the right course is for the government to spend as much money as possible. Doing so will not only restore prosperity by stimulating aggregate demand but will alleviate the suffering and economic insecurity that accompany business downturns. When the economy is strong, however, the right course is . . . well, then it's also for the government to spend as much money as possible. Doing so is necessary to redress the imbalance between private splendor and public squalor, in Galbraith's famous phrase. With all this wealth we can afford to try . . . anything. Everything.

The precise economic conditions that call for reducing or merely stabilizing government spending remain unspecified, despite liberals' heroic efforts to ascertain them. No matter how many people have good jobs and rising incomes, it will always be imperative for the government to expand its social welfare efforts. In 2005 Jonathan Cohn argued in *The New Republic* that the country's circumstances meant "[T]here's a compelling case for the government spending a great deal more money than it does now." His assertion would be more persuasive if, during a century of publication—through recessions and booms, war and peace—*The New Republic's* editors had encountered even one set of circumstances that convinced them there was *not* a compelling case for the government to spend a great deal more money.[27]

THE NEW POLITICS AND NEOLIBERALISM

The 1966 mid-term elections saw the beginning of Ronald Reagan's political career and the end of Pat Brown's, when Reagan won 58% of the vote against California's liberal Democratic governor who was seeking reelection to a third term. Furthermore, Republicans gained more seats in the U.S. House of Representatives than they had lost in 1964. According to Michael Barone, "The new House clearly lacked a majority for Great Society measures."[28] The election was the first sign of the most rapid political decline since the Republicans' in the 1930s. The 1964 Democratic presidential nominee received 61% of the popular vote and 90% of the Electoral College vote. The party's 1972 nominee received 37% of the popular vote, and 3% of the electoral vote.

Liberalism was beset by several crises during these years. The war in Vietnam caused fierce debates about how or whether liberals should carry forward the containment doctrine they had formulated during the Truman Administration. Riots in slums and campuses raised questions about where or whether one could locate the limits of liberals' solicitude for black nationalists and adolescent revolutionaries.

When it came to fashioning the right relationship between capitalism and the welfare state, liberals were torn. Some, practitioners of what came to be called the New Politics, believed that the New Deal had not gone far enough in restructuring American capitalism for the sake of social justice. Others, the neoliberals, believed that the New Deal had gone too far in its reliance on government programs.

Neither effort made a lasting difference because neither succeeded, intellectually or politically. The New Politics agenda was always murky, and the strategy for assembling a constituency that would carry it to political dominance was hazy and wishful. Neoliberalism made more sense, but had no success in winning over conservatives, who were more skeptical about government activism than the neoliberals, or converting "paleoliberals," who had no interest in curtailing the welfare state.

By the time he wrote his memoirs in 2000, Arthur Schlesinger described himself as an "unreconstructed and unrepentant"

New Dealer, a description that pushed back against the prevailing winds of the Reagan-Gingrich era.[29] In 1978, however, when Ted Kennedy's victory in the 1980 presidential election seemed at least as plausible as Reagan's, Schlesinger embraced the New Politics critique of the New Deal. "With all its faults, the old liberalism had at least arrayed itself against the immovable and impenetrable institutions," he said in his biography of Robert Kennedy. "Yet the old liberalism had failed to beat the structures. And its distinctive institutions tended to leave out those too poor or demoralized to form organizations of their own. . . . In different ways, welfare, public housing, farm price supports, one creation after another of the old liberalism, had congealed into props of the existing order."[30]

The practitioners of the old liberalism thought America had problems to be solved. They were confident that the sort of highly educated, public-spirited young men who flocked to Washington in 1933 and 1961 could solve them. The advocates of the New Politics thought America had sins to be expiated. The enormity of the sins, the suffering of those who had been sinned against, and the emptiness of the lives led by the sins' beneficiaries, meant that the smug complacency of the old liberals had to be replaced by fevered moral urgency. What it meant to "beat the structures" or remove the props from the "existing order" was never made clear, but this lacuna was not the sort of detail allowed to forestall a gratifying rant. Schlesinger uncritically records that in 1967 Robert Kennedy told an audience of students, "Don't you understand that what we are doing to the Vietnamese is not very different than what Hitler did to the Jews?"[31]

Schlesinger was an active supporter of George McGovern's 1972 presidential campaign. The McGovern Democrats came to a fork in the road between the old liberalism and the New Politics—and took it. That year's Democratic platform wrapped gauzy rhetoric about personal fulfillment and participatory democracy around expensive promises to every interest group that could fit under the party's tent. The Democrats, wrote Tom Geoghegan at the time, were caught between two worlds. In one, "politics is expected to deal with the whole man and his sense of helplessness." In the other, "a faceless bureaucracy indemnifies anyone or any group big enough to make trouble for it." In short, "Government has failed—give us more government."[32]

Some veterans of the McGovern campaign concluded his defeat was not an anomaly: It was unlikely the voters would ever entrust the dramatic expansion of the government's power to redistribute income and regulate economic activity to the sort of liberals who called Americans "the most frightening people on this planet," as Schlesinger did in 1968.[33] They began to entertain surprisingly skeptical thoughts about the old liberal imperative to give us more government. McGovern's campaign manager, Gary Hart, was elected to the Senate from Colorado, and promptly declared that his class-of-1974 Democrats were not "a bunch of little Hubert Humphreys." He later explained that he meant that those Democrats "were not automatic regulators, new-agency creators, and higher-tax-and-spend people."[34]

This political impulse eventually acquired a name, neoliberalism, and a magazine, *The Washington Monthly*. In "A Neoliberal's Manifesto," the *Monthly's* editor, Charles Peters, decried the "shortage of self-criticism among liberals." The neoliberals, he said in his 1983 article, "no longer automatically favor unions and big government or oppose the military and big business." Rather, "Our hero is the risk-taking entrepreneur who creates new jobs and better products." The neoliberals "are against a fat, sloppy, and smug bureaucracy. We want a government that can fire people who can't or won't do the job." Peters called for means testing all government transfer programs, including veterans' benefits and Social Security. Finally, he said, "The snobbery that is most damaging to liberalism is the liberal intellectuals' contempt for religious, patriotic, and family values." This con-tempt is "the least appealing trait of the liberal intellectuals," many of whom "don't really believe in democracy."[35]

On cue, Arthur Schlesinger promptly wrote a book review expressing his contempt . . . for the neoliberal heretics. He allowed that they had "useful points to make," but that "neoliberalism was a hoax from the start," one whose "anti-government line" was "a bow to fashion and a bid for publicity." He called on all liberals to re-embrace the one, true faith in "affirmative government," and for "the end of the neoliberal nonsense."[36]

TAXING THE RICH

Within a few years, the neoliberal nonsense did indeed end. Lib-eralism proved impervious to internal efforts to make it more skeptical about expanding old government programs and adding new ones to correct capitalism's shortcomings. The failure of even this tentative attempt to incorporate a limiting principle into lib-eralism makes the challenge of funding the limitless welfare state more imposing. Assurances that the welfare state will pay for itself haven't closed the sale. The first line of retreat for liberals has been to assure voters that if, and to the extent, funding the welfare state really is a problem, it is somebody else's problem—somebody *richer's* problem.

In 2006, for example, the film director Rob Reiner was pro-moting a ballot proposition in California to guarantee that every 4-year-old in the state would attend preschool. The proposi-tion called for creating a new top bracket for the state income tax—11% rather than 9.3%—affecting couples making more than $800,000 per year and individuals making more than $400,000. The projected $2.4 billion increase in tax revenues would have been devoted to the preschool program. Reiner was optimistic in advance of the vote. The "American public has no problem raising taxes if it's for something good," he told the columnist E.J. Dionne, who joined Reiner in the hope that "California, which started the tax revolt in the late 1970s, could inaugurate a new era of public investment in things that matter."[37]

After Prop. 82 was defeated, with only 39% of Californians voting for it, Dionne was forced to acknowledge that "there remains a deep skepticism about government spending, even for the best purposes. . . . Attacks on tax and spend sound old and tired, but they still have force." Taking a more conciliatory tone than many liberal writers, Dionne said that "taxpayers aren't selfish just because they place a heavy burden on those who would ask them to part with some of their money."[38]

The failure of measures like Prop. 82 is distressing to liberals, since the political arithmetic looks so promising on paper: Confining tax increases to the most prosperous 2% of the population in order to award valuable prizes to the other 98% will result in making 49 people happy for every one you make angry, which seems like a good formula for winning an election. Despite its failure to banish the political problem of funding the welfare state, liberals have stuck with this approach, preferring it to the alternatives: selling tax increases applicable to a broad swath of the electorate; or curtailing welfare state spending until it matches the tax burden Americans are comfortable with.

In a debate before the 2008 Pennsylvania primary, for example, Hillary Clinton said, "I am absolutely committed to not raising a single tax on middle-class Americans, people making less than $250,000 a year."[39] Barack Obama's reply at the time was less categorical, but on the eve of the Democratic convention his top two economic advisors signaled, in a *Wall Street Journal* op-ed, that the Democratic nominee had embraced the Clinton position with one small modification: The Obama tax plan "would not raise any taxes on couples making less than $250,000 a year, nor on any single person with income under $200,000—not income taxes, capital gains taxes, dividend or payroll taxes."[40]

The difficulty, as *The American Prospect*'s Ezra Klein put it delicately, is that "when everyone below the 95th percentile is untouchable, and effectively middle class, you're in a bit of an odd discourse, distribution-wise."[41] According to the Census Bureau's data, Clinton and Obama had made everyone below the *98th* percentile untouchable, since only 1.92% of American households had an income of $250,000 or more in 2007. (The portion of all households with an income of $200,000 or more was 3.64%.)[42]

FINANCIAL HARMONY

There is no evident escape from this odd discourse. Liberals need to hunt where the ducks are. The problem is that they're hunting both for votes and for tax revenues. Their electoral strategies require votes (and campaign contributions) from the 30.1% of households with an income between $75,000 and $250,000. Given the positive correlation between household income and voting turnout, these families make up significantly more than 30.1% of the electorate. Liberals' welfare state aspirations, however, cannot be realized merely by making the rich less rich. Enacting any significant portion of the liberal agenda will also require making the merely comfortable noticeably less comfortable—and liberals are terrified that imposing tax increases on upper middle-class voters will doom them when those voters go to the polls.

This is not a new dilemma. In *The Ethics of Redistribution*, published in 1952 and based on lectures delivered in 1949, Bertrand de Jouvenel observed that both American and European leftists are convinced "that our societies are extremely rich and that their wealth is merely maldistributed. . . ." The necessary and obvious corrective is for the government to turn "caviar into bread." Heavy taxes on a small number of extremely wealthy people will deprive them of some of their luxuries, enabling the government to provide large numbers of poor people with necessities.[43]

Jouvenel argued that the income distribution of modern societies is, in fact, thicker in the middle than at the top. As a consequence, high taxes on the rich will yield disappointing revenues, funding only a fraction of liberals' ambitions. He makes his point with a thought-experiment, a simple redistributive program that consists of a 100% tax on all income over a specified ceiling. The proceeds are transferred to all households with incomes below a specified floor. For a ceiling to be "financially harmonious" with a floor, the amount of money collected from all households above the ceiling must be just enough, once redistributed, to bring every household with an income below the floor right up to it.

In the real world, of course, a 100% income tax will wind up yielding the government zero revenue, since people will defer or disguise income rather than go to the trouble of earning money that will be immediately transferred to the tax collector. This is the one postulate of supply-side economics about which there is no controversy. By the same token, if the government makes up the entire shortfall between each poor family's income and a specified floor, it is imposing what amounts to a 100% tax rate on those people, too: Every dollar they earn will cause the government to reduce their compensatory stipend by one dollar. Many will accede to this massive incentive to stop working altogether, or to disguise and defer their income. Such actions will dramatically increase the amount needed to bring every household's income up to the floor. In other words, an income ceiling and floor would stop being in financial harmony the minute a redistributive program based on them went into effect. Jouvenel is concerned with the contours of the income distribution, rather than feasible tax and welfare policy options, so he leaves this practical consideration out of his thought-experiment.

Jouvenel's analysis of the distribution of income in the United Kingdom in 1948 led him to conclude that "such surpluses as we might be willing ruthlessly to take away—always assuming that this would have no effect upon production—are by a long way inadequate to raise our nether incomes to a desirable level." Confiscating and liquidating yachts and private jets won't do much to alleviate poverty. An income floor that corresponds to a standard of living regarded as decent by those who are keen on redistribution will require heavy assessments on a much larger group of people, most of whom will be astonished to learn that they are officially rich. "The executive, the public servant, the engineer, the intellectual, the artist are to be cramped," says Jouvenel. "Is this desirable? Is this right?"[44]

An examination of the Census Bureau's data suggests that America's income distribution remains thick in the middle. In 2007, a household income of $250,000 left you better off than 98.08% of all other households, an income of exactly $200,000 was more than 96.4% of all others, an income of $150,000 was higher than 92% of the rest of the country's, and an income of $100,000 defined a group just slightly larger than the most prosperous quintile, being greater than that received by 79.8% of all Americans.[45]

It should be noted that the Congressional Budget Office provides income distribution statistics that are probably more accurate than the Census Bureau's, but also harder to use for our purposes. CBO relies on the analysis of income tax returns rather than survey data, as the Census Bureau does, and the CBO approach generally yields higher totals for the most affluent households. Furthermore, CBO defines income more broadly than the Census Bureau by including the value of Medicare, Medicaid, employer-provided health insurance, capital gains from the sale of assets, and the employer's share of an employee's payroll tax and corporate taxes.

When CBO defines the boundaries of income quintiles and the highest 10, 5 and 1 percent of the income distribution, it adjusts income for household size. It does this by dividing household income, using its encompassing definition, by the square root of the number of people in the household. Thus, a household of one person with an income of $100,000, a household of two with an income of $141,421, a household of three with an income of $173,205, and a household of four with an income of $200,000 are all considered by CBO, for the purposes of segmenting the income distribution, to have an income of $100,000. Using these methods, CBO estimated that in 2005 the most prosperous 1 percent of American households had incomes of at least $307,500; the highest 5 percent had at least $126,300; the highest 10 percent received at least $92,400; and the highest 20% received at least $67,400. There is no way to know how many of the households counted by CBO as having an income of exactly $307,500 were single people receiving that amount, or couples with an income of $434,871, or families of four with an income of $615,000, which makes it impossible to employ them for carrying out Jouvenel's thought-experiment.[46]

If the confiscatory tax Jouvenel hypothesizes had been applied to all income above $250,000, using the Census Bureau's 2007 data, the yield to the government would have been $377 billion. That is, the 2,245,000 households receiving an income of at least $250,000 in 2007 had a mean income of $418,063, yielding a total income of $939 billion. Of this total, $561 billion was the amount that would have given each household an income of exactly $250,000, leaving $377 billion, after rounding, as the amount received in excess of $250,000.

We can apply the same computation to other income ceilings and get even larger notional windfalls for the Jouvenel thought-experiment. A 100% tax bracket on income above $200,000 would yield $529 billion. A ceiling of $150,000, affecting the most prosperous 8% of American households, captures $841 billion. Dropping the ceiling down to $100,000 affects the upper 20.2% of the income distribution, taking $1.588 trillion from them.

An income floor of $20,000, which is close to the federal "poverty line" for a family of four ($20,650 in 2007) would require a transfer of $197 billion. The 22,233,000 households living on less than $20,000 in 2007, 19% of the total, had an aggregate income of $247 billion. For each of those households to have an income of exactly $20,000 would see them with an aggregate income of $445 billion, yielding a $197 billion transfer, plus rounding, to fill the cup right to the brim.

It will be noted that an income floor of $20,000 is, quite easily, in financial harmony with a ceiling of $250,000. The amount we could capture with the 100% tax bracket on income in excess of $250,000 is more than double what we need to secure the $20,000 floor. (Unfortunately for our purposes, the Census Bureau does not break households with annual incomes above $250,000 into smaller categories. Otherwise, it would be possible to specify the ceiling, presumably somewhere between $300,000 and $400,000, in exact harmony with a $20,000 floor.) Calculating the transfer required by a higher income floor, we see that the $377 billion yielded by a $250,000 ceiling is also adequate to provide for a floor of $25,000, which would require $328 billion.

Confirmation of Jouvenel's claim that redistributionists want a higher income floor than they can plausibly pay for comes from Jared Bernstein, who worked for the liberal Economic Policy Institute before being named Vice President Biden's economic advisor. Bernstein considers it "unjust in an affluent, highly productive economy to label *only* those facing the most severe material deprivation as poor." He argued in 2007 that "families who are unable to meet basic needs . . . face a material disadvantage that government should recognize and address," and recommends an income *twice* the official poverty level to define the portion of the population the government needs to help.[47]

We are talking, then, about an income floor around $40,000, which would have required a transfer of $894 billion in 2007. The $841 billion yielded by applying the 100% tax bracket to all income in excess of $150,000 would have fallen a little short, meaning that the income ceiling in financial harmony with the income floor suggested by Bernstein would be in the neighborhood of $140,000.

Of course, as Jouvenel predicted, American liberals aren't even whispering about plans for a society where no one lives on more than $140,000 or less than $40,000. Both Hillary Clinton and Barack Obama promised forcefully to impose no tax increases of any kind on families making less than $250,000. On the contrary, Obama proposed to *cut* taxes for "95% of workers and their families," meaning that upper-middle class households will be paying a smaller amount of money to support the welfare state.[48]

But even the goal of a society where no one lives on more than $250,000 or less than $25,000 is too ambitious. The tax increases Obama called for after he won the Democratic nomination were miles short of being confiscatory. According to his campaign advisors Jason Furman and Austan Goolsbee, the Obama tax plan called for a top bracket of 39.6%, and a top rate for federal taxes on capital gains and dividends of 20%.[49] By contrast, the top rate was cut from 91% to 70% in 1964, then from 70% to 50% in 1981, and has been lower than 40% since 1986. The liberal historian Sean Wilentz says that "never, in our lifetimes," are we going to see top marginal income tax rates of 70% again, something that "if you stood looking to the future in 1980, would have been amazing."[50]

Thus, for any imaginable political future, there is a huge disparity between the welfare state liberals want to build and the tax system they are prepared to call for. And it gets worse. We've agreed to play by the rules of Jouvenel's thought-experiment, pretending that a 100% tax bracket won't even slightly diminish the tax base or expand the welfare rolls. But we can't ignore the fact (which Jouvenel doesn't ignore) that the households receiving income above any given ceiling already pay taxes. The 100% tax we impose for the purpose of transferring money from every household above the ceiling to every household below the income floor is going to deprive the government of *all* the revenues from taxpayers above the ceiling, revenues that are used for every government activity besides the transfer program. The state is always bigger than the welfare state.

It's unrealistic to count the money raised from the 100% tax bracket even once, but we have done so for the purpose of carrying out Jouvenel's thought-experiment. It is impossible, however, to count that money twice. An income floor and ceiling that are in financial harmony will not allow all the households with incomes above the floor but below the ceiling to be mere spectators to the transfer of income from the rich to the poor going on over their heads. Those families, too, will have to surrender more to the government, which needs to make up for all the tax revenue it used to receive from those above the ceiling, funds devoted to national defense, infrastructure, public health, law enforcement, education, and every other government activity. According to the Congressional Budget Office, households in the top 1% of the income distribution paid 27.6% of all federal taxes in 2005—income, social insurance, corporate and excise taxes. The top 5% of the income distribution accounted for 43.8% of the federal government's tax receipts.[51]

An enormous amount of money is going to have to be replaced, then, if the government is going to continue all the functions it performs apart from the income transfer program. Those funds can't come from above the income ceiling—all that money has been taken by the government already—and they can't come from below the floor, since a tax increase that affected those households would defeat the purpose of establishing a floor and a program to make sure no one falls below it. Thus, the transfer program not only requires a 100% tax on all households with incomes above the ceiling, but a heavy tax increase on all households below the ceiling and above the floor.

How heavy? According to the CBO, households in the top tenth of the income distribution accounted for 54.7% of all federal taxes in 2005. The next most prosperous tenth provided 14% of federal taxes, while the quintile just south of this group paid 16.9%. In all, the top 40% of the income distribution paid 85.8% of all federal taxes, meaning the lowest, second and middle quintiles, combined—the least prosperous 60% of the population—paid 14.2%. The thought-experiment redistribution program would obviate the need for some welfare state programs—which does not guarantee, as a matter of practical politics, that it would eliminate the programs themselves—thus reducing the amount of the tax burden formerly paid by those above the income ceiling that will now have to be assumed by those below it. On the other hand, the CBO numbers cover only federal taxes, so states, counties and municipalities will be raising taxes on those below the ceiling to make up for the revenue *they* no longer receive from those above it. Even with all the favorable assumptions Jouvenel builds into his thought-experiment, its implementation would require a dramatic tax increase on families who expected, based on the description in the brochure, to be bystanders observing the transfer of income from people richer than they are to those who are poorer.

PROPERTY RIGHTS

If we discard Jouvenel's for-the-sake-of-the-argument assumption about the irrelevance of high taxes to the continuation of

186 Liberalism's Continuing Inability to Make Payroll

economic activity, the redistribution of income grows even more daunting. The growth of the welfare state will, beyond a certain point, require some combination of high taxes, heavy borrowing and muscular regulations that reduces the amount of wealth the private economy produces, and ultimately reduces the amount available for the government to distribute through welfare state programs. The "difference principle," advanced by John Rawls in *A Theory of Justice*, takes note of this problem by eschewing the kind of redistribution that leaves the poor with a bigger slice of a smaller pie. Rawls's goal, a society where the least-advantaged members have the highest possible standard of living, can be thwarted by too much egalitarianism. Insisting, for example, that medical researchers shouldn't get to have large research budgets unless everyone else gets comparable subsidies will, in the name of equality, worsen the lives of people with serious diseases that never get cured because too little is invested in research.[52]

There is another respect in which Rawlsianism's problems are liberalism's. All the elaborate theories about the just distribution of income are implicitly based on the false premise that incomes *are* distributed. Rawls offers a complex chain of syllogisms to establish the morally optimal departure from absolute equality, but makes no room in it for the legitimate acquisition, possession and voluntary exchange of wealth. Property would be private in an entirely contingent sense in a Rawlsian society; any claim I have to keep what's mine will always be trumped by the social imperative to adhere to the just allocation of all economic assets.

This critique was central to the argument of *Anarchy, State and Utopia*, written in 1974 by Rawls's colleague at Harvard, Robert Nozick.[53] We can update Nozick's argument about the legitimacy of Wilt Chamberlain prospering from the sale of tickets to basketball fans by noting that the highest paid baseball player, Alex Rodriguez, signed a ten-year contract in 2007 for $275 million. That average annual salary of $27,500,000 works out to $75,342 a day—every day of the calendar year, that is, not every day of the baseball season. Leaving aside the additional money Rodriguez makes from commercial endorsements and appearance fees, as well as the interest, dividends and capital gains on wealth he has already accumulated, his *daily* compensation is $7,733 higher than the mean *annual* income in 2007 for an American household, which was $67,609.

If a cabinet-level Department of Wealth Allocation, charged with determining the just and optimal allotment for each American, had decreed that a baseball star receive an income 407 times higher than the average household's, most people would demand a congressional investigation. Nozick's point against Rawls is that we do, and should, use a very different moral calculus to judge the economic outcomes that are the byproduct of millions of individuals' decisions to buy and sell thousands of different goods and services. "The socialist society would have to forbid capitalist acts between consenting adults," Nozick argues, because if the socialist's ideal distribution of income could be realized even for one day, it couldn't be made to last beyond the end of the day, except through "continuous interference" in everyone's lives, since their purchases will increase the income of some more than others.[54]

The Department of Wealth Allocation's assessment will have little in common with the array of incomes resulting from millions of individual economic decisions. Rather than worry about economic outcomes, Nozick concentrates on processes. The government should make sure that people who have arrived at mutually agreeable terms can voluntarily exchange what they wish to, and hold on to what they have acquired as a result of those exchanges. If it does so, the disparity between the star athlete's income and the schoolteacher's or pipefitter's neither vindicates nor violates some abstract principle of distributive justice. As long as the New York Yankees aren't coerced into hiring Rodriguez, baseball fans aren't coerced into buying tickets to see him play, and advertisers aren't coerced into paying for commercials on the broadcasts of Yankees games, A-Rod's $27.5 million salary is a victimless "crime"—a non-problem that should elicit a non-solution.

INDECENT HIGH-LIVING

In *The Ethics of Redistribution*, Jouvenel set his redistributive thought-experiment in motion by observing that egalitarianism has two related preoccupations, "indecent low-living and indecent high-living." Misery is a scandal, and extravagance is a scandal. Above all, the side-by-side existence of misery and extravagance is *the* scandal that everywhere animates the political Left.[55]

Liberals will sometimes try to deflect accusations about class warfare by insisting they bear the rich no malice. Their interest in the rich is as limited and practical as Willie Sutton's interest in banks: that's where the money is. According to Chait, "Liberals want to make the rich pay higher tax rates not because they hate them. . . . It's because somebody has to pay for the government, and the rich can more easily bear higher rates."[56]

Liberalism's posture toward the rich *seems*, however, to involve something more—something angrier—than observing that they have lots of money, with which the welfare state can do lots of good. In his acceptance speech to the 1936 Democratic convention, Franklin D. Roosevelt spoke of "economic royalists" and "privileged princes" of "economic dynasties," who have "created a new despotism." In his final speech of that campaign, FDR said, "I should like to have it said of my first Administration that in it the forces of selfishness and of lust for power met their match. I should like to have it said of my second Administration that in it these forces met their master." According to the account of the campaign rally by the historian David Kennedy, "Bedlam broke out on the arena floor as the partisan audience roared its approval."[57] We may reasonably infer that this reaction to FDR's speech reflected something more spirited than calculations about the higher government revenues progressive taxes might yield.

American liberals, like leftists in other countries, rarely work up much anger, however, against famous athletes, actors or musicians who enjoy life in the capstone of the income pyramid. Stardom confers a kind of democratic legitimacy on the stars' aristocratic lives and status. In economic terms, the purchases that diminish our modest incomes in order to increase their vast ones are direct and unmediated. We pay to see Kobe Bryant, Angelina Jolie or Bruce Springsteen, and if we like what we see we'll keep paying, making them even richer. The popularity of the sycophantic television show, "Lifestyles of the Rich and Famous," rested on the "and famous" part of its title. Nobody wanted to see a show about venture capitalists' houses in the Hamptons. The guided tours of famous actors' and musicians' homes gave us a chance to see our entertainment dollars at work, as the camera lingered over their antique automobiles or sweeping ocean views.

The stardom of the stars is treated, in the broader sense, as an expression of the will of the people rather than an affront to it. Fame is fleeting. We who have elevated this tiny minority so high reserve the right to knock them down a peg or five, passing judgment at any moment on their professional or personal missteps, instantly turning a star from a hero into a laughingstock, and reminding the whole firmament that their eminence depends on our revocable opinions.

The entire weight of the accusation of indecent high living is left to fall on rich people who are not stars. Heirs to large fortunes qualify, as do those who've made it to the top in business or finance. The dispensation given to the few who are chosen by the many to lead gold-plated lives doesn't extend to them. (This distinction suggests a certain shrewdness in the efforts of Paris Hilton and Donald Trump to reposition themselves as famously rich rather than just exceedingly rich.) The voluntary exchanges that legitimate, according to Nozick, the athlete or movie star's enormous income take place in public view. For the heiress or the CEO, those transactions take place offstage, raising suspicions. The heiress owes her prosperity to her great-grandfather's business success—success that, in many quarters, has the burden to prove itself a great fortune that does not rest on a great crime—abetted unto the present day by a retinue of lawyers and bankers who navigate the tax code to make sure that the rich will only grow richer.

As for the CEO, "Incestuous corporate boards regularly approve compensation packages for chief executives and others that are out of logic's range," according to Sen. James Webb of Virginia. He complained in 2006 that "the average CEO of a sizeable corporation makes more than $10 million a year." Though true, this is a salary received by some professional athletes who are never going to be chosen for their sport's hall of fame, or even for this year's all-star game.[58]

The AFL-CIO maintains an "Executive PayWatch Database," which provides information on how much the CEOs of hundreds of American corporations "raked in," using a calculation that includes salary as well as the present value of bonuses, stock options and other incentives. The database shows that for the ten largest U.S. corporations, as measured by 2007 gross revenue, the average CEO compensation was $22,041,814. (The ten companies were: Walmart, ExxonMobil, Chevron, General Motors, Conoco-Phillips, General Electric, Ford, Citigroup, Bank of America, and AT&T.) For the four highest-paid members of the 2009 New York Yankees the average salary is $22,975,000. (The four ballplayers include: Derek Jeter, Alex Rodriguez, C.C. Sabathia, and Mark Teixeira.)[59] It's true that some of those big companies have gone through huge difficulties; it's also true that Rodriguez, Sabathia and Teixeira had never played in the World Series at the time they signed their contracts.

Again, however, we sanction the star's wealth in a way we don't sanction the executive's. People understand and accept the connection between purchasing their Yankees tickets and A-Rod's salary. Sen. Webb appeals to popular suspicions that, by contrast, something sinister taints the long chain of transactions connecting the purchase of a tank of gas to the compensation of Rex Tillerson, the CEO of ExxonMobil. (According to the AFL-CIO's database, Tillerson's total compensation in 2007 was $27,172,280. For running a company with 107,100 employees that made $40.6 billion in profits on revenues of $373 billion in 2007, Tillerson received 98.8% as much as Alex Rodriguez.) The indecent high-living of the CEO further incites liberal anger because, unlike the star or even the heiress, his wealth not only stands in contrast to indecent low-living, but we can accuse him of causing it. Our dissatisfactions as consumers or workers can be directed against the occupant of the executive suite.

None of these grievances, however, dispatches Nozick's objection as it applies to heirs, executives, financiers *or* movie stars and ballplayers. If their wealth is the result of licit, voluntary transactions, we should not treat it as an affront to some abstract principle of distributive justice, such as Rawls's, or to the inchoate sentiments about economic fairness that motivate non-tenured liberals. Nor can we, following Chait, assume that justice is on the side of social reformers who want to finance their projects by treating the rich as an ATM. The fact that they can "more easily bear" higher taxes would justify 70%, 91%, or 99.9% tax brackets—taxing the rich to the point where they can bear such rates no more easily than my barber or your accountant. As F.A. Hayek argued in *The Constitution of Liberty*, the rule of law requires universality. Once you make different people pay different tax rates, or obey different speed limits, there's nothing to stop the government from enacting the most arbitrary, capricious, or burdensome policies it can get away with. The liberal "principle" that people with higher incomes should pay higher tax rates is as vague, flexible and, therefore, useless as every other liberal principle. It's impossible to obey a principle if it's impossible to say what it would mean to violate it, and no liberal argument for progressive taxation ever stipulates the point at which higher rates on the prosperous become excessive and indefensible.

TAXING CORPORATIONS

The revenue measure liberals like to pair with taxing the rich is taxing corporations. Together, the policies target the two villains in what George F. Will calls "liberalism's master narrative—the victimization of the many by the few."[60] By virtue of punishing the victimizers, these tax policies are morally just. By virtue of mining the allegedly vast and inexhaustible vein of wealth possessed by the rich and the corporations, the policies are economically sound. And by virtue of the tautology that the many outnumber the few, these policies in a democracy are politically self-perpetuating.

The trouble is that financing liberalism's limitless ambitions by taxing corporations is even more intellectually dishonest than relying on taxation of the rich. The argument for sticking the rich with the tab for the welfare state is that they can afford it. This isn't true—unless one defines the welfare state's mission far more narrowly than liberals do, or the rich more broadly than anyone does. But at least it *could* be true. The top-heavy income distribution liberals imagine is logically possible; it's just not empirically accurate. If it were, then we could pay for a big welfare state with heavy taxes on the rich and negligible taxes on everybody else.

The idea that making corporations pay for the welfare state is an alternative to making ordinary citizens pay for it, however, isn't even a logical possibility. The distinction between taxes paid by corporations and taxes paid by flesh-and-blood voters falls apart when analyzed. As Irving Kristol pointed out, corporations don't pay taxes, they *collect* them. To the extent a corporation pays its taxes by charging more than it otherwise would for the goods and services it sells, the corporate tax is really a sales tax imposed on its customers. To the extent a corporation pays its taxes by spending less than it otherwise would for the goods and services it buys, the tax is really a value-added tax imposed on its suppliers and employees. Finally, to the extent a corporation pays its taxes by reducing its profits, the tax is imposed on its shareholders, either in the short term through reduced dividends or in the long term by the diminished value of a company that has curtailed its investment in all the factors that promote growth, such as facilities, research and technology. (Many of the "investors" who will suffer, such as non-profit institutions with an endowment, or retirees receiving payments from a pension fund, may not even realize they're shareholders.) We have met our Fortune 500 sugar daddy, and it is us.[61]

There is nothing esoteric about this analysis. One must assume, therefore, that liberals understand that taxing corporations is a *way* to tax people, rather than a way to avoid taxing them. That, indeed, is the point. Liberalism confronts the political fact that lots of Americans suspect that the welfare state's benefits—or at least a much bigger welfare state's benefits—are not worth its costs. Though they themselves have no doubts on this question, liberals rarely try to disabuse their countrymen of the idea that taxation for the welfare state is money ill-spent. Such efforts would involve persuading people that they're better off surrendering a larger portion of their income to a government that provides a comprehensive welfare state, and worse off by keeping that income and living in a society with a limited welfare state.

Rather than demonstrate that voters' skeptical ideas about the welfare state are unfounded, liberals design their rhetoric and policies to alter voters' *perceptions* of the welfare state. They do not, that is, take on the burdens and risks of arguing that the benefits of the welfare state are X, the costs are Y, and X is greater than Y. Instead, liberals concentrate on making X appear to be greater than it is and Y less than it is. Taxes "paid" by corporations are ideal for this purpose. The citizens who really pay the tax, as consumers, employees or shareholders, have no way to ascertain how much they're paying, and usually no awareness they're paying anything at all.

BLACKENING THE SKIES WITH CRISS-CROSSING DOLLARS

The effort to sell the welfare state by making its benefits overt and its costs covert extends far beyond the reliance on corporate taxes. It is an approach that informs the liberal project to defederalize America by tilting power and resources away from the states and toward the national government. As the economist James Tobin wrote in *The New Republic* in 1964:

> We are a nation. Connecticut citizens do have an interest in the quality of rivers in Massachusetts, of highways in Wyoming, and life in Harlem. We cannot leave it wholly up to 50 state legislatures to determine whether or how national resources are used to meet national needs.[62]

To say that the federal government should pay for better schools in Indiana or better highways in Idaho means, of course, that taxpayers in Oregon and South Carolina are going to pay for them. This arrangement holds obvious appeal for politicians: Governors and mayors are happy to bestow benefits on people who can vote for them, using taxes paid by people who cannot vote against them. It is impossible, of course, for every state, city, county and school district to come out ahead by sending money to and receiving it from Washington, D.C. Some jurisdictions will wind up being net importers of dollars and some will be net exporters. The shipping costs of letting the money stay in Washington for a while, to be counted and tended by federal employees, guarantees that the total amount imported by the states, cities, etc. will always be less than the total amount exported.

It is not, however, impossible for every jurisdiction to *seem* to come out ahead, for all of them to look like importers rather than exporters. All that's required is the successful management of perceptions—the dollars must arrive more conspicuously than they depart. Ribbon-cutting ceremonies for new bridges and schools paid for by grants from the federal and state government are common. Clear statements to taxpayers of how much they have paid for projects in distant jurisdictions are not.

Christopher Jencks, also writing in *The New Republic,* said that "local and state electorates" have repeatedly shown their aversion to paying for better school systems. As a result, "friends of education have called for massive federal aid."[63] This analysis is unintentionally revealing. Local and state electorates comprise the same voters as the federal electorate. There's no good reason to think those voters' sentiments about paying for education undergo a radical change as they move from the section of the ballot where they vote for federal officials to the one where they vote for state and local ones. There is a good reason, however, to think that voters opposed to state and local expenditures will acquiesce in federal ones: They expect that the benefits of "massive federal aid" will be enjoyed locally while the costs are imposed distantly.

This is the political logic of turning "the skies black with crisscrossing dollars."[64] Simplicity promotes clarity, while complexity promotes confusion. Liberals could have chosen otherwise, but have consistently acted like people who believe that clarity is the enemy and confusion the friend of the welfare state. The goal, accordingly, is to make the welfare state as complex as possible. A complex welfare state will have many ambitions, many initiatives to advance them, and will not be fastidious about programs overlapping or duplicating one another. This proliferation increases the number of voters who identify themselves as the beneficiaries of at least one government program. The tax and regulatory systems, meanwhile, should also be as baroque as possible. Such complexity increases the number of voters who can only guess at what they pay for the welfare state, and increases the likelihood that their guesses will fall well below the actual amount.

SOCIAL INSURANCE

The ultimate political goal of blackening the sky with crisscrossing dollars is to promote the belief that not only every state, county and city, but every household, can be a net importer of the enormous but nevertheless finite number of dollars vacuumed up and airdropped by the government. Liberals have made this mathematical impossibility the political foundation for America's social insurance system. Understanding this strategy explains what is otherwise baffling: Income redistribution is very hard, as our discussion of the Jouvenel thought-experiment demonstrated. Liberals respond to this problem, which they cannot solve, by dramatically expanding it. If it's hard to defend the taxes needed for a welfare state that helps the poor, the thing to do is to build a welfare state that helps people whether or not they're poor.

Liberals believe that the government must intervene to compensate for all the ways our economic system is rigged in favor of the rich. At the same time, they furiously denounce any proposed reductions in social insurance benefits paid *to* the rich. Sen. John Edwards, for example, told the 2004 Democratic convention that we are descending toward two Americas, "one for people who are set for life, [who] know their kids and their grandkids are going to be just fine; and then one for most Americans, people who live paycheck to paycheck."[65] Curtailing or even eliminating Social Security and Medicare benefits for the people who are set for life in order to concentrate on helping people who live paycheck to paycheck would seem like one sensible response to this trend. If the rich, and only the rich, are getting richer, then coals-to-Newcastle government programs to pay for their pensions and medical insurance would appear to be both unaffordable and indefensible.

In reality, means testing social insurance is the third rail of liberal discourse. Paul Kirk, the chairman of the Democratic National Committee in 1985, spoke uncritically about means testing with some reporters, only to issue a press release a few *hours* later: "I was wrong. Our party . . . is unalterably opposed to any cuts in Social Security benefits. I should not have mentioned the subject of a means test."[66] Kirk's transgression was his obliviousness to the political logic of social insurance. According to the journalist Chris Suellentrop, liberals "support Social Security because it's redistributive. In other words, it's welfare for old people. . . . Liberals are willing to keep paying rich people Social Security in the hopes that the payments will keep those rich people from figuring out that Social Security is a redistributive transfer program."[67]

The point, again, is the management of perceptions. A simple program to help poor people, including those who are old, would make it easy to distinguish the households that are net exporters of dollars from the ones that are net importers. Liberals don't want to run that risk. They don't trust the prosperous citizens in the net exporter households to be generous and public-spirited enough to keep voting for welfare programs once it becomes clear to them that they are financing benefits bestowed on others.

"Liberalism needs government," says Cohn, "because government is how the people, acting together, provide for the safety and well-being of their most vulnerable members."[68] The journey from this premise to the conclusion that reducing Warren Buffet's Social Security benefits would be an outrage is an interesting one. In a society that is remarkably prosperous by global and historical standards, shouldn't "most vulnerable members" be construed as referring to the most vulnerable 5, 10, or 25% of the population—not necessarily those who are abjectly miserable, but people who are at least confronting serious threats or problems? When it turns out, time and again, that the effective meaning of liberal welfare and social insurance programs is to elicit compassion and government subventions for the most "vulnerable" 75, 90, or 95% of the population, it's hard not to feel scammed.

Like Cohn, Paul Starr of *The American Prospect* says the welfare state is about the poor. Its "objective should be, above all, to eliminate poverty and maintain a minimum floor of decency to enable individuals to carry out their own life plans." But giving benefits to everyone, not just the most vulnerable, serves social and political purposes. Socially, "the long-term tasks of nation-building and of fostering a common culture and a sense of shared citizenship also strongly argue for public and universal schooling, old-age pensions, and other services that serve an integrative as well as egalitarian purpose," according to Starr. Politically, the imperative to construct democratic majorities that support programs for the poor "will often mean support for programs that provide universal benefits." We may say that such programs "target" the most vulnerable 100% of the population.[69]

Wilbur Cohen, who devoted half a century in government to designing and defending America's social insurance programs, explained the risk of not universalizing benefits in 1972, during a debate with Milton Friedman on Social Security:

> I am convinced that, in the United States, a program that deals
> only with the poor will end up being a poor program. . . . Ever
> since the Elizabethan Poor Law of 1601, programs only for the
> poor have been lousy, no good, poor programs. And a program
> that is only for the poor—one that has nothing in it for the
> middle income and the upper income—is, in the long run, a
> program the American public won't support.[70]

The government provides Social Security and Medicare to people who don't need them for the sake of people who do.

Starr and Cohen are confident that people can be *induced* to support programs to help the poor, but have no interest in relying on the prospect they can be *persuaded* to support them. Liberals distrust their own forensic abilities as much as they distrust the decency of their fellow citizens. It's easy to garner support for government programs from their beneficiaries. The hard thing is to persuade people who know they aren't beneficiaries that the programs are wise and necessary.

We have already noted, in our discussion of communitarianism, the implausibility of nurturing the mystic chords of unity by having the same government agency dispense benefit checks to millions of strangers. Starr's hope for nation-building and fostering a common culture through public and universal schooling is less far-fetched. There's a lot to be said for public education. Some of it is said by Democrats—such as the Clintons, Obamas, and Bidens—who enroll their children in expensive private schools, apparently with no apprehensions that they will be warped into selfish Republicans by the time they graduate.[71]

The supposed necessity of universalizing social insurance in order to secure majority support for programs that only a minority really needs is more serious than liberalism's concern with civic unity, but equally spurious. Were it otherwise, the Earned Income

Tax Credit (EITC), for which all families with an income above $41,646 were ineligible in 2008, would be as politically besieged as Aid to Families with Dependent Children was before 1996. In reality, EITC enjoys bipartisan support in Congress and is politically unassailable. "If means testing makes Social Security as unpopular as the EITC," writes Mickey Kaus, "Democrats have nothing to fear."[72]

Disregarding the evidence that their efforts to enlarge Americans' sense of the public obligation to the poor are succeeding, liberals prefer to rely on the people's credulity rather than their civitas. A welfare state based on the people's public-spiritedness, as well as liberals' ability to appeal to it, would be constructed without fear that people who are net exporters of governmentally redistributed dollars will easily realize this about themselves. Such a regime would simply, even elegantly, provide for the well-being of society's most vulnerable members.

It might also, however, realize liberals' fears about the limits of the people's generosity. A welfare state that relies on people's credulity, by contrast, won't. Such a welfare state can't abide simplicity because gullibility can be trusted only so far. It would be asking too much, for example, to assert that government programs can pay out more than they take in and somehow remain solvent indefinitely. People can be led to believe a lot of things, but probably not the magic beans theory of public finance.

Programs that promise every household can be a net importer of dollars will never withstand scrutiny. If they are complicated enough, however, they will defeat scrutiny by wearing it down. The conservative writer Ramesh Ponnuru, wondering at liberalism's reliance on social insurance measures designed to leave net exporters with the impression that they're net importers, asks, "Is the theory that rich people can't do math?" And that is indeed the theory, with the proviso that the math should be calculus rather than arithmetic. Since Social Security is now in its eighth decade and its fiscal precariousness has never engendered its political precariousness, one must conclude that this liberal theory has established a formidable track record.[73]

CHAPTER FIVE

CONSERVATISM'S CONTINUING INABILITY TO MAKE A DIFFERENCE

As we observed in Chapter One, the world has never seen a shrinking welfare state. Have conservatives, determined to reduce America's, given themselves an impossible assignment? In 2006 Ramesh Ponnuru wrote, "Conservatism is in crisis," one which "can be boiled down to two propositions. The first is that, at least as the American electorate is presently constituted, there is no imaginable political coalition in America capable of sustaining a majority that takes a reduction of the scope of the federal government as one of its central tasks. The second is that modern American conservatism is incapable of organizing itself without taking that as a central mission."[1]

It's not that elections don't make a difference. Table 1.8 shows that the federal government's real, per capita outlays on Human Resources grew 12.57% per year during Lyndon Johnson's elected term in the White House, while increasing at an annual rate of 0.90% during Ronald Reagan's presidency. Whether the welfare state doubles every six years, as it would if the growth rate from 1965 to 1969 were sustained, or every 80, as it would if the Reagan trajectory were extrapolated, is more than a detail.

It's not surprising that the leading candidates for the 2008 Republican presidential nomination invoked the Reagan legacy. All presented themselves as Reagan's heirs when appealing to the conservative voters who dominate GOP primaries. Mitt Romney said, "We must return to the common-sense Reagan Republican ideals."[2] "What we're lacking is strong, aggressive, bold leadership, like we had with Ronald Reagan," Rudy Giuliani declared.[3]

The biographical commercial on John McCain's website linked him to *both* of the most important conservative politicians of the 20th century: "I am confident that the reason why I hold a lot of the philosophical views that I have [is] the inspiration of Barry Goldwater and Ronald Reagan, there's no doubt about it. . . . One of the things that caused our defeat in 2006, was we strayed from many of [Reagan's] principles, we forgot who we were and who we are."[4]

The implicit criticism by these candidates—that George W. Bush had led Republicans away from Reagan's conservative principles—was less than fair. It's true, returning to Table 1.8, that expenditures on Human Resources grew more than three times as fast under Bush as under Reagan. For that matter, those outlays grew twice as fast under Bush as they did under Bill Clinton (and the Gingrich Republicans in Congress). On the other hand, the similarities between Bush and Reagan concerning the growth of the welfare state are more important than the differences. Human Resources outlays grew more slowly under Bush than under Jimmy Carter, more slowly than under John Kennedy and LBJ from 1961 to 1965, and significantly less rapidly than they had under George H.W. Bush, Richard Nixon and Gerald Ford.

There is a more fundamental problem with the contest to lay claim to Reagan's mantle. For welfare state spending to have grown less than 1% a year for eight years was an exceptional achievement, whether we compare Reagan to other presidents or to other nations' governments. And yet . . . 0.90% is a very small number, but it is still a positive number. Reagan's "triumph" was to yield ground more slowly than any other political leader in the battle that conservatives consider their central mission.

To understand the crisis of conservatism, then, we need to understand what did and did not happen in the Reagan era, which we'll define expansively to include the efforts of the Gingrich Republicans after their victory in 1994.

A SMALLER SLICE OF A LARGER PIE

We noted in Chapter One that the growth of the welfare state, here and abroad, is the result of two trends: economic growth, and the political willingness to devote an increasing portion of economic output to social welfare programs. The two decades following Reagan's election in 1980 are a partial exception to this rule. During those years economic growth accounted for almost all the increase in welfare state spending—the portion of GDP devoted to federal Human Resources outlays barely budged.

Per capita Human Resources outlays, expressed in fiscal year 2000 dollars, were $2,659 in 1981 and $3,942 in 2001, an increase of 48.3%. Over the same period, per capita GDP increased by 50.9%, from $22,834 to $34,464. Had the portion of GDP devoted to Human Resources stayed exactly level over those two decades, the federal government would have spent $3,826 per capita in 2000 dollars. The fact that this portion increased from 11.10% in 1981 to 11.43% in 2001 accounted for the other $116—9.0%—of the $1,283 increase.

Looking at the two decades more closely reveals that the four-year presidency of George H.W. Bush was the only period when the portion of GDP used for federal Human Resources expenditures really grew. Between 1981 and 1989 it declined from 11.10% to 9.97%, then increased to 12.04% in 1993. The percentage reached 12.09% in fiscal year 1995, then began a steady decline after the 1994 midterm elections brought Republican majorities to Capitol Hill, reaching as low as 11.01% in 2000 before increasing to 11.43% in 2001.

Tenths and even hundredths of a percentage point are not rounding errors when discussing something as vast as the American economy. Had the percentage of GDP devoted to Human Resources expenditures remained at 11.1% throughout the Reagan presidency, the federal government would have spent an additional $196 billion for those purposes during those eight years, which works out to $267 billion in FY 2000 dollars. Had the 9.97% of 1989 obtained throughout the four years George H.W. Bush was president, the federal government would have spent $338 billion *less* on Human Resources programs, which works out to $396 billion in FY 2000 terms. And, finally, had the 12.04% rate of 1993 applied to the subsequent eight years, the federal government would have spent an additional $322 billion on Human Resources ($327 billion in FY 2000 dollars), better than $40 billion per year.

We observed in the last chapter that although liberals are, at best, skeptical about capitalism, they also depend on it to generate the wealth they want the government to spend on social reforms. Conservatives, by the same token, are always praising capitalism, but find themselves in the awkward position of having their fight against the welfare state severely complicated by the markets' dynamic growth. Watching conservatives try to reduce the welfare state after 1980 was like looking at people trying to walk down an up escalator. Many hard political battles were required to reduce the welfare state's claim on the nation's economic output by a tenth between 1981 and 1989. By 1989, however, real per capita GDP was 22.3% larger than it had been in 1981. For the conservatives' troubles, Human Resources outlays were 7.4% higher when Reagan left office than when he was inaugurated.

ENTITLEMENTS

It's useful, up to a point, to segment the welfare state's growth into presidential terms. It would be wrong, however, to leave the impression that federal spending on Human Resources is an exercise in zero-based budgeting, where Congress and the president start every fiscal year with a blank page and determine how many billions are going to be spent on each of the dozens of different welfare state programs. In reality, most of the federal government's Human Resources outlays reflect political decisions made years ago and written into the laws and regulations controlling such entitlement programs as Social Security and Medicare. Year-to-year variations in Human Resources outlays will be determined, then, by the interaction of established benefit formulas with changing economic and demographic circumstances.

Recall, for example, that Max Sawicky scorned the "pathetic" growth of the welfare state under Bill Clinton in the pixels of *The American Prospect*. While the growth rate from 1993 to 2001 *was* slower than under any president except Reagan, that fact cannot be entirely ascribed to Newt Gingrich's boldness and Clinton's acquiescent triangulation. The strong economy of the 1990s reduced the number of people applying for unemployment compensation and food assistance programs. Measured in constant dollars and adjusting for the increase in the national population, outlays for those purposes declined between 1993 and 2001 by 38.0% and 24.9%, respectively. Demographically, the people who became eligible for Social Security and Medicare during the 1990s were born in the 1930s, when birth rates were unusually low. The portion of the American population between 65 and 74 years in age declined from 7.25% in 1990 to 6.53% in 2000. In a nation that numbered 281 million by 2000, and that devotes so much of its welfare state spending to programs for the elderly, this decline of three-quarters of one percent made a difference. Social Security outlays, measured in constant dollars and relative to the size of the entire U.S. population, grew at an annual rate of 1.15% under Clinton, while Medicare outlays grew at a rate of 3.17%; both figures are lower than for any other presidency.[5]

We noted in Chapter Two that the New Deal sought not merely political victories but *permanent* victories that would place America's welfare state "beyond the vagaries of public opinion and the reach of elections and party politics," in the words of Sidney Milkis. He quotes one New Dealer, Joseph Harris, writing in 1936 that "we may assume the nature of the problems of American life are such as not to permit any political party for any length of time to abandon most of the collectivist functions which are now being exercised."[6]

The durability of liberalism's victories is shown most clearly by the political invulnerability of entitlement programs—the descriptor itself is a testament to the matter-of-fact understanding that streams of benefits from the government should be regarded as inalienable rights. The architects of America's social insurance system designed it to reinforce that sense of entitlement, to remove any reluctance the people might have about demanding the benefits that were "theirs." In 1941 Luther Gulick, an advisor to several New Deal commissions, suggested to Pres. Roosevelt that the decision in 1935 to couple Social Security benefits to a regressive payroll tax had been unfortunate. His point was that paying for Social Security out of the government's *general* revenues would have better served two liberal goals: tax progressivity, and Keynesian deficit spending to stimulate aggregate demand. In an oft-quoted reply, FDR said, "I guess you're right on the economics. They are politics all the way through. We put those pay roll contributions there so as to give the contributors a legal, moral, and political right to collect their pensions and their unemployment benefits. With those taxes in there, no damn politician can ever scrap my social security program. Those taxes aren't a matter of economics, they're straight politics."[7]

FDR's prediction about the imperviousness of social insurance to meddling by damn politicians—and, by extension, the damn voters who elect them—has held up for 70 years. The political resilience of the entitlement programs explains, better than any other factor, why conservatives led by Ronald Reagan in the 1980s and Newt Gingrich in the 1990s were able to slow the growth of the welfare state, but not to stop or reverse it. The Reagan administration made good on his promise to curb the size of the federal establishment—in those areas where it was politically feasible to do so. Between 1981 and 1989 federal outlays on Education, Training, Employment and Social Services programs, adjusted for inflation and population growth, shrank by 27.9%. Income Security outlays fell 7.4%. But these two functions accounted, together, for only 34.1% of the constant-dollar spending on Human Resources during the Reagan years. By contrast, Social Security and Medicare accounted, together, for 57.9% of Human Resources spending. Medicare outlays, adjusting for inflation and national population growth, were 46.8% higher in 1989 than 1981, while Social Security outlays, reckoned the same way, were 12.7% higher.

The contest between liberals who want to expand the welfare state and conservatives who want to shrink it would seem to be a classic zero-sum game, a tug of war where one side gains precisely to the extent the other loses. The Clinton years, however, were an era of negative-sum politics; both liberals and conservatives had good reason to be chagrined. As a result, no one recalls that decade of peace and prosperity as an Era of Good Feeling.

Liberals hoped that Clinton's election in 1992 meant not only the conclusion but the repudiation and dismantling of Reaganism. Whatever the New Covenant—Clinton's hazily defined and rapidly forgotten domestic agenda catchphrase—might have meant in theory, it was not, in practice, the next volume of the New Deal/Great Society trilogy. Even with Democratic congressional majorities during his first two years in office, Clinton found it difficult to enact welfare state expansions of the sort that defined the presidencies of FDR and LBJ. His hopes to secure national health insurance, the last big piece of the New Deal and Great Society puzzle, stalled in 1993 and finally sank in 1994. Other ambitious plans were also abandoned or scaled back as the need to reassure financial markets and Ross Perot's voters, nearly one-fifth of the 1992 electorate, made deficit reduction a higher priority than government expansion. In April 1993, three months after his inauguration, Clinton was already bitter about the limited prospects for his legacy. "I hope you're all aware we're all Eisenhower Republicans," he said to one group of advisors. "We're Eisenhower Republicans here, and we're fighting with Reagan Republicans. We stand for lower deficits and free trade and the bond market. Isn't that great?"[8]

Conservatives, on the other hand, hoped that the elections of 1994 meant the consummation of Reaganism, and that didn't happen either. Republicans held majorities in both the House and Senate for the first time in 40 years, made up of legislators who were far more ideologically militant than the Eisenhower Republicans of 1953. And yet, as during Reagan's presidency, the welfare state grew slowly but did not shrink. In *The Enduring Revolution*, a book on the Contract with America, Major Garrett, a television reporter for Fox News, argues that the Gingrich Republicans achieved important policy victories that have been overshadowed by their more vivid political defeats. Specifically, he argues that the government shutdown in late 1995 resulted in a budget framework that checkmated Democrats' hopes for a new Great Society. The unexpected gusher of capital gains taxes during the dot-com boom was diverted to deficit reduction and debt retirement rather than new and bigger welfare state programs.[9]

There are two problems with this argument. The first is that any bright-line distinction between politics and policy distorts the innumerable ways they seamlessly influence each other in the real world. Garrett's book says as much. Clinton won a political victory when the Gingrich Republicans overplayed their hand in 1995 and shut down the federal government by refusing to extend the federal debt limit unless Clinton acquiesced to their plans for long-term spending reductions. After it became clear that the public blamed the GOP for the shutdown, Republicans realized that the federal debt limit was one of those weapons that can be effectively brandished but never safely discharged. After 1995, Clinton was regularly able to wrest more welfare state dollars from the Republicans than they wanted to spend just by hinting that their failure to comply would result in another shutdown.[10]

As was the case during the Reagan presidency, the welfare state's political resiliency derived from well-fortified entitlement programs. Republicans set themselves up for Democrats' most effective counterpunches by trying to curb Medicare. Clinton "used Medicare's popularity against Republicans," according to Garrett.[11] The GOP furiously insisted that their plan would have cut the rate of Medicare's *growth*, not actually reduce the program itself, going so far as to include in their 1996 platform the raw statement, "Bill Clinton lied about the condition of Medicare and lied about our attempts to save it."[12] None of these efforts did them or their plans for Medicare any good. By the end of Clinton's presidency the Republicans were "demoralized, frustrated and listless," according to Garrett. "They wanted to change Medicare but they didn't know how."[13]

The other problem with Garrett's argument is that to call the 1.49% annual growth rate of the welfare state under Clinton—or, for that matter, the 0.90% rate under Reagan—a conservative victory amounts to defining effectuality down. Conservatives lost the game but covered the point spread: They did better than expected, and better than opponents of the welfare state in other countries. Labeling these defeats moral victories does not disguise the fundamental reality, however. Nor does it change the fact that such victories are themselves ultimately demoralizing.

THE LIBERTARIAN ARGUMENT AGAINST THE WELFARE STATE

The fact that even Ronald Reagan could not "curb the size and influence of the federal establishment," as he promised in his 1981 inaugural address, indicates that the battle between liberals and conservatives over the welfare state is fundamentally asymmetric. What's at stake in their political contest is not whether the permanent liberal project of expanding the welfare state will or won't go forward, but whether it will proceed rapidly or slowly. Liberal victories advance liberalism; conservative "victories" postpone liberalism.

The dismal prospects for conservatism cannot be explained by the strength and cohesion of the liberal arguments for the welfare state; their deficiencies were discussed in Chapters Three and Four and have been the subject of many other books and articles. Conservatives have written most of them, but not all. *The End of Liberalism* is a devastating indictment of liberals' governance because its author, Theodore Lowi, is sympathetic to the ends they pursue.[14]

The very shapelessness of liberal thinking makes it difficult to refute. A modern liberal, Jacob Hacker, writes approvingly that the New Deal did not set out to supplant the market economy with a different system, but was "guided by an abiding conviction: Capitalism needed to be 'made good.'"[15] What it means for capitalism to *be* good, or just better, is a perpetually hazy and open question, however, so that making capitalism good is never going to be distinguishable from messing around with it.

This deficit in rigor, however, turns out to be a very manageable political problem. As the British jurist A.V. Dicey wrote in 1914, "The beneficial effect of State intervention, especially in the form of legislation, is direct, immediate and, so to speak, visible, whilst its evil effects are gradual and indirect, and lie out of sight. . . . Hence the majority of mankind must almost of necessity look with undue favor upon governmental intervention."[16]

According to James Q. Wilson, conservatives have tried to fight back with three different arguments against the welfare state: libertarianism, supply-side economics, and welfare economics.[17] Of these, libertarianism confronts the welfare state most directly and rejects it categorically. Despite the many accommodations he had made to the welfare state during his presidency—some prudential, some imprudent—Ronald Reagan distilled the essence of the principled argument against the welfare state in his January 1989 farewell address: "I hope we have once again reminded people that man is not free unless government is limited. There's a clear cause and effect here that is as neat and predictable as a law of physics: As government expands, liberty contracts."[18]

Libertarians sometimes call themselves "classical liberals," a designation that contests the legitimacy of the liberalism practiced by advocates of Big Government. In the introduction to his popular and influential book, *Capitalism and Freedom*, for example, Milton Friedman stipulates that rather than "surrender the term to proponents of measures that would destroy liberty," he intends to use "the word liberalism in its original sense—as the doctrines pertaining to a free man."[19] The issue goes beyond competing claims to some prime semantic real estate. The libertarian position is that the older liberalism, devoted to securing liberty by limiting government, wasn't broken and didn't need to be fixed. It was fully capable of adapting to the transformation from agrarian to industrial society without modifying the fundamental belief that *the* threat to individual liberty was a powerful and intrusive government.[20]

As the remarks from Reagan and Friedman indicate, the true libertarian believes that all other political considerations are

214 Conservatism's Continuing Inability to Make a Difference

secondary to liberty. If it turned out that Big Government promoted prosperity and limited government undermined it, the libertarian would still favor limited government as the alternative that upheld freedom. Libertarians also believe, however, that this dilemma is one they'll never confront. Freedom Works, as one pro-market advocacy group titles itself. It works because the "spontaneous order" of voluntary exchanges of goods and services, guided by market prices, directs resources to their best use more reliably and flexibly than any board of experts.

We noted in the last chapter that several left-of-center thinkers have accepted the idea of spontaneous order through markets. We should also note that others do not. Matthew Yglesias, for example, wrote in 2008 that "the idea of [a] state committed to neutral and effective administration of justice around laissez faire lines seems like an illusion. The alternative to reasonably effective democratic institutions and a viable left-wing political movement isn't free markets but the capture of the state by large economic interests as during the Gilded Age or, indeed, the Bush administration."[21] The invisible hand is really a hidden hand, according to Yglesias. The question is not *whether* government will be used to secure the advantage of some against others. That's a given. The real issue is *which* interests will gain by availing themselves of government power. Yglesias says the basic choice is whether the already rich and powerful will bend government to strengthen their position even further, or whether the less advantaged will use government to tilt the imbalance in their favor.

Even if we reject this assessment and treat the idea that the government should be a neutral, disinterested umpire as a standard worth aspiring to, rather than an illusion to discard, Yglesias does point us to the difficulty of mixing libertarian principles, capitalist prosperity and democracy. The economist Tyler Cowen, far friendlier to libertarianism than Yglesias, says the "fundamental paradox of libertarianism" is that "human beings have deeply rooted impulses to take newly acquired wealth and spend some of it on more government and especially on transfer payments." Looking at the sort of international evidence we examined in Chapter One, Cowen calls greater prosperity and bigger government "a package deal," and says that "libertarianism is in an intellectual crisis today" because, "The major libertarian response to modernity is simply to wish that the package deal we face [wasn't] a package deal."[22]

The electoral success of libertarianism would require persuading reliable majorities of voters to take either: a) the principled view, that the tangible benefits offered by the welfare state would require a government so big it would jeopardize liberty—end of discussion; or b) the enlightened view, that the welfare state's immediate benefits will be outweighed by its ultimate costs. Suffice to say that the voters have proven to be a disappointment in this regard. As Louis Menand wrote, Barry Goldwater campaigned against Big Government in 1964 in the belief "that he could run for President on a program of political abstractions. People don't vote for abstractions. They vote their hopes and their fears, and they tend to see those in concrete terms."[23] As a result, says Cowen, "much of libertarianism has become a series of complaints about voter ignorance, or against the motives of special interest groups. The complaints are largely true, but many of the battles are losing ones." Indeed, he says, the biggest battle is a losing one: "the welfare state is here to stay, whether we like it or not."[24]

Even if the voters were high-minded or far-sighted enough to be fully receptive to the libertarian argument, that argument does not provide the guidance they seek. The welfare state's liberal advocates say the government should be as big as necessary, while its libertarian opponents say the government should be as small as possible. Libertarians are not much better at explaining how small is small enough, however, than liberals are at explaining how big is big enough. The liberal will always be able to find one more social welfare program to add, no matter how many are already up and running, while the libertarian will always be able to find one more to cut, no matter how many have been dismantled. The economist Murray Rothbard denounced Milton Friedman for supporting school vouchers, for example, in the belief that a serious libertarian would oppose public funding for education by *any* mechanism.[25]

The problem is bigger than a fight over ideological purity. Journalists are familiar with the "to be sure" paragraph, which appears after the writer has laid out the piece's argument. The "to be sure" paragraph checks off the duty to acknowledge a contrary viewpoint, and is a convenient segue to the conclusion that the contrary viewpoint is markedly inferior to the journalist's.

When the libertarian case against the welfare state is incorporated into the speech of a conservative politician, there is always a "to be sure" paragraph. The one in Reagan's 1981 inaugural, for example, stated:

> Now, so there will be no misunderstanding, it's not my
> intention to do away with government. It is rather to make
> it work—work with us, not over us; to stand by our side, not
> ride on our back. Government can and must provide oppor-
> tunity, not smother it; foster productivity, not stifle it.[26]

The "to be sure" paragraph in Reagan's 1980 acceptance speech was even more concrete:

> It is essential that we maintain both the forward momentum
> of economic growth and the strength of the safety net beneath
> those in society who need help. We also believe it is essential
> that the integrity of all aspects of Social Security [is] pre-
> served.[27]

Op-ed writers, trying to win a debate, concede as little as possible in their "to be sure" paragraphs. Politicians trying to win an election must concede all the ground necessary to secure a majority. Conservative politicians, facing an electorate accustomed to relying on welfare state programs, employ "to be sure" paragraphs that promise the continued existence of those programs and accept that they are among the government's inescapable responsibilities. Effectively, conservatives concede that the libertarian premises that undergird the critique of the welfare state are going to be honored at a high level of abstraction, but not followed very far in practice. "We mean it, but we don't *mean it* mean it." As government expands, liberty contracts, and as government contracts, liberty expands—but, don't worry, voters, the sort of contractions of government that would expand liberty by weakening the safety net or stop government from providing opportunity are not part of our plans.

ARGUMENTS PLUS BENEFITS: SUPPLY-SIDE ECONOMICS

The strongest case that the 1980s were a major conservative defeat was made by David Stockman, OMB director during Reagan's first five years in the White House. In his memoirs, *The Triumph of Politics: How the Reagan Revolution Failed*, Stockman portrays himself as the journalist Timothy Noah portrayed him in 2003: "a true believer in supply-side economics and the last powerful conservative to make a serious attempt at radically shrinking the size of government."[28] That matter-of-fact assessment suggests that supply-side economics and the effort to shrink government were related in simple and harmonious ways. The record, however, argues the relation was complex and often tense. Supply-siders, for example, frequently invoke the tax cuts proposed by Pres. Kennedy in 1962 and enacted in 1964, which reduced the top marginal rate from 91% to 70%, as a precursor to their own efforts. It's worth remembering, however, that the most important conservative politician in America in 1964, Barry Goldwater, voted against those tax cuts, saying, "If we reduce taxes before firm, principled decisions are made about expenditures, we will court deficit spending and the inflationary effects that will inevitably follow."[29]

The supply-side argument, which won over many conservatives by the time Reagan was elected president, held that insisting on firm, principled and politically difficult budget cuts prior to any tax cuts was excessively fastidious economic policy and, politically, a self-inflicted wound. By 1980 conservatives believed that they had spent the past half-century winning arguments with liberals while losing elections to them. Observing in 1965 that its contradictions had "proved damaging to liberalism as a theory, although it has not hindered liberalism as a political movement," Joseph Cropsey concluded evenly, "it is instructive to note how wide is the gap between theoretical sufficiency and political efficacy."[30]

Conservatives believed liberals filled that gap with tangible benefits, which persuaded a decisive swath of the electorate to disregard the flaws in liberals' syllogisms. Rather than continuing to develop logically sound and politically ineffectual syllogisms of their own, conservatives needed to fight fire with fire. Liberalism had flourished by making government spending the independent variable and taxes the dependent one: Give the people a cluster of attractive and successful social welfare programs, the logic went, and voters will accept the taxes required to support them. Supply-side conservatives tried to make taxes the independent variable and spending the dependent one: Give the people a cluster of appealing tax cuts and count on their attachment to *them* to set spending at the level defined by the resulting revenue stream.

National Review made the economic argument in the immediate aftermath of Reagan's 1980 election with a simple equation: The government's tax revenue equals the tax rate multiplied by the tax base. The right kind of tax cuts, in conjunction with wiser regulatory and monetary policies, will expand the economy—the tax base—allowing reduced tax rates to deliver unreduced tax revenues to the government. As for the politics, *NR* said that the supply-side insistence on passing the tax cuts first "represents an economics of hope, not the economics of belt-tightening that has been losing elections for the last fifty years." Reversing the sequence Goldwater demanded holds the promise of expanding the Reagan coalition, "unlike the traditional Republican economic approach," and *NR* viewed that political strength as necessary for meeting both the nation's domestic and foreign challenges.[31]

What's striking about this argument is that the spending cuts advocated by legions of conservatives for decades are spoken of not as something that gets done second, after the tax cuts, but as something to be done at some hazy point in the distant future that sounds a lot like never. By the time Reagan had been inaugurated, *National Review* modulated its supply-side argument, incorporating the older objective of attacking Big Government, and presenting the idea of cutting taxes first as a no-lose political tactic:

> The political genius of immediate tax cuts, a la Kemp-Roth, lies in the potential leverage they exert on merely human congressmen. Tax cuts, naturally, are easier to put through than budget cuts. Kemp-Roth says, okay, put through the tax cuts. Then either, or a mixture, of two things happens: a) an economy stimulated by the tax cuts pours revenue into the federal coffers, making subsequent budget cuts milder and politically more palatable; or b) that doesn't happen, and

sudden inflationary pressures make deep cuts to reduce the deficit much more feasible politically.[32]

One of the lingering controversies about the Reagan legacy is whether an economy stimulated by the Kemp-Roth tax cuts did or did not pour revenue into the federal coffers. The best answer appears to be, using *NR's* language, that a mixture of the two things happened. That is, the federal government was neither rolling in money nor running on fumes during Reagan's presidency. Supply-side theory focused on the stimulus derived from cutting income tax rates. We can see that the Reagan years, 1981–1989, were unexceptional in the historical context of 67 years of federal receipts of individual income taxes (Table 5.1)[33.]

From 1981 to 1984, the first three years of Reagan's presidency, real, per capita income tax receipts declined by 12.2%. During a serious recession and the initial recovery from it, a smaller tax rate was being applied to a diminished tax base. This development was not simply a consequence of fiscal policy. The Federal Reserve Board moved aggressively at the start of the Reagan presidency to curtail inflation by making money scarcer and its price, interest rates, higher. As a result, according to an article by Sen. Daniel Patrick Moynihan in 1983, "Real interest rates reached the highest levels in our nation's history, and the economy fell off the cliff. At the end of September 1981, the steel industry was operating at 74.5 percent of capacity; by the end of 1982, it was operating at 29.8 percent of capacity."[34]

As that tax base strengthened during the expansion of the 1980s, income tax receipts rose, although it took until 1987, the sixth year of Reagan's presidency before they surpassed their level in 1981. By 1989, real, per capita income tax receipts were 22.9% higher than they had been in 1984, and 7.9% higher than in 1981.

Individual income taxes were not a particularly important source of revenue for the government until World War II. From

TABLE 5.1   Per Capita Federal Receipts From Individual Income Taxes, 1940–2007, In Constant, Fiscal Year 2000 Dollars

1940	69	1963	1,153	1986	2,040
1941	97	1964	1,150	1987	2,216
1942	222	1965	1,119	1988	2,176
1943	409	1966	1,230	1989	2,305
1944	1,178	1967	1,308	1990	2,303
1945	1,060	1968	1,397	1991	2,201
1946	857	1969	1,680	1992	2,160
1947	849	1970	1,631	1993	2,237
1948	820	1971	1,463	1994	2,311
1949	628	1972	1,519	1995	2,436
1950	633	1973	1,570	1996	2,634
1951	810	1974	1,672	1997	2,881
1952	989	1975	1,543	1998	3,169
1953	1,020	1976	1,533	1999	3,290
1954	982	1977	1,691	2000	3,559
1955	930	1978	1,800	2001	3,407
1956	997	1979	1,983	2002	2,858
1957	1,044	1980	2,023	2003	2,568
1958	972	1981	2,137	2004	2,527
1959	995	1982	2,063	2005	2,780
1960	1,073	1983	1,900	2006	3,001
1961	1,057	1984	1,876	2007	3,227
1962	1,134	1985	2,019		

1934 through 1941, individual income taxes supplied only one-sixth of federal tax revenue; excise taxes accounted for a third. By 1944, individual income taxes had assumed a role in federal revenues that was nearly three times as large, accounting for 45% of the total. In the subsequent 62 years the percentage has stayed close to that plateau, fluctuating between 39% and 50%.

It's necessary to consider how income taxes relate to other sources of revenue for the federal government because, unsurprisingly, Congress declined in 1981 to turn the American economy into a laboratory for testing the supply-side hypothesis that lower marginal income tax rates would catalyze a new era of rapid economic growth. Once the income tax rate structure was on the legislative table, Congress began to consider other aspects of the federal government's tax policies, including business depreciation schedules, the indexing of tax brackets to keep up with inflation, and rules governing the tax treatment of contributions to Individual Retirement Accounts. The legislative process could not be mistaken for a graduate seminar; interest groups sought and won tax benefits. By the time the bill reached Pres. Reagan's desk, many "tax-cut ornaments," in James Q. Wilson's phrase, had been "hung onto the Kemp-Roth Christmas tree."[35]

We should, then, be aware of the total federal revenue picture: individual and corporate income taxes, payroll taxes for social insurance, excise taxes, estate and gift taxes, customs duties, and miscellaneous receipts. We can take this encompassing view in Table 5.2.

This table shows that not until 1986 did real, per capita federal tax receipts surpass the level they had reached in 1981, the year Reagan took office. By 1989, they were 14.4% larger than they had been eight years earlier. Overall, the federal government's individual income tax receipts, measured in real, per capita dollars, grew at an annual rate of 5.88% from 1940 to 2007. Total federal tax receipts, measured the same way, grew 4.01% per year. As with the measurement of Human Resources outlays, this aggregate picture of steady growth contains a great deal of fluctuation. Federal taxation increased dramatically during World War II, particularly the income tax. Things were quieter after 1945, but not uneventful (Table 5.3).

We can also see in Table 5.3 that the Reagan record was middling in terms of federal tax revenues. Three postwar presidencies saw individual income tax receipts grow more rapidly than they did under Reagan, and five saw them grow more slowly. We find the same thing if we look at all federal tax revenue: The

TABLE 5.2   Per Capita Federal Receipts From All Taxes, 1940–2007, In Constant, Fiscal Year 2000 Dollars

Year	Amount	Year	Amount	Year	Amount
1940	507	1963	2,582	1986	4,496
1941	644	1964	2,659	1987	4,823
1942	996	1965	2,678	1988	4,932
1943	1,509	1966	2,903	1989	5,126
1944	2,615	1967	3,164	1990	5,092
1945	2,605	1968	3,110	1991	4,964
1946	2,093	1969	3,598	1992	4,952
1947	1,823	1970	3,479	1993	5,067
1948	1,765	1971	3,175	1994	5,356
1949	1,592	1972	3,323	1995	5,581
1950	1,584	1973	3,510	1996	5,832
1951	1,934	1974	3,700	1997	6,170
1952	2,344	1975	3,518	1998	6,586
1953	2,381	1976	3,471	1999	6,838
1954	2,316	1977	3,814	2000	7,178
1955	2,118	1978	3,973	2001	6,824
1956	2,311	1979	4,217	2002	6,171
1957	2,345	1980	4,286	2003	5,766
1958	2,229	1981	4,480	2004	5,873
1959	2,148	1982	4,281	2005	6,459
1960	2,438	1983	3,950	2006	6,921
1961	2,412	1984	4,191	2007	7,122
1962	2,481	1985	4,431		

Reagan years saw it grow more slowly than it did under Kennedy and Johnson, Carter and Clinton, and more quickly than it did under Truman, Eisenhower, Nixon, Ford and during both Bush presidencies.

The broader pattern is too reliable to be an accident: During Republican administrations, federal tax revenues are basically flat, after adjusting for inflation and population growth; during Democratic administrations they grow better than 3% annually. (The one exception is the Truman administration, which looks, statistically, more like a Republican presidency. Taxes fell after World

TABLE 5.3   Annual Growth Rates of Real Per Capita Federal Income Taxes and Total Federal Taxes, by Presidential Term and Presidency, 1940 to 2007

Presidential Term; Presidency	First and Final Years	Number of Years	Annual Growth Rate of Real Per Capita Individual Income Tax Receipts	Annual Growth Rate of Real Per Capita Total Federal Tax Receipts
FDR III	1941–45	4	81.74%	41.81%
FDR IV/Truman	1945–49	4	–12.26%	–11.59%
Truman	1949–53	4	12.89%	10.60%
FDR IV/Truman	**1945–53**	**8**	**–0.48%**	**–1.12%**
Eisenhower I	1953–57	4	0.60%	–0.38%
Eisenhower II	1957–61	4	0.29%	0.71%
Eisenhower	**1953–61**	**8**	**0.44%**	**0.16%**
Kennedy/Johnson	1961–65	4	1.44%	2.65%
Johnson	1965–69	4	10.70%	7.66%
Kennedy/Johnson	**1961–69**	**8**	**5.97%**	**5.12%**
Nixon I	1969–73	4	–1.67%	–0.61%
Nixon II/Ford	1973–77	4	1.76	1.97%
Nixon/Ford	**1969–77**	**8**	**0.08%**	**0.71%**
Carter	**1977–81**	**4**	**6.03%**	**4.10%**
Reagan I	1981–85	4	–1.41%	–0.27%
Reagan II	1985–89	4	3.36%	3.71%
Reagan	**1981–89**	**8**	**0.95%**	**1.70%**
George H.W. Bush	**1989–93**	**4**	**–0.74%**	**–0.29%**
Clinton I	1993–97	4	6.53%	5.05%
Clinton II	1997–2001	4	4.28%	2.55%
Clinton	**1993–01**	**8**	**5.40%**	**3.79%**
George W. Bush I	2001–05	4	–4.95%	–1.36%
George W. Bush II	2005–07	2	7.72%	5.01%
George W. Bush	**2001–07**	**6**	**–0.90%**	**0.72%**

War II, and because Republicans won congressional majorities in the 1946 midterm elections. They rose during Truman's elected term, when there were Democratic majorities on Capitol Hill, and a war in Korea.) There's little doubt that the liberal objective of securing more money with which the government can do more good works is better served by the Clinton-era formula, multiplying a larger tax base by an increased tax rate to yield significant growth in tax revenue, than by the supply-side approach.

STARVING THE BEAST

There's also, however, little doubt that the conservative objective of constraining the welfare state is not well served when the U.S. Treasury faces a sea of black ink. Did the slow but steady increase of federal revenues under Reagan vindicate *National Review's* prediction that supply-side tax cuts would facilitate budget cuts, both if they worked and if they didn't? Each of the options in *NR's* assurance that supply-side tax cuts were a win-win proposition for conservatives rested on a hypothesis about the political attitudes and actions that would be engendered by the economic outcomes of the tax cuts. Option A supposed that if the tax cuts resulted in revenues pouring into the federal coffers, then voters would be, in some combination: a) grateful to and enthusiastic about Republicans as the party of prosperity; b) receptive to, or at least acquiescent in, other parts of the conservative agenda, including the reduction or elimination of social welfare programs; and c) receptive to the idea that greater prosperity meant that more people could provide for more of their own health, education and welfare needs without government programs to guarantee economic security. Option B hypothesized that if the tax cuts did not stimulate the economy, then deep budget cuts would be transformed from being political impossibilities to tolerated inevitabilities by the prospect of massive, long-term federal budget deficits. This second approach to fiscal policy came to be known as "starving the beast."[36]

Neither hypothesis turned out to be a particularly good prediction about Americans' political behavior. The logic of Option

A points back to *National Review*'s initial assessment of supply-side economics as an alternative to the politically unpopular "economics of belt-tightening," rather than a way to make those economics politically feasible. That is, if the economic stimulus provided by tax cuts was going to make budget-cutting mild and politically palatable, why not graduate to the next level of optimism and hope that tax cuts would *really* stimulate the economy and make budget cutting completely unnecessary, or even make budget increases possible? The ultimate victory of "the economics of hope" would be no belt-tightening at all—and even some belt-loosening—not just a smaller dose of the distasteful medicine conservatives had been struggling to sell for 50 years.

Supply-siders themselves turned out to be one of the biggest reasons why tax cuts did not render budget cuts politically palatable. Throughout the Reagan presidency, avid supply-siders took the position that the avoidance of spending cuts was necessary to vindicate tax cuts, to buy them the political time they needed to work their magic on the economy. From this point of view, tax cuts didn't make spending reductions politically palatable—they made them politically impossible. In 1981, when the Reagan administration was contemplating Social Security cutbacks, Jack Kemp objected, showing what the political theory of supply-side economics meant in practice: "What happened to the party of growth and opportunity? At the first sign of trouble, we're being stampeded into the slash and cut medicine that kept us in the minority for decades. This is just more root canal politics. I won't apologize for the deficit for a minute, but we can't be panicked by it either."[37]

National Review's Option A didn't pan out. Instead, something nearly the opposite happened—tax cuts became a reason to rule out spending cuts. Supply-siders urged other conservatives to table the whole limited-government part of the agenda, even as a discussion item, until revenues poured into federal coffers. According to David Frum, "Spending cuts were no longer to be seen as a precondition for tax cuts; they had become the antithesis of tax cuts, the one thing that could destroy the political consensus that made the tax cuts possible."[38]

Conservatism's actual capacity to scale back the welfare state, then, came to rest heavily on *NR*'s Option B. Revenues didn't pour into federal coffers, at least not as fast as expenditures poured out of them, leading to higher federal deficits, causing "sudden inflationary pressures," that were supposed to "make deep cuts to reduce the deficit much more feasible politically." Daniel Patrick Moynihan insisted during and after the Reagan presidency that conservatives *never* expected Option A to work. Instead, "a massive loss of revenue" from the tax cuts "was intended." The Reagan administration had a "hidden agenda," he argued in 1983:

> The President genuinely wanted to reduce the size of the federal government. He genuinely thought it was riddled with "waste, fraud, and abuse," with things that needn't or shouldn't be done. He was astute enough to know there are constituencies for such activities, and he thought it pointless to try to argue them out of existence one by one. He would instead create a fiscal crisis in which, willy-nilly, they would be driven out of existence.[39]

The U.S. Treasury saw more revenue growth under Reagan than any other *Republican* president, but that doesn't really settle the economics department question of whether supply-side policies "worked," in the sense of multiplying an expanded tax base by a diminished tax rate to yield a slightly larger sum of tax revenue. One complication is that Pres. Reagan was both a tax-cutter and a tax-raiser. In 1982 Reagan acceded to congressional "deficit hawks" and signed the Tax Equity and Fiscal Responsibility Act, which raised taxes by nearly 1% of GDP, making it, by some measurements, the largest peacetime tax increase in U.S. history.

Reagan signed additional tax increases into law throughout his presidency, whose cumulative effect, according to the conservative economic journalist Bruce Bartlett, was to generate tax revenues for the federal government equal to 2.6% of GDP.[40]

BENEFICIARIES AND BENEFACTORS: THE LIBERAL CONFIGURATION

As we have seen, the welfare state was shrewdly designed to summon into existence permanent political forces that would favor the welfare state's expansion and oppose its contraction. The ideal is for every American household to consider itself, correctly or incorrectly, a net importer of dollars after the welfare state has exacted all its taxes and conferred all its benefits. It is not possible, of course, for every household to actually come out ahead when the government reallocates a finite number of dollar bills among a finite number of households. Some will be net importers and some will be net exporters.

The first requirement for the political vigor of the welfare state is that all the net importers of the dollars it rearranges understand themselves to be such—to be beneficiaries of the welfare state who want it to continue and grow. This may sound like a marketing challenge as formidable as selling parkas in Alaska, but it's a point liberals have labored to get across. People have interests, but they also have pride, and will resent measures that further their interests while damaging their pride. Net importers of the welfare state's dollars might not necessarily regard themselves as its beneficiaries if they feel that the benefits belittle them even while augmenting their incomes. They might fear being stigmatized in the eyes of other citizens as lazy, improvident or incompetent. And if they conclude, or even suspect, that there is a measure of justice in such evaluations, they'll be burdened by self-contempt as well as the contempt of others.

As a consequence, the political success of the welfare state required that liberals undertake a sustained effort to de-stigmatize the receipt of its benefits. They argued that there was no justification for people who weren't benefiting from welfare state programs to denigrate those who were, or for those beneficiaries to accuse themselves of any kind of failure. Consider the case put forward in 1936 by Harry Hopkins, one of FDR's closest advisors and the director of such critical New Deal agencies as the Federal Emergency Relief Administration and the Works Progress Administration:

> I am getting sick and tired of all these people on the W.P.A. and local relief rolls being called chiselers and cheats. These people are just like the rest of us. They don't drink any more than us, they don't lie any more, they're no lazier than the rest of us—they're pretty much a cross-section of the American people. . . . I have gone all over the moral hurdles that people are poor because they are bad. I don't believe it. A system of government on that basis is fallacious.[41]

In short, the old, censorious distinction between the deserving and undeserving poor has to be repudiated. Glenn Loury made this clear in his critique, from the left, of the Clinton-era formulation that no one who works hard and plays by the rules should be poor. "But where," he asked, "does that leave the great number of people who are unable (or unwilling) to 'work hard and play by the rules?' By implication, they (and their children) deserve to be poor." It is notable that in Loury's rhetorical question, the distinction between whether an individual's poverty is a consequence of the inability or the refusal to work hard and obey the rules is, literally, parenthetical.[42]

The way to reassure those who hesitate to take welfare state benefits that have been proffered, and to rebuke those who criticize the willingness to accept government help, is to insist that those benefits are morally indistinguishable from the relief given to victims of natural disasters. In both cases, we are alleviating suffering that can in no way be blamed on the sufferers' behavior. Net importers of the welfare state's dollars who have been assured, over and over, that they are the beneficiaries of entitlements rather than any kind of charity, will be reliably vocal, not diffident, in their defense of the welfare state.

The second requirement is that as many net exporters as possible of dollars to the welfare state mistakenly imagine themselves to be net importers. They will make common cause with people who really are net importers, even though their interests are divergent, and in some respects opposed. As we saw in the last chapter, liberal rhetoric and the intimidating complexity of the social insurance system encourage the misperceptions of this second group, and do nothing to disabuse those who harbor them.

This leaves a final group: net exporters of the dollars redistributed by the welfare state who cannot be misled into imagining themselves to be net importers. The third requirement for the political vigor of the welfare state is that these net exporters either acquiesce in being, on balance, benefactors rather than beneficiaries of the welfare state, or that their refusal to acquiesce in this arrangement should be as politically inconsequential as possible, and their opposition to the welfare state easy to resist or denigrate.

One argument to this end is that it is possible to be a net exporter of the welfare state's dollars and still be a net beneficiary of its operations. For one thing, people's circumstances change, so that the prosperous net exporter may spend some months or years as a net importer due to time spent preparing for a career at a college or technical institute, or, later, unemployment or disability. Even for net exporters who don't encounter these problems, the existence of a safety net provides the peace of mind that comes with owning an insurance policy.

Furthermore, liberals argue that life in a society that has been rendered less economically anxious and more socially cohesive by the welfare state is, in part, a public good, enjoyed even by people who contribute more tax dollars to the welfare state than they receive benefit dollars from it. The economist Jared Bernstein asks, "What if our economic happiness is based not solely on our own well-being but on that of others? What if 'utility' is interdependent—if my happiness depends on yours?" Answering these rhetorical questions, Bernstein says, "I'm not suggesting that we should jump for joy on April 15 because we have the opportunity to invest in our interdependence. But I am saying that we might want to think of our tax system as a conduit through which we strengthen our connections to one another, our communities, and lift the prospects and opportunities of the least fortunate among us."[43]

Prosperity is economically important to liberalism because it generates the wealth the welfare state rearranges. It is politically important because it mollifies those net exporters of dollars to the welfare state who can't bring themselves to take Bernstein's advice and vicariously enjoy how money that used to be theirs is now being spent on and by people who receive government benefits. Prosperity leaves the net exporters more willing to accede to the strong political forces that demand the growth and oppose any reduction of the welfare state. The welfare state's taxes leave those households with less disposable income but economic growth more than makes up the difference. The household is running a deficit in its transactions with the welfare state but a surplus in its overall dealings with the economy.

BENEFICIARIES AND BENEFACTORS: THE SUPPLY-SIDE CONUNDRUM

The generous benefits modern prosperity has conferred on the upper-end of the income distribution are widely condemned as the consequence of Reaganism, but one of this trend's results has been to make the conservative political project of resisting the growth of the welfare state even harder. The Congressional Budget Office's data show a big upward shift in the relative position of the nation's most prosperous households (Table 5.4).[44]

Note that this table shows *pre*tax data—it's what the tax cuts of 1981, 1986 and 2001 had to work with, not their after-tax consequences on the distribution of income. We can see that distribution in Table 5.5.

CBO calculates two more important statistics—the total effective federal tax rate and the share of total federal tax liabilities paid by each segment of the income distribution. The former is the real tax rate paid, on average, by households in each quintile, decile or percentile measured—the portion of their pretax income collected by the federal government once individual income taxes, social insurance taxes, corporate income taxes and excise taxes have been added up. The latter is the portion of all federal taxes borne by each segment of the income distribution (Table 5.6).

TABLE 5.4   Congressional Budget Office Data on Pretax Income Distribution, 1979 and 2005

	1979 Average Pretax Income in 2005 Dollars	1979 Share of Total Pretax Income	2005 Average Pretax Income in 2005 Dollars	2005 Share of Total Pretax Income
Lowest Quintile	15,700	5.8%	15,900	4.0%
Second Quintile	34,000	11.1%	37,400	8.5%
Middle Quintile	51,000	15.8%	58,500	13.3%
Fourth Quintile	69,000	22.0%	85,200	19.8%
81st through 90th percentiles	89,700	15.0%	120,600	14.2%
91st through 95th percentiles	110,600	9.8%	161,900	9.9%
96th through 99th percentiles	162,300	11.4%	269,700	13.0%
100th percentile	517,800	9.3%	1,558,500	18.1%
All Households	59,700	100.0%	84,800	100.0%

TABLE 5.5 Congressional Budget Office Data on After-Tax Income Distribution, 1979 and 2005

	1979 Average After-Tax Income in 2005 Dollars	1979 Share of Total After-Tax Income	2005 Average After-Tax Income in 2005 Dollars	2005 Share of Total After-Tax Income
Lowest Quintile	14,400	6.8%	15,300	4.8%
Second Quintile	29,100	12.3%	33,700	9.6%
Middle Quintile	41,500	16.5%	50,200	14.4%
Fourth Quintile	54,300	22.3%	70,300	20.6%
81st through 90th percentiles	68,700	14.8%	96,100	14.2%
91st through 95th percentiles	82,900	9.5%	125,400	9.6%
96th through 99th percentiles	117,400	10.6%	200,500	12.1%
100th percentile	326,400	7.5%	1,071,500	15.6%
All Households	46,400	100.0%	67,400	100.0%

The *National Review* idea—multiply a lower tax rate by a bigger tax base—did work, but it *really* worked for the most prosperous sections of the income distribution, and just sort of worked

TABLE 5.6 Congressional Budget Office Data on Total Effective Federal Tax Rates and Shares of Total Federal Tax Liability, 1979 and 2005

	1979 Total Effective Federal Tax Rate	1979 Share of Total Federal Tax Liability	2005 Total Effective Federal Tax Rate	2005 Share of Total Federal Tax Liability
Lowest Quintile	8.0%	2.1%	4.3%	0.8%
Second Quintile	14.3%	7.2%	9.9%	4.1%
Middle Quintile	18.6%	13.2%	14.2%	9.3%
Fourth Quintile	21.2%	21.0%	17.4%	16.9%
81st through 90th percentiles	23.4%	15.7%	20.3%	14.0%
91st through 95th percentiles	25.0%	11.0%	22.5%	10.8%
96th through 99th percentiles	27.6%	14.2%	25.7%	16.2%
100th percentile	37.0%	15.4%	31.2%	27.6%
All Households	22.2%	100.0%	20.5%	100.0%

everywhere else. The highest percentile of the income distribution saw its share of pretax income increase by 95.7% between 1979 and 2005, its share of after-tax income increase by 108.7%, and its share of the total federal tax liability increase by 79.6%. The least prosperous 60% of the population, by contrast, went from paying nearly one fourth—22.5%—of all federal taxes in 1979 to one seventh—14.2%—in 2005. These tax cuts were hardly of a sort to significantly improve the lives—or earn conservatives the political loyalty—of the households making up this three-fifths of the income distribution. Their share of pre-tax income fell from 32.7% in 1979 to 25.8% in 2005, and of after-tax income from 35.6% to 28.8%. The average after-tax income for a middle quintile household, adjusted for inflation, was 21% higher in 2005 than in 1979, an increase whose impact on the family budget is neither imperceptible nor transformative. For the second quintile the increase was 15.8%, and for the bottom quintile it was 6.3%.

Supply-side tax cuts would be an unbeatable political tactic in the conservative battle against the welfare state—if the United States of America were a publicly traded corporation, governed on the basis of one share, one vote. The directors of USA, Inc. would secure support for their position and policies with tax cuts that bestowed big benefits on big shareholders. It's far harder to use those tax cuts to assemble a coalition in a democracy governed on the basis of one citizen, one vote. The poorest 60% of the population saw its share of the federal tax burden fall by a third between 1979 and 2005. The effective federal tax rate on the lowest quintile was cut nearly in half; for the second quintile it was reduced by just less than a third, and by almost one-fourth for the middle quintile.

These reductions didn't do conservatives much good politically because they didn't—couldn't—do the bottom 60% of the income distribution much good economically. If you had exempted everyone in those three quintiles from *all* federal taxes in 2005, the disposable income of the average household in the bottom quintile would have increased by $600—$50 a month—or 3.9%. For the second quintile the increase would have been an extra $3,700 a year, an increase of 11.0%. For the average household in the middle quintile, the permanent tax amnesty would have left them $8,300 ahead for the year, a 16.5% increase.

It's doubtful that a political coalition for limited government can be purchased so cheaply. On the contrary, exempting the poorest three-fifths of the nation from all federal taxes would do a lot more to stimulate the growth of the welfare state rather than constrain it. Once a majority of the electorate thinks government benefits are things they receive and taxes are things other people pay, they'll have a huge incentive to demand expanded benefits, paid for by higher taxes.

At the top of the income distribution, the ability of tax cuts to engender political support for conservatism is greater, but still limited. Rich people are a small portion of the electorate. They support Republicans and conservatives disproportionately anyway, so the number of additional votes to be won by offering them tax cuts is modest. In 2004, according to CNN, George Bush won 63% of the votes cast by the 3% of the electorate making $200,000 or more, while John Kerry won 63% from the 8% of the electorate making less than $15,000.[45] That election was not a departure from historical patterns. The political scientist Marvin Wattenberg's analysis of election data showed Dwight Eisenhower winning 75% of the votes cast in 1956 by Americans in the top decile of the income distribution, and Ronald Reagan winning 75% of this group's votes in 1984. Voters in the upper-middle class, which Wattenberg defined as the seventh, eighth and ninth income deciles, voted 57% for Eisenhower and 64% for Reagan.[46]

Finally, supply-side tax cuts have been applied to an economy where the size of income gains has had a very high correlation to the level of household income. This fact makes the policy vulnerable to liberals' accusation that the tax cuts give the most help to the people who least need it. It also, however, undermines conservatives' efforts to tilt the dollar exporter/importer ratio in their political favor by giving the most help to people who least *appreciate* it.

The rich may be presumed to know something about money and therefore to be aware that the gains they made at the end of the 20th century and beginning of the 21st had much more to do with changes in the economy than changes in the tax code. If, for example, 1979's effective federal tax rate of 37% had been applied to the top 1% of the income distribution in 2005, rather than the 31.2% rate those households did pay, their average after-tax income would have been $982,400 instead of $1,071,500—201% greater than the average after-tax income for the top 1% of the country in 1979, in other words, as opposed to 228% more. Given how much better top percentile households fared as a result of changes in pretax income, the number of prosperous Democrats and independents persuaded by that 27% bonus from the revised tax code to re-register as Republicans cannot be large. Leave the effective tax rates of 1979 in place for the next 26 years and the average after-tax income of the 96th through the 99th percentiles would have increased only to $195,200, rather than to $200,500. For the 91st through the 95th percentiles, the 2005 average goes to $121,400, rather than the actual $125,400.

RE-EQUALIZING INCOMES

In *The End of Equality*, Mickey Kaus argued that increasing economic inequality is an inevitable consequence of the increasingly sophisticated production of increasingly sophisticated goods and services:

> When the middle class consisted of workers tightening bolts
> on the assembly line, the difference between a superlative

bolt-tightener and a merely competent bolt-tightener wasn't
much, economically. As long as the bolts didn't come loose,
management had no compelling reason not to pay both workers the same. But train those workers as computer repairmen,
and the picture changes. The differences between a good
repairman and a mediocre repairman are probably substantial,
and worth rewarding. Train workers as computer *programmers*,
and the picture changes even more. The difference between a
really good programmer and a merely adequate programmer
can be enormous, and management will be strongly tempted
to recognize this enormous difference with an enormous difference in pay.[47]

The compelling reason or strong temptation Kaus cites is
the possibility of other employers hiring away your firm's best
employees. There's very little prospect of getting into a bidding
war over the services of a superlative bolt-tightener, since the marginal value of that excellence is so small. If one does depart, and
is replaced by a merely competent bolt-tightener, the damage to
the firm in terms of the reduced quality of the final product or
the additional cost of producing it will be negligible. The marginal value of an A-plus as opposed to a C-minus computer
programmer, however, is very high. Other firms, some of them
competitors, will know it. And the A-plus programmer will know
they know it.

Increasing inequality of incomes has sociological causes, not
just economic ones. Divorced or never-married women raising
children are about as likely to be poor today as they were 25 or 50
years ago. There are more such households now, however. One
study concluded that if two-parent families had been as common
in 1998 as they were in 1960, 28.4% of black Americans would
have been poor, as would 11.4% of whites. The actual 1998 percentages were 45.6% and 15.4%, respectively. At the same time,

divorce rates have declined in the upper reaches of the income distribution. In the long run, children raised in two-parent families have an advantage at school and in the labor market over those raised by one severely frazzled parent.[48]

In the short run, two-parent households are increasingly likely to be two-income households, and the resulting economic unions compound economic inequality. The compensation gap between truck drivers and cashiers, on the one hand, and lawyers and investment bankers, on the other, is growing, for the same reason computer programmers are pulling farther ahead of bolt-tighteners. The gap between a trucker married to a cashier, and a lawyer married to a banker, is even wider. This source of economic inequality—"assortative mating" in sociologese—would be mitigated if there were more marriages between truckers and lawyers, or cashiers and bond traders, but it's impossible to imagine the policy changes that would advance that cause, and nearly as difficult to imagine the social ones.

Kaus defines "Money Liberalism" as the effort "to prevent income differences from corroding social equality by the simple expedient of reducing the income differences—or, more accurately, *suppressing* the income differences continually generated in a capitalist economy." And, he says, the "precarious prospect of reequalizing incomes" is Money Liberalism's lost battle.[49] The use of taxes and transfer payments to reequalize income is particularly unpromising. If we return to the CBO data comparing 1979 and 2005, and ask what effective tax rates would have been needed in 2005 to give each segment of the income distribution the same share of total after-tax income that it had in 1979, the results take us far beyond repealing the Reagan and Bush tax cuts (Table 5.7).

The 1979 Déjà vu Act isn't just a New Deal—instead of giving the players different cards, we're taking poker chips away from some and giving them to others. Many poker chips. The plan

TABLE 5.7   Consequences of Enacting the 1979 Déjà vu Income Redistribution Act, Giving Each Segment of the Income Distribution the Same Percentage of Total National After-Tax Income in 2005 as it Received in 1979

	Average After-Tax Income in 2005	Total Effective Federal Tax Rate in 2005	Average After-Tax Income in 2005 Under Déjà vu Act	Total Effective Federal Tax Rate in 2005 Under Déjà vu Act
Lowest Quintile	15,300	4.3%	21,900	−37.7%
Second Quintile	33,700	9.9%	43,000	−15.0%
Middle Quintile	50,200	14.2%	57,600	1.5%
Fourth Quintile	70,300	17.4%	76,200	10.6%
81st through 90th percentiles	96,100	20.3%	100,100	17.1%
91st through 95th percentiles	125,400	22.5%	123,500	23.7%
96th through 99th percentiles	200,500	25.7%	175,800	34.8%
100th percentile	1,071,500	31.2%	513,400	67.1%
All Households	67,400	20.5%	67,400	20.5%

calls for redistributing $756.2 billion—7.8% of the $9.71 trillion American households received in 2005—from the top decile of the income distribution. Of that, $629.0 billion comes from the wealthiest 1% of the population, $115.7 billion from the next-richest 4%, and $11.6 billion from the next 5%. The destinations for those three-quarters of a trillion dollars include $159.1 billion for the poorest quintile of the income distribution, $204.6 billion for the second quintile, $164.0 billion for the middle quintile, and $132.3 billion for the fourth quintile. The final $44.9 billion goes to the ninth decile—people who are doing well, but whose share of the nation's after-tax income was about one-tenth smaller in 2005 than it had been in 1979. The 1979 Déjà vu Act has the middle quintile of the income distribution paying a sliver of all federal taxes, while enrolling the second quintile in a negative income tax program that augments their pretax income by, on average, nearly one-sixth. The negative income tax increases the average income of a lowest quintile household by almost two-fifths. The fourth quintile and the ninth decile are still taxpayers, but their total effective rates are reduced by two-fifths and one-sixth, respectively.

Recall, from Chapter Four, that liberals' stated aspirations for raising taxes on the wealthy stop well short of *marginal* rates of 67%, to say nothing of taking away 67 cents of the first and every subsequent dollar of income. Given that it would be applied to employer-paid taxes and insurance premiums, the 1979 Déjà vu Act would impose higher effective tax rates on the top 1, 5 and 10 percent of the income distribution than America has ever tried before. In 1989 Joseph Pechman of the Brookings Institution calculated the effective tax rate on the top percentile of the income distribution in 1966 as 39.6%—a calculation that included state and local, as well as federal taxes. He shows the rate descending steadily over the next quarter-century.[50]

Sweden, naturally, appears to be the only country that has ever had a tax regime even approaching the Déjà vu tax code. And, as Kaus says, "Asking Americans to out-tax Sweden is like asking us to play cricket better than the English or cook pasta better than the Italians."[51] Moreover, whether or not it is worse than the disease, the déjà vu cure would merely restore the income distribution to its condition in the late 1970s, which few liberals at the time hailed as a paradigm of social justice. The 1976 Democratic platform, for example, pledged "a government that will be committed to a fairer distribution of wealth, income and power." In particular, it promised to "strengthen the internal revenue tax code so that high-income citizens pay a reasonable tax on all economic income."[52]

Liberals are very angry about the enrichment of the rich. A few days after he was elected to the Senate in 2006, Jim Webb took to the pages of the *Wall Street Journal* to decry "our society's steady drift toward a class-based system, the likes of which we have not seen since the 19th century. America's top tier has grown infinitely richer and more removed over the past 25 years." The "average American worker is seeing a different life and a troubling future," while the "ever-widening divide is too often ignored or downplayed by its beneficiaries. A sense of entitlement has set in among elites, bordering on hubris."[53] When Webb reiterated this point in his response to Pres. Bush's 2007 State of the Union message, the columnist E.J. Dionne praised him for making clear that "there is a class war going on, and that the wrong side is winning it," because "the fruits of a growing economy are not being shared by all Americans."[54]

Such rhetoric blurs the distinction between economic inequality and economic hardship. The CBO numbers show that each slice of the income distribution was better off in 2005 than it had been in 1979, both in terms of pretax and after-tax income. The poor, however, were just a bit better off, the middle class modestly better off, and the rich dramatically better off.

It is not self-evident how, exactly, asymmetrical economic progress *is* a problem—liberal discourse assumes or asserts, but rarely tries to demonstrate, that growing inequality demands a regulatory and redistributive solution. If the only home improvement I could afford this year was a new dishwasher, while my neighbor put in a new kitchen, it's not obvious how these changes leave me worse off, or give me a legitimate reason to feel aggrieved, or a reason to expect the government to rectify my "grievance."

The Webb-Dionne formulation clearly implies, as well, that the disproportionate gains of the wealthy are not solely, or even primarily, the result of the transition to a society with more computer programmers and fewer bolt-tighteners. Rather, the real story is one of sinister political changes rather than unintended economic ones. "We've had a deliberate shift of resources from middle- and working-class Americans and the poor, to the very rich, supported by our tax codes, twisted political values and the 'winner-take-all' ethic that's prevailed at the highest levels of business and government for the last 30 years," Joan Walsh wrote in 2009.[55] That analysis fits into the Yglesias framework—the alternative to a politically dominant Left is not a free market but an unfettered and ravenous oligarchy. The rich have wrested income shares away from everybody else. It's time, and it's fair, for everybody else to wrest them back.

In addition to the tax and transfer cure, liberals have advocated other responses to growing inequality, including job-training, stronger unions and protectionism. Kaus argues that none of these remedies are better bets for improving the incomes of those in the lower quintiles than the tax and transfer cure, mostly because it is beyond the power of public policy to restore the economic leverage bolt-tighteners enjoyed during the unique economic circumstances in the quarter-century after World War II, when American industries had unprecedented advantages against all their international competitors.[56]

Curiously, though, asymmetrical economic growth makes the liberal political problem easier and the conservative one harder. It means that the net exporters of dollars to the welfare state constitute a diminishing group, but the number of dollars they can export is larger. Liberals, consequently, can avail themselves of the convenience of one-stop taxing. And it means that there are more net importers of dollars from whom liberals can assemble a coalition of voters to expand the welfare state. The situation is a bit like the state governments that impose high taxes on cigarettes to discourage smoking, then realize after a few years that the state budget has become heavily dependent on the revenue stream from those taxes. If either smokers or avaricious capitalists actually gave up their noxious habits, the fiscal consequences would be dire.

Liberals who want to maximize the number of dollars they extract from the affluent *will* need to keep in mind the uncongenial possibility that the higher taxes that express their disapproval of economic inequality generally, and the lifestyles of the rich and infamous in particular, might cause the goose to lay fewer golden eggs. Liberals who call for the rich to pay a "reasonable tax" on all their income never explain how they determine what's reasonable. In particular, they never specify the point beyond which taxes imposed on the rich become unreasonable. The one coherent attempt to do so was John Rawls's difference principle, according to which the only reason to think that we're treating the rich too harshly will be if the *poor* start to suffer.

Conservatives defend the changing patterns of income distribution, but would find it easier to round up votes against the welfare state if economic growth were especially pronounced in the broad middle rather than the prosperous right tail of the curve. The net exporters would then be a much larger group, and conservatives would have a sizeable audience prepared to consider the disadvantages they suffer as a result of the welfare state. If Sean Wilentz is right to say that Reaganism rendered 70% income tax brackets politically impossible, this conservative victory owes more to the acceptance of older arguments that limitless taxation is unfair in principle than to supply-side innovations about expanding the tax base or starving the Big Government beast. Ruing the unpopularity of an estate tax that 98% of Americans will never pay, *The New Republic*'s Peter Beinart wrote in 2006 that Democrats who insist that it applies only to the rich "unwittingly concede the GOP's point. Yes, the tax is unfair, they imply, but to someone else. And thus, they lose the moral high ground."[57]

WELFARE ECONOMICS: THE BEST AND HIGHEST USE

David Stockman is coy, in his memoirs, about whether Sen. Moynihan was right to call the big federal deficits of the 1980s the intended result all along, rather than just an acknowledged possibility. For Stockman, true belief in supply-side economics did not mean expecting the tax cuts to pay for themselves, obviating hard choices about government spending. At the very least, he acknowledged the possibility that the cuts would not pay for themselves, thus compelling those difficult choices. Supply-side economics, Stockman wrote, "could add up only if deep dents were kicked in the side of the welfare state. This meant remaining in the political trenches year after year until the middle of the decade. The work of shrinking back the spending boundaries of the state had to proceed in tandem with the automatic fall of its revenue claim on the national economy, as the multi-year tax cuts achieved full maturity."[58]

Stockman's broader conclusion, however, argues that the politicians' failings, including his own and Pres. Reagan's, were epiphenomena. The big story is that the sort of dents Stockman wanted to kick in the welfare state were *always* politically impossible. Stockman says that while a "dictator" would have been able to enact the budget cuts he sought, "the politics of American democracy made a shambles of my anti-welfare state theory," because that theory "rested on the illusion that the will of the people was at drastic variance with the actions of the politicians." In reality, "The Reagan Revolution amounted to the clearest test of [conservative] doctrine ever likely to occur in a heterogeneous democracy like our own. And the anti-statist position was utterly repudiated. . . . The abortive Reagan Revolution proved that the American electorate wants a moderate social democracy to shield it from capitalism's rougher edges."[59]

James Q. Wilson's long review of Stockman's book was a critique, not just of Stockman's memoirs, but of his tenure at OMB. Wilson makes clear that the problem with being disillusioned is that it means you were illusioned to begin with. He argues that Stockman started out with exaggerated ideas about how much the welfare state could be scaled back, and ended up with exaggerated ideas about how little it could be reduced.[60]

Wilson contends that Stockman, as he portrays his own thoughts and actions in his memoirs, had two kinds of illusions, political and theoretical. The political illusion was the belief that 1981 was an opportunity for conservatives to shrink the welfare state corresponding to the opportunities liberals had in 1935 and 1965 to expand it. In fact, Wilson argues, "The 1980 elections produced no special moment in American history." Americans had lost patience with Jimmy Carter and elected a conservative Republican president, a Republican Senate and a Democratic House where conservatives held more sway than they had for many years.[61]

The Republicans in 1980 had neither sought nor received a mandate for kicking deep dents in the side of the welfare state, however. In his acceptance speech at the Detroit convention, for example, Ronald Reagan promised a federal hiring freeze and a thorough review of every federal program to eliminate waste and inefficiency. He promised to turn every program that the states and localities can run more effectively back to them, along with the funding sources to pay for them. But that was about it, and that was all pretty general. There was nothing in the Republican platform or Reagan's campaign to make it clear to voters that electing Reagan and the Republicans meant hitting the Great Society and the New Deal with a wrecking ball.

The 1994 Contract with America was only a bit more forthcoming on the subject of shrinking government. Of its ten provisions, the one that explicitly sought a smaller welfare state called for a "personal responsibility act" to reduce welfare eligibility and benefits, a promise the Republican Congress fulfilled in 1996. Another provision called for a constitutional amendment to require a balanced budget, and for a line-item veto, a measure that would almost certainly require a constitutional amendment as well. The purpose of these reforms, according to the Contract, was to "restore fiscal responsibility," but these procedural changes did not commit the Republicans to any specific spending cuts or ask the voters to endorse any. The other eight provisions addressed disparate issues, including crime, national defense and term limits. None of them would have kicked even shallow dents in the side of the welfare state.[62]

As we have seen, conservatives in the business of winning elections speak very guardedly about reducing or eliminating welfare state programs. (Barry Goldwater in 1964 isn't really an exception, because he wasn't really in the business of winning that election.) Conservatives have been honing their arguments against big government for nearly a century. And yet, according to Wilson, "it is hard to find any support for a broad movement toward a minimal state."[63]

Conservative activists and theoreticians will not relinquish the hope that the policy consequences of the 1932 election might yet be reversed and the New Deal undone. They are as angry at conservative politicians, whom they consider too unprincipled and maladroit to advance this goal, as they are at liberals. These activists and theoreticians, some of whom are tenured, make the willingness to run suicide missions the sole criterion for judging the courage of politicians, who are never more than an election away from having no votes to cast and no policies to shape. Casualties of the electoral battles never get to fight the policy ones, of course. No conservative, either in the trenches or the commentariat, has yet devised a strategy for politicians to kick deep dents in the side of the middle-class entitlement programs without forfeiting a presidency or a congressional majority.

Stockman's theoretical illusion, according to Wilson, was to rely on a "mélange" of conservatism's three different arguments against the welfare state, rather than consistently put forward the

clearest and strongest. It's a surprising failure because the best presentation of that argument was made by . . . David Stockman, in an
article he wrote for *The Public Interest* in 1975, titled, "The Social
Pork Barrel."[64] Wilson calls the article "brilliant" and "vivid," a
"manifesto for how best to reconstruct the welfare state."[65]

The theory Stockman relied on in that article was welfare economics, the idea that the welfare state, like any corporation, shoe
store, or household, has finite resources at its disposal. A well-
designed and well-run welfare state should direct those resources
to where they can do the most good by assisting the people who
need help most urgently. The corollary of that principle is that the
welfare state should stop using its resources in ways that are not
the best and the highest, which means reducing or eliminating
programs to help people who don't need it urgently. This theory,
unlike libertarianism, does not look to the ultimate disappearance
of the welfare state, but wants it to function fairly and efficiently.

David Stockman was the executive director of the House
Republican Conference when he wrote "Social Pork Barrel."
The year after it appeared Stockman won a House seat from a
district in rural Michigan. It's significant, then, that his *Public
Interest* article was not a Republican attack on Democrats, but a
critique of both parties. New welfare state programs are always
Democratic initiatives opposed by Republicans. But the opposition never lasts long, according to Stockman. The problem is
the Capitol Hill belief that anything worth doing is worth doing
435 times, in every congressional district in the country. Federal
subsidies are sprayed like a fine mist over the entire political map,
and all but the fiercest congressional opponents of a program are
transformed into supporters, happy to remind their constituents
about all the benefits they have secured for their district.

This process, according to Stockman, is bad politics and
bad policy. It's bad politics because the principled opposition of
conservatives to the growth of the welfare state is undermined as

Republicans are bought off with benefits for their constituents. The social pork barrel is bad policy because it guarantees that the welfare state will be *much* less fair and efficient than it could and should be.

Stockman cites as an example the Elementary and Secondary Education Act, created in 1965 to direct federal funding to public schools that serve "the poorest of the poor." If the poorest of the poor were evenly distributed throughout all 435 congressional districts, the policy imperative to help them would coincide with the political imperative for incumbents to get re-elected. They aren't so conveniently dispersed, in reality, but concentrated in the country's major metropolitan areas. If ESEA funding were directed to the people who need it most, only a fraction of the 435 congressmen would have a stake in the program. The solution was to redefine the policy problem in a way that addressed the political problem. By 1975, Stockman reported, 80% of the nation's school districts received ESEA funding, and once the funds reach the local level the school superintendents had enough discretion over their use to guarantee "substantial dissipation of [ESEA] funds across a broad range of the public school population."[66]

Stockman's article was not only hard on Republicans but surprisingly easy on the welfare state. At several points he contends that if we had a more efficient welfare state, one that helped people who really need it rather than maximizing political support by helping a lot of people who don't, we could easily afford big expansions of the welfare state, such as national health insurance.

As a result, Stockman's criticism of the Democrats is not that they want to expand the welfare state, but that they want to do so with the same lack of discipline and indifference to fairness and efficiency that weakens the welfare state we already have. Stockman makes three allegations about what he calls "Capitol Hill liberalism," but all of them apply with equal force to the liberalism of word and deed practiced beyond Capitol Hill. First, liberalism is vague and sentimental, too concerned with demonstrating that liberals' hearts are in the right place, and insufficiently concerned about whether programs really work, or make the best use of their resources. This is the liberalism that emphasizes feeling good at the expense of doing good.

Second, liberalism "contains only a vague notion of who really needs public assistance." Such terms as "middle-class," "average American," or "working families" are invoked constantly but never defined. They "can encompass almost the entire electorate" and, for political purposes, frequently do.[67]

Third, the consequence of liberalism's indifference to whether or not programs are effective, and to whether or not they help people who really need it, is that "inclusion rather than exclusion is the normal liberal prescription." As a result, "most federal social programs scatter benefits over a much wider portion of the income spectrum than their avowed objectives would suggest." Stockman derides one of the projects Hubert Humphrey pursued after returning to the Senate in 1970, a federally funded program to provide every American public school student with a free lunch every school day. Since school lunch programs for the poor were already in place when Humphrey was advocating this expansion, "the only apparent benefit of the proposal," according to Stockman, was that it would give families with incomes above the median and children in public school, "the privilege of buying school lunches on an annual purchase plan every April 15th."[68]

MEANS TESTING: CONSERVATIVE OPPOSITION

"If conservatives could design their ideal welfare state," the political scientist Paul Pierson has written, "it would consist of *nothing* but means-tested programs."[69] It would be better to say that if conservatives have to acquiesce in a welfare state, they would prefer that it be pervasively means tested. The logic of libertarianism welcomes every reduction of the welfare state, and views every part of the welfare state that remains as a reduction waiting to be enacted.

Conservatives who employ Stockman's argument about the social pork barrel to make the welfare state fair and efficient through comprehensive means testing will confront three different kinds of resistance—one from libertarians, one from liberals, and one from Americans whose social insurance benefits will be reduced. None of these fights will be easy.

Acquiescence to the popularity and resulting political invulnerability of the welfare state is the outer limit of conservative enthusiasm for it. In 1993 Irving Kristol said conservatives must face the question: "what kind of welfare state do they want—because in our dynamic, urbanized, industrial society, some kind of welfare state is a permanent feature of the political landscape."[70] James Q. Wilson made the same point in his essay on Stockman in 1985: "The people want no cuts in spending in many broad policy areas, including health, education, law enforcement, and environmental protection." As a result,

> Libertarianism and the minimal state . . . are not viable ideas. A large, heterogeneous, democratic nation cannot be governed on the basis of a conception of the public good that requires, for its success, that the nation be small, homogeneous, and undemocratic. Telling people who want clean air, a safe environment, fewer drug dealers, a decent retirement, and protection against catastrophic medical bills that the government ought not to do these things is wishful or suicidal politics.[71]

Even William Buckley, who launched *National Review* in 1955 to be a magazine that "stands athwart history, yelling Stop," ended up counseling much more selective yelling. Conservatives "need to make prudent accommodations," he wrote in 2001. "What conservatives are going to have to get used to is that certain fights we have waged are, quite simply, lost. It is fine, in our little seminars, to make the case against a federal Social Security program, but it pays to remind ourselves that nobody outside the walls of that classroom is going to pay much attention to our Platonic exercises."[72]

Committed libertarians view discussions about how conservatism makes its peace with the welfare state's permanence as a betrayal of the imperative to protect liberty by limiting government. Michael Tanner of the Cato Institute wrote an unambiguously titled book on this theme: *Leviathan On the Right: How Big Government Conservatism Brought Down the Republican Revolution*. According to Tanner, "Republicans should stand for limited government and individual liberty simply because it is the right thing to do."[73]

Politics, and life in general, would be easy to navigate if the "simply the right thing to do" consideration were dispositive, a necessary *and* sufficient basis for making choices. In a complex world, however, the claim that no other considerations matter is dubious. To the extent libertarians are actually interested in curtailing government, the right-thing-to-do strategy rests on an unfalsifiable proposition: The welfare state *will* crumble if conservatives push against it hard enough, so the continuing existence and growth of the welfare state proves only that conservatives have been slacking off and need to redouble their efforts.

Lacking any basis on which to say that the game is lost, the logic of libertarianism ultimately celebrates futility. Rather than engage in the messy enterprise of being politically consequential, unwavering devotion to clear, simple principles lets libertarians prove to themselves that they are morally serious. Engaging in politics on these terms culminates in the equation of realism with cynicism, and irrelevance with integrity. Power tends to corrupt, but so does powerlessness.

In 1980 supply-siders said to libertarians, "We've tried it your way, again and again, and it's just not working." The "Reagan gambit," in David Frum's words, was to jettison conservatism's "flinty frugality" and "change the subject from spending to taxes."

> Later, after the tax cuts had worked their magic, there would be plenty of time to start chopping at the excesses of big government. Reagan's domestic policy was, then, essentially a gamble—a gamble that with the proper tactics he could bring the federal government under control, without mobilizing against him the pro-spending constituencies that had triumphed over presidents Nixon, Ford, and Carter.[74]

Frum, as well as the data earlier in this chapter, argue that this supply-side gamble did not pay off. Tax cuts, along with breaking the back of inflation and eliminating some onerous and unnecessary regulations, *did* contribute to the restoration of economic vigor after the 1970s' stagflation. Furthermore, the tax revolt reminded liberals that angry voters would locate liberalism's limiting principle for them, even if liberals themselves had no interest in joining the search party. The weight of the evidence, however, points to the conclusion that supply-side tax cuts did not render the conservatives' aspiration to shrink the welfare state either politically possible or necessary.

Conservatives partial to the social pork barrel argument say to libertarians *and* supply-siders, "We've tried it both your ways, and neither of them worked." To persuade them, the means testers will have to be clear about what they mean by the "it" they want to try a different way. The intra-conservative argument for means testing is that some parts of the welfare state might get smaller, but the entirety will never get small. Unless conservatives start making half-a-loaf strategies, they won't end up with anything but crumbs.

MEANS TESTING: LIBERAL OPPOSITION

If the conservative goal is to reduce the welfare state as much as politically possible, and conservatives turn to means testing as the least unpromising way to pursue it, then there is every reason to expect liberals to oppose it as aggressively as they would any other downsizing plan. We have already seen how heavily liberalism has invested in the strategy of blackening the sky with criss-crossing dollars, how the imperative to help the most vulnerable among us bequeaths a welfare state committed to directing enormous benefits to the least vulnerable.

It is possible, then, that means testing would be nothing more than the next front in the endless war between conservatives who want to shrink the welfare state and liberals who want to expand it. There's little reason to be in suspense about the outcome of that contest. As a sportswriter once said, if they staged a rematch the smart money would still be on Goliath. The harm inflicted by curtailing welfare benefits through means testing will always be more easily apprehended than the harm of letting those benefits grow without limit, meaning conservatives are condemned to fight uphill and, as usual, lose.

This outcome would be not only a conservative loss, however, but one for liberals and the country as a whole. A debate over means testing would be an excellent opportunity to suggest that when all else fails, Americans should try responsible governance. The oldest baby boomers, born in 1946, turned 62 in 2008, and became eligible for early Social Security pension benefits. In 2011 they'll be eligible for Medicare and can receive full pension benefits in 2012, if they chose to defer their retirement. The ranks of beneficiaries will grow for many years; the Census Bureau projects that 40.2 million Americans will be 65 or older in 2010, representing 13% of the entire population. By 2025 there will be half-again as many people 65 or older, 63.9 million, amounting to 17.9% of the population.[75]

The baby boomers' retirement will be the best documented, least surprising policy challenge in American history—and still we are not prepared for it. "Herb Stein's Law" has not been repealed, however: If something can't go on forever, it won't. Entitlements can't go on, indefinitely, laying claim to a bigger portion of the federal budget and the GDP.

Liberals are determined to build a much bigger welfare state. Every four years the Democratic platform groans under the weight of all the ingenious and compassionate plans for new government initiatives. The trouble is that before adding even a single new program, maintaining the welfare state we already have, especially Social Security, Medicare and Medicaid, will cause the portion of GDP devoted to federal spending on Human Resources to increase relentlessly. In 2007 the Congressional Budget Office reported that federal spending on those three programs equaled 8.4% of GDP. It estimated that if no changes were made to them, that portion would increase to 14.2% in 2030 and 18.1% in 2050. Incorporating into its projections "some changes in policy that are widely expected to occur and that policymakers have regularly made in the past" raises the 2030 projection to 14.5% of GDP and the 2050 one to 18.6%.[76]

The three biggest entitlement programs would be absorbing nearly the same portion of national economic output as the entire federal government did in 2007. Keeping them going will require tax increases equal to 6% of GDP in the next 20 years, and another 4% in the 20 years after that. Such enormous increases to keep the existing welfare state functioning are going to make the sort of expansions liberals have in mind politically and fiscally impossible.

A handful of liberal writers are candid enough to acknowledge this fact, and conscientious enough to call it a problem. William Galston, for example, called for a bigger welfare state in an essay for *The American Prospect* in 2008. He also said, however, "[W]e will need a new approach toward the large entitlement programs—especially Medicare and Medicaid—that drive so much of the long-term increase in the federal budget. . . . [W]hatever we do in this area, we will have to rethink the comfortable assumption that a 21st-century social contract can simply add a new wing to the existing edifice."[77]

If a "new era of public investment in things that matter," as E.J. Dionne characterized liberals' aspirations, will at last vindicate and resume the New Deal/Great Society agenda, liberals are going to have to sort out whether all the things that matter matter with equal urgency. If so—if Human Resources expenditures are indistinguishable, interchangeable units—then the federal government's additional pension and medical insurance payments to retired baby boomers, many of whom are otherwise prosperous, will be an entirely satisfactory result for liberals.

And if not, then not. The journalist Matt Miller has tried, with little success, to get liberals to fashion policy on the basis of rigor rather than sentiment and wishful thinking. He notes the enormous entitlement increases already baked into the fiscal cake. "Then there's the plethora of other Democratic priorities, from covering the uninsured, to wage and child-care subsidies for the working poor, to R&D and infrastructure backlogs." All the leading Democrats want to repeal the Bush tax cuts, as they apply to households making more than $250,000 per year. The trouble, according to Miller, is that you can repeal them only once.[78]

Coming up with six new ways for the government to spend each additional dollar of tax revenue may be good politics but cannot be good governance. Asking liberals to acknowledge that there can be only 100% of anything, however, including GDP at the disposal of the welfare state, is like trying to row a skiff up Niagara. The political (and financial) capital liberals consume with tax increases that shore up our existing entitlement programs is capital they can't consume again with the additional tax increases needed to expand child-care, develop green technology, protect workers from the consequences of globalization, etc. How *does* America render entitlements solvent, pay for liberals' numerous initiatives for those who aren't elderly, and do all this without resorting to the sort of massive tax increases that would trigger political fury and an economic debacle? Miller posed that question to one Clinton Administration veteran, who said, "I don't think that conversation has yet taken place in the heads of most Democratic economists."[79]

It would be a good conversation to start. Liberals who want a bigger welfare state and conservatives who want a smaller one have a big thing to fight about, but nothing really to talk about. Liberals who understand the finitude of the resources available to the welfare state, and conservatives who understand the futility of dismantling it, do have things to talk about, however. If those conversations are going to take place in good faith, conservatives must stipulate that America will and should have a welfare state, and that the withering away of the welfare state is not the goal of the conservative project, not even in the distant future. Such a conservatism, according to Wilson, presents "not an argument for a small government or a weak government or a government indifferent to the poor . . . [but] an argument for a fair and competent government." The liberals sitting across the table, in turn, must abandon the belief that everything is good to do, and that with all this money we can afford to try anything we have the audacity to hope for. In its place, this liberalism would affirm, in Wilson's words, "It is not enough that a program have a noble purpose or a laudable motive; to warrant a claim on resources, it should actually produce the intended effect and do so at a reasonable cost."[80]

MEANS TESTING: VOTER OPPOSITION

The framework for such a conversation would be the reconstitution of the welfare state so that, in David Stockman's formulation, it favors weak claimants over weak claims. Means testing welfare state programs involves giving the most help to people who have the strongest claims, by virtue of their being the most vulnerable among us. It also reduces or eliminates government aid to the people who have the weakest claims, by virtue of their being the least vulnerable among us.

A democracy prosperous enough to have a welfare state, in other words, is prosperous enough to have many people who don't need most of what the welfare state provides. The large numbers of people who don't need government aid will have large numbers of votes, however. Their claims, weak on the merits, will be pressed successfully by affluent claimants who are not only strong in numbers, but who can bring campaign donations and public relations aptitudes to bear on the welfare state to make it redistribute more income in their direction. As David Frum wrote in 1994:

> Far more than in the 1980s, governors and mayors face
> voters who profess to prefer budget cuts to tax increases.
> But those same voters continue to expect lavishly equipped
> suburban high schools, subsidized tuition at state colleges,
> toll-free highways, and environmental improvement at oth-
> ers' expense. What could be more tempting to a politician

than to teach voters to blame taxes and regulations not on the requirements of the middle class but on the inordinate demands of the poor? What could be more reckless than to attack bloated education, highway, and farm budgets, which largely benefit the middle class? Trouble is, the refusal to take that apparently reckless course dooms all other conservative hopes to futility. If you cannot say 'no' to middle-class constituents, you cannot lighten the crushing load of government upon society.[81]

It's possible to see the resolution of negotiations between those conservatives who favor means testing, and those liberals who acknowledge the need to set priorities in view of the finite resources available to the welfare state. The truce would be a welfare state that is "both better targeted *and* more robust" in the words of Josh Patashnik of *The New Republic*.[82]

How much better targeted and how much more robust would be crucial and difficult questions, of course, ones more likely to frame a long-term argument than a permanent resolution. For liberals, this framework would mean taking Yes for an answer. Seventy-five years of their rhetoric about defending the most vulnerable among us really has persuaded the American people, who are prepared to support government programs for the poor because they're the right thing to do. The welfare state doesn't need to keep buying votes it already has.

For conservatives, it means affirming that a decent society is obligated to prevent the small minority of citizens who are chronically unable to fend for themselves, and the larger minority occasionally and transitionally unable to do so, from leading miserable lives. Government programs will be one necessary expression of that concern. Conservatives will work from that premise to limit welfare state programs to poor people through means testing and strengthen, for people who aren't poor, incentives like Health Savings Accounts and 401(k) plans to keep them out of poverty and, thus, ineligible for the means-tested programs.

Such an accommodation will be difficult to achieve and easy to scuttle. At every point of disagreement, the conservatives can threaten to blow up the talks by going to the voters and denouncing the taxes necessary for a robust welfare state. Liberals, in turn, can always threaten to go to the voters and denounce the benefit restrictions necessary for a targeted welfare state. The reality is that the welfare state we have cannot be maintained without either sufficient taxes, better targeting or, most plausibly, both. The hallmark of futile negotiations is that each side regards this overarching reality as a problem for the people on the *other* side of the table, rather than one for everyone at the table.

In *The Pact*, the historian Steven Gillon recounts how a fragile accommodation on entitlement reform *was* reached between Bill Clinton and Newt Gingrich in 1997, and how it fell apart in 1998. The framework for reforming Social Security and Medicare would have been elevated, finally, from think tank seminars to agendas being set by the country's most powerful politicians:

> In private conversations with Gingrich and with Texas Republican Bill Archer, powerful head of the House Ways and Means Committee, [Clinton] promised to "provide political cover" for Democrats and Republicans by announcing his support for raising the minimum age required for Social Security and for reducing the [cost of living] adjustments. The president was willing to oppose the leadership of his own party and support the Republican demand for private accounts. Although most Republicans planned to use the [emerging federal] surplus for a massive tax cut, Gingrich privately accepted the administration's position that the surplus should be used first to save Social Security "for all time," with any remaining amount used for a tax break.[83]

By the end of 1997, according to Gillon, Clinton and Gingrich had not only agreed on this framework for reforming Social Security but also a calendar for winning congressional approval by the end of 1998. The outcome of Medicare reform was less well defined and the schedule for enacting it envisioned a vote in late 1999, perilously close to the start of the 2000 presidential campaign. The outlines were similar, however. Gingrich and Clinton agreed to form a National Bipartisan Commission on the Future of Medicare. Clinton planned to "use the commission to develop bold, controversial proposals, and he was willing to pressure Democrats into accepting painful compromises in order to get a deal with the Republicans," according to Gillon.[84] The Commission's ultimate recommendations were, indeed, controversial and would have required all of Clinton's skills to sell to congressional Democrats. In Josh Patashnik's summary, the Commission, headed by Democratic Sen. John Breaux and Republican Rep. Bill Thomas, proposed "to convert Medicare from a universal fee-for-service plan into a defined-benefit subsidy toward the purchase of a public or private health insurance plan."[85]

But, of course, 1998 was not the year Social Security and Medicare were rendered solvent by being better targeted to those who need them most. Instead, 1998 was the year Bill Clinton faced impeachment and Newt Gingrich was driven out of Congress. The ignition of the Monica Lewinsky firestorm was not inevitable. The gallons of gasoline sloshing around the Clinton-Gingrich entitlement concordat meant, however, that it was always highly flammable; its ultimate success a real possibility, but never a safe bet.

When Clinton and Gingrich met to discuss entitlement reform in October 1997, they did so without informing Hillary Clinton, Vice President Gore, or Democratic congressional leaders. According to Clinton's advisor Paul Begala, the House Democratic leader, Richard Gephardt, was categorically opposed to a Democratic president making deals with Gingrich, someone who "was undermining everything that he [Gephardt] got into public life for: social security, medicare, caring for the poor, a decent society." Al Gore feared a challenge from Gephardt in the 2000 Democratic presidential primaries, in which liberal voters would be heavily overrepresented. Gore would have opposed entitlement changes that gave Gephardt one more reason, beyond the North American Free Trade Agreement and welfare reform, to accuse the Clinton-Gore administration of selling out liberal principles. Gingrich, by the same token, kept the meeting secret from all but a handful of his own senior staffers to prevent other House Republicans from finding out about it. Many of them, according to Gillon, "found it unconscionable that Gingrich, the architect of the Republican Revolution and the most fierce and effective congressional partisan of the past decade, was working with the president."[86]

Within hours of the Lewinsky story hitting the front pages in January 1998, the rapprochement between Clinton and Gingrich on Social Security and Medicare was null and void. The careful, detailed plans to build a "'60-percent' coalition made up of moderates in both parties" were rendered useless.[87] Rather than antagonize the most liberal Democrats in Congress, the ones who detested the idea of *any* cuts in entitlement spending, Clinton was now dependent on their good will if he hoped to avoid impeachment or a forced resignation. Rather than antagonize the most conservative Republicans, the ones who wanted every dollar of the budget surplus directed toward tax cuts and away from welfare state programs, Gingrich had no choice but to join them in regarding Bill Clinton as morally unfit for the presidency, rather than a man Republicans could do business with. "Impeachment empowered the groups in both parties that were least interested in [entitlement] reform," according to Gillon: "liberal Democrats who opposed privatization and conservative Republicans who supported large tax cuts."[88]

Not only was 1998 a lost opportunity for entitlement reform, but it was also the beginning of a lost decade. Negotiations are impossible between adversaries who equate cooperation with capitulation. It's surprising, given the hard feelings between Democrats and Republicans in Washington in 1997, that Clinton and Gingrich could arrive at the outlines of a tentative deal on entitlement. By 2005, when George W. Bush tried to make Social Security reform the history-book achievement of his second term, partisan feelings were even more rancorous. The Clinton impeachment battle in 1998, and *Bush v. Gore* in 2000, had banished the spirit of reciprocity from Capitol Hill. Republicans in 2005 took the position that Social Security reform meant partial privatization and Democrats took the position that any kind of privatization was a deal breaker. Negotiations had no way to proceed past that unsplittable difference.

According to the historian Howard Quint, "Optimism is most usually the effect of an intellectual error."[89] Optimism about rendering America's entitlement programs solvent always is. Clinton and Gingrich were able to agree on a framework for changing Social Security and Medicare because of an opportunity, the surprising appearance of federal budget surpluses in Clinton's second term. The political rationale for George W. Bush's starve-the-beast tax cuts was that there were *never* going to be surpluses "as far as the eye could see." They existed only because they caught Washington by surprise, and once the surprise was over, they were certain to be spoken for and consumed, either by larger welfare state expenditures or lower taxes.

Democrats, of course, dreaded the prospect that the slice of GDP represented by the projected surpluses would be steered away from the welfare state toward tax cuts. Al Gore pleaded with voters in 2000 to elect Democrats to put those surpluses in a "lockbox" reserved for Social Security, the most popular welfare state program, rather than electing Republicans who viewed the

surplus as tax cuts waiting to happen. When Bush won his disputed victory over Gore in 2000, and won big tax cuts in 2001 on
what was nearly a party-line vote in both houses of Congress, the
chances that Democrats would be in a mood to deal on Social
Security in 2005 were reduced to zero. Patashnik justifies their
refusal even to acknowledge that Social Security *had* solvency
problems: "Bush asked Democrats to cut Social Security benefits after he had spent four years cutting taxes for the wealthy
and stubbornly refusing to help close the gaping holes in the
social safety net. In this context, one can hardly blame liberals for
refusing to give away one of their few sources of political leverage
in exchange for nothing."[90]

Well, one can try. The Social Security cuts Bush wound up rec-
ommending when he embraced the idea of "progressive indexing"
were "cuts" in the Washington sense of the term: increases, but
ones smaller than expected. Low-wage workers would continue to
see benefits indexed for wage growth; high-wage workers would
have them indexed to prices, which grow more slowly over time.
High-wage workers would have had the chance to close the gap
by investing a slice of their withholding taxes outside the Social
Security trust fund.[91] Putting "most of the burden of rescuing
Social Security on the affluent" is not a policy change liberals
should regard as "nothing."[92]

If the planets ever line up again for entitlement reform, it will
be a matter of necessity rather than opportunity: the prospect of
huge federal deficits to pay for the programs' scheduled benefits,
rather than 1997's prospect of huge federal surpluses to cushion
the shock of reducing those benefits. Until and unless that occurs,
each of our two ideological adversaries will keep a firm grip on
one end of the domestic policy wishbone. Liberals speak to and
for the public's aversion to a smaller welfare state. Conservatives
speak to and for its aversion to higher taxes. Neither side wants to
relinquish its hold on that part of public opinion that is the source

of its own political strength. Each hopes that the public's contradictory desire for a welfare state that confers generous benefits
while imposing modest taxes will ultimately be resolved in its own
favor. It is not possible, however, for them to go on indefinitely
pulling the wishbone in opposite directions without guaranteeing
the whole country bad luck.

CONSERVATISM AND THE LEGITIMACY OF THE WELFARE STATE

During Newt Gingrich and Bill Clinton's secret meeting on entitlement reform in October 1997, Clinton's chief-of-staff, Erskine
Bowles, suggested the tentative agreement between the two prin-
cipals had made them "partners." According to Gillon:

> Gingrich demurred. "I would prefer to say we are a coalition,
> not partners," he said. It was an important distinction for
> Gingrich. "Partners are on the same team," he reflected. "We
> were never going to be on the same team."[93]

It turned out they weren't even going to be in the same coalition
after three months.

Yet the progress Gingrich and Clinton made on recasting
America's welfare state tells us about the process the next attempt
to find an accommodation between liberals and conservatives is
likely to go through, and the substance it is likely to produce.
Liberalism, as we have seen, not only lacks a limiting principle
but is fundamentally hostile to the idea of formulating one. An
accommodation with conservatives that does anything beyond
trimming the welfare state at the margins will be one liberals are
pre-programmed to detest.

Conservatives will arrive at the table in an equally wary mood.
In 1993 Irving Kristol called for a "conservative welfare state," on

the pragmatic grounds that "the welfare state is with us, for better or worse, and that conservatives should try to make it better rather than worse." Making it better, for Kristol, meant enlisting the welfare state in the culture wars by rendering it "consistent with the basic moral principles of our civilization and the basic political principles of our nation." The only entitlement "reform" required by that battle was to make Social Security, if anything, even "a bit more generous."

> Our Social Security system is enormously popular. If the American people want to be generous to their elderly, even to the point of some extravagance, I think it is very nice of them. After all, the elderly are such wonderful, unproblematic citizens. They are patriotic, they do not have illegitimate children, they do not commit crimes, they do not riot in the streets, their popular entertainments are decent rather than degrading, and if they find themselves a bit flush with funds, they happily distribute the money to their grandchildren.[94]

The only conservative parsimony Kristol did call for, then, was to limit and even reject the claims pressed on the welfare state by people who had illegitimate children, committed crimes, rioted, favored degrading entertainment, etc.

The libertarian position, of course, is that a conservative welfare state is a contradiction in terms. The effort to achieve one is going to be a waste of time and ultimately counterproductive—accommodating the welfare state will change conservatism for the worse much more than conservatism will change the welfare state for the better. As Michael Tanner of the Cato Institute puts it:

> [T]here is no evidence that if conservatives agree not to try to roll back the welfare state, liberals will agree to restrain its growth. More likely, conservatives will simply become

involved in a bidding war, in which they will inevitably look like the less caring party. Having surrendered on principle, they will be left with little more than arguments about efficiency or limited resources. That sort of green eye-shades conservatism seldom stands up against the Left's call for greater compassion.[95]

If Tanner is right, and a conservative accommodation with the welfare state's advocates is impossible, then the only hope for the cause of limited government is a long series of sweeping electoral repudiations of the welfare state, an outcome for which there is no precedent in the history of any modern democracy. Hedging against the possibility that the day when every school child can recite Hayek's *The Constitution of Liberty* might not arrive soon, we should note the general rule that agreements *can* be struck between parties who don't like or trust one another. The key is that both have strong incentives to regard making and keeping the agreement as an improvement to living outside it. If liberals and conservatives decide they can do business with each other it will be because conservatives accept they'll never sell voters on the huge benefit reductions they ultimately seek, and because liberals decide they'll never sell the huge tax increases they ultimately need.

There will be an additional barrier for conservatives. As we saw in Chapter Two, they not only regard the welfare state as a cluster of misdirected policies but also as an enterprise at odds with America's fundamental constitutional principles. In this view, the Supreme Court's capitulation to the New Deal in 1937 was, in the words of the most prominent libertarian legal theoretician, Richard Epstein, "an intellectual and political mistake that ought to be undone if only we could find the way."[96] According to the American Enterprise Institute's Michael Greve, who has co-edited books with Epstein, "The New Deal was a genuine transformation," and "if conservatives concede the legitimacy of that constitutional transformation, how can they contest other transformations, past or proposed?"[97] The road to Sweden is paved with prudent concessions.

According to this argument, the two goals proclaimed in Reagan's 1981 inaugural address define one mission, indivisible; conservatism will never "curb the size and influence of the federal establishment" without reinstating "the distinction between the powers granted to the federal government and those reserved to the states or to the people." The delegitimization of the New Deal is another unsplittable difference between conservatives and liberals. Given the enormity of the political undertaking, conservatives have been ambivalent for a long time about whether to embark on it. Even William F. Buckley's famous mission statement in the first issue of *National Review*, boldly assertive in every other respect, hedged on this point: "Conservatives in this country—at least those who have not made their peace with the New Deal, and there is a serious question of whether there are others—are non-licensed nonconformists."[98]

Conservatives have painted themselves into a corner. It's impossible to regard the idea of restoring the jurisprudential status quo ante 1937 as anything other than a quixotic, self-marginalizing gesture. Imagine a conservative movement strong enough to win the number of presidential and senatorial elections needed to populate the federal courts, including the Supreme Court, with majorities prepared to overturn the long list of Big Government-affirming precedents dating from 1937. Such a conservative movement wouldn't really *need* the courts' help. It would have defunded all the offending welfare state programs and shut down all the disdained federal agencies long before the cases challenging them ever reached the Supreme Court.

To abandon the critique of the New Deal's legitimacy, however, leaves conservatives acquiescing in liberalism's gravest and defining error—the demolition of the legitimacy barriers existing in the pre-1937 Constitution and the refusal to erect any new ones in their place. As Greve argues, accepting *that* liberal victory would make conservatives complicit in the perpetuation of liberalism's new regime, founded on History instead of Nature. In that polity, the government's powers are protean rather than enumerated, the people's rights subject to perpetual revision rather than inalienable, and the consent of the governed advisory rather than dispositive.

If the true meaning of the conservative critique of the welfare state is that the entirety of it, and every last program in it, is constitutionally illegitimate, then conservatives have no choice but to seek its demolition. Like Luther, there they stand, and can do no other. This is the disposition of two libertarians, Robert Levy and William Mellor. Their book, *The Dirty Dozen*, is a catalogue of the Supreme Court decisions that have left us "afflicted by a vast enlargement of federal power, condoned by a Supreme Court that has selectively protected some—but not all—of our constitutionally guaranteed rights."[99]

Levy and Mellor bestow the dishonor of leading off their devil's list on *Helvering v. Davis*, the 1937 decision upholding the constitutionality of the Social Security Act's provisions for the aged. They argue that programs that "collect money from some taxpayers and redistribute the money to other taxpayers" are unconstitutional, because they are not among the powers enumerated in Article I of the Constitution. A Constitution that authorizes taxing and spending to promote the general welfare, apart from those enumerated powers, abolishes "any meaningful restriction on congressional enactments," and makes "a mockery of the notion of limited federal government."[100]

Michael Greve, however, argues that *Helvering* was correctly decided, because "there is no constitutional obstacle to federal insurance programs, provided that they are structured properly—for example, like Social Security." (Greve doubts the constitutionality of the unemployment insurance provisions of the Social Security Act, because they put the federal government in the position of "commandeering" the compliance and conduct of state governments. The program for retirees, on the other hand, is purely federal.) More broadly, says Greve, "New Deal programs that served a discernible public purpose were never [in danger of being ruled unconstitutional]. Nothing in the Constitution precluded the New Deal from paying unemployed artists to adorn U.S. post offices with Soviet-Realist murals."[101]

The Greve position has several advantages over Levy and Mellor's. First, without counseling judicial passivity, it treats the Constitution more like the rulebook of a sport than the script of a play. That is, Greve's argument makes room for the possibility that there will be many good policy projects not required by the Constitution, and many bad ones not prohibited by it. Every policy should be constitutional, but not every policy debate should be reduced to a constitutional one.

"It is possible," Levy and Mellor acknowledge, that welfare state programs, including Social Security, "are both desirable (a policy judgment) and unconstitutional (a legal judgment)."

> If that's the case, then either the programs have to be amended to comply with the Constitution or the Constitution has to be amended to authorize the program. Instead, our politicians today enthusiastically redistribute our taxes without asking the crucial question: Where in the Constitution is the federal government authorized to rob Peter in order to pay Paul?[102]

By this analysis, the National Security Act of 1947, which established the Air Force as a distinct branch of the military, is constitutionally dubious. Section 8 of Article I grants Congress the power to "raise and support armies," "provide and maintain a navy," "make rules for the government and regulation of the land and naval forces," and "provide for calling forth the militia." To insist that the Philadelphia convention's understandable omission of an explicit authorization for any other branch of the military means that the Air Force has been living in sin for the past 60 years, and can be made an honest woman only by a constitutional amendment explicitly authorizing its existence, reduces principled constitutionalism to a jurisprudential obsessive-compulsive disorder.

Second, Greve's approach keeps a difficult political project from being turned into an impossible one. A conservative campaign to persuade voters that Social Security is unconstitutional is more likely to diminish the Constitution's popularity than Social Security's. In the event conservatives secure a Supreme Court majority in favor of that proposition before they secure a popular majority, they'll manage, above all, to turn voters against conservatism.

There can be no conservative welfare state if conservatives insist there can be no constitutional welfare state. In exchange for a lottery player's chance at wiping it out entirely, such conservatives forfeit any prospect of placing the welfare state on sounder footing, financially, functionally or philosophically. Instead, liberals committed to expanding the welfare state to any extent possible by any means necessary will have the unfettered ability to chart its future course.

Third, conservatism's stronger policy and constitutional arguments against Big Government are ones against the regulatory state rather than the welfare state. Conservatives should strive to see that Big Government has the smallest possible footprint. Robbing Peter to pay Paul is not ideal; siccing a dozen regulatory agencies to superintend, second-guess and reconfigure every aspect of Peter's contractual dealings with his customer Paul, his employee Paula, or his neighbor Fred is significantly worse. For

Congress to give those agencies amorphous grants of power that engender massively complicated and constantly mutating regulations is worse still.

The Earned Income Tax Credit has the government taking money from some citizens and redistributing it to others. According to Levy and Mellor's analysis, this basic fact puts it in violation of the Constitution. Yet the EITC is, from every perspective, superior to minimum wage laws. As Cass Sunstein points out, the tax credit does not reduce job opportunities for low-wage workers; it does not distort the labor market, encouraging the substitution of capital for labor in situations where it otherwise makes no economic sense; and it does not misdirect a large portion of its benefits to teen-agers and spouses bringing a second or third paycheck into a household that already has a middle-class income.[103]

Greve wishes that Sunstein had followed his policy argument to a constitutional conclusion and rejected the 1937 Supreme Court decision in *West Coast Hotel v. Parrish*, which upheld a state minimum wage law: "[T]he poor who deserve a living wage would also benefit if they could rake food off the supermarket shelves without paying for it, or if they could make themselves at home in your living room without an invitation."[104] It's a strong argument, likely to be unavailing. But its prospects of winning a hearing are far better if one starts by making Greve's distinctions between the constitutionally permissible and impermissible parts of the New Deal, than by working from Levy and Mellor's insistence that there *are* no constitutionally permissible parts.

WHERE DO PROGRESSIVES WANT TO PROGRESS *TO* AND WHAT DO CONSERVATIVES WANT TO CONSERVE?

"Although conservatism and liberalism confront each other directly as movements," Joseph Cropsey wrote, "their names appear not to take notice of each other."

"Conservatism" stands for conserving the inheritance, "liberalism" for devotion to liberty. The tension between movements appropriately called by these names should disappear if the inheritance is liberty. In the United States the inheritance is indeed liberty yet the tension is real.[1]

The liberal/conservative dichotomy made more sense in Victorian England, where the inheritance was not liberty. By 1882, after the struggle between Benjamin Disraeli and William Gladstone had dominated British politics for 15 years, Gilbert and Sullivan could offer these lines in "Iolanthe":

I often think it's comical,
How Nature always does contrive
That every boy and every gal
That's born into the world alive
Is either a little Liberal
Or else a little Conservative![2]

"Conservatism" and "progressivism," by contrast, *do* take notice of each other. The conservative looks fondly and protectively to the past. His concern is to prevent a rupture that separates us, and the future we're building, from the heritage that should inform and civilize that future.

The progressive is more optimistic about the future, believing in history's inherent tendency to generate greater freedom, prosperity, enlightenment and concord within and between nations. The progressive may like the past for the qualities that make tourism and visits to museums satisfying, but considers the past, generally, more ignorant, dogmatic and intolerant than the present. Rather than worry about becoming disconnected from civilizational roots, the progressive thinks the more urgent concern is to prevent the past from impinging on the future in a way that postpones or prevents our rendezvous with destiny.

In Chapter Two we noted three difficulties with the progressive's commitment to progress. First, it is impossible to have an intelligible debate about something unknowable, and nothing is less knowable than the future. Second, the laudable qualities progressives ascribe to the future are all so general and innocuous as to be impossible to argue or even care about. Third, progressives could not insist that their faith in progress was objectively true while debunking every other political faith as self-interest or superstition on stilts. Subjecting their own political preferences to the abrasive skepticism they had directed at the ones embraced by their political opponents rescued progressivism from the accusation of special pleading, but at the cost of rendering it trivial and incoherent.

James Ceaser shows that the latest, and presumably final, stage in liberal theorizing is to embrace and celebrate triviality and incoherence. The clunky, though useful, term for this position is "idealistic non-foundationalism," which reconciles compassion and social justice with an epistemology that regards such ideals as arbitrary, idiosyncratic personal preferences. When challenged to explain why and how we should be guided by the "evolving standards of decency that mark a maturing society"—how we can be so confident that a particular evolution or maturation is, in fact, an improvement, or on what basis we can assert that today's standards are more decent than yesterday's—the non-foundationalist answer, according to Ceaser, is that

> the deeper theoretical foundations, of the sort conservatives invoke, do not really exist in the sense of providing any objective standard; these are merely temporary vocabularies. And more important, we would be better off if these theoretical arguments were not brought into politics as claims of truth. The ideal democratic community can be—should be—constructed without them.[3]

The non-foundationalist position, according to Ceaser, is that we have nothing more to guide us than "our currently shared ideals," which "represent the consensus position among the most enlightened thinkers. If enough of these thinkers tell themselves and those who follow them that something is 'true,' then it must be so."[4] In *The Future of Liberalism*, for example, Alan Wolfe argues that the liberal temperament is more important than any of liberalism's substantive or procedural commitments. Liberalism is "best treated" as "a set of dispositions toward the world" that "tell us not so much what to think as how to think."[5] These dispositions, as celebrated by Wolfe, turn out to be as bromidic as a faculty senate revision of the Boy Scout Oath:

> "Liberalism" . . . seeks to include rather than exclude, to accept rather than to censor, to respect rather than to stigmatize, to welcome rather than reject, to be generous and appreciative rather than stingy and mean. Temperamentally, liberals are impatient with arguments rooted in fear and self-protection. . . . [T]he fact that some societies lack liberalism's generosity of spirit is all the more reason for liberals to insist on reform,

not only in the public and political sense but in the private and human one."[6]

If liberalism suffers from the absence of theoretical foundations, conservatism wrestles with a surplus. The purpose of conservatism is to conserve. Conservatives disagree, however, about what, exactly, they exist *to* conserve. Ceaser identifies four different foundations for American conservatism: 1) Traditionalism, which prefers "what grows in politics—hence 'culture,' originally an agricultural term—to what is made wholesale by human reason;" 2) Libertarianism, and its assurance that "spontaneous order" will emerge from uncoerced human action; 3) Natural Right, the belief that human reason can ascertain universally valid principles of human conduct, such as the Declaration's self-evident truths; and 4) Faith, the desire to resist the forces of secularization and vindicate the role of religion in shaping American culture.[7]

As we saw in Chapter Five, in the debate over the welfare state—or, more generally, big government as opposed to limited government—the conservatism based on libertarianism has opposed the liberal project most forcefully. Libertarianism's belief that the government that governs least, governs best has exposed it to the charge of being indistinguishable from anarchism. The debate over the welfare state, thus construed, pits liberals who are "for" government, who "like" it, against conservatives who are "opposed" to government because they "dislike" it. James Fallows, for example, says that conservatives believe "government is simply evil, that it is wasteful, oppressive, misguided and inefficient."[8]

Some conservatives do resemble Fallows' straw man, but the more crowded and thoughtful wing of the conservative movement understands its work in terms of defending government rather than opposing it. For them, government is not simply evil, but good and necessary. It is also, however, inherently precarious. What makes *big* government dangerous is not the augmentation of something wicked but the deformation of something fragile. As Alfred Marshall, the leading English economist of the 19th century, argued:

> Government is the most precious of human possessions; and no care can be too great to be spent on enabling it to do its work in the best way: A chief condition to that end is that it should not be set to work for which it is not specially qualified, under the conditions of time and place.[9]

In the context of American politics, the stakes are even higher. Assigning the government tasks for which it is not specially qualified—such as designing Model Cities or guaranteeing the right to rest, recreation and adventure—jeopardizes not just government, per se, but the American experiment in self-government. What is most regrettable about progressivism is the progress it has made in forgetting the tenuousness of self-government. In *The Federalist Papers*, the challenge is described as a conundrum: to enable the government to control the governed while obliging it to control itself. At the outset of the Civil War, Lincoln asked whether the vulnerability of the experiment in self-government is not better regarded as tragic flaw: "Is there, in all republics, this inherent and fatal weakness? Must a government, of necessity, be too strong for the liberties of its own people, or too weak to maintain its own existence?"[10]

However else conservatives understand their mission, whatever philosophical commitments or policy proposals they bring to the table, the American experiment in self-government is the precarious undertaking conservatives defend. The past and, in many ways, astounding triumphs of that experiment do not guarantee its perpetual success going forward. Asked in the 1970s about the significance of the French Revolution, the Chinese premier Zhou En-lai is said to have answered, "It's too soon to tell."[11]

Conservatives agree, furthermore, that defending self-government more often requires opposing than accommodating liberalism. The danger liberalism poses to the American experiment comes from its disposition to deplete rather than replenish the capital required for self-government. The operation of entitlement programs leaves the country financially overextended, while the rhetoric and rationale for those programs leave it politically overextended. They proffer new "rights," goad people to demand and expand those rights aggressively, and disdain truth-in-advertising about the nature or scope of the new debts and obligations those rights will engender. The moral and social capital required by the experiment in self-government is the cultivation, against the grain of a democratic age, of the virtues of forbearance, resolve, sacrifice and restraint. People who have acquired those virtues accept and understand, "There will be many long periods when you put more into your institutions than you get out," according to David Brooks.[12]

For self-government to be viable, both citizens and rulers must regard themselves as custodians who will determine whether self-government endures, rather than consumers of what government provides and redistributes. The American conservative looks at the triumphs of progressivism—and envisions a future ominously similar to the ruinous paths chosen by France or Argentina. Avoiding that fate requires rejecting policies and attitudes that discourage the multiplication of wealth while encouraging the division of it. And it means rejecting the snarling but unrugged individualism that demands ever-larger entitlements, and the progressivism that incites and sanctions those demands.

The conserving the American conservative wishes to undertake, then, is ultimately a commitment to stewardship of the experiment in self-government. The economic, political, social and moral capital it requires needs to be replenished and defended against those who would dissipate it cavalierly. The refusal to answer or engage the question of what *would* be enough—specifying the point at which the welfare state has done all we can expect and can no longer be beneficially expanded—leaves liberalism inviting, if not demanding, that dissipation . . . permanently. Conservatives will have discharged a significant portion of their duty to protect our experiment in self-government if they can induce liberals to fulfill *their* duty by treating this question seriously—or make them pay a political price for refusing to.

ACKNOWLEDGMENTS

I began work on this book as a research fellow of the Claremont Institute, and concluded it as a visiting scholar at Claremont McKenna College's Henry Salvatori Center. I'm indebted to Larry Arnn, Brian Kennedy and Bruce Sanborn of the Claremont Institute; and Mark Blitz of the Salvatori Center. Portions of this book were initially published in the *Claremont Review of Books*. For invaluable advice and assistance I'm grateful to *CRB's* editor, Charles Kesler, and his staff: Kathleen Arnn, Christopher Flannery, John Kienker, Richard Samuelson and Joseph Tartakovsky.

Many books on politics owe their existence to the John M. Olin Foundation. This one does, too, not because of a grant for its completion, but because of the friendship and encouragement I received from my colleagues there: Caroline Hemphill, James Piereson, Janice Riddell and Betty Sturdy.

Three political scientists, Thomas Engeman and John Williams of Loyola University and Ralph Rossum of Claremont McKenna College, helpfully reviewed and improved a preliminary version of this book. Other scholars who focused my thinking on public policy questions are John Gueguen and Jerry Nagel. Conversations with Gregory Simoncini over two decades have left me a net importer of political insights.

Carol Mann of the Carol Mann Agency and Roger Kimball of Encounter Books encouraged and reassured a first-time author. Encounter's Lauren Miklos, Heather Ohle, Emily Pollack and Sam Schneider patiently and helpfully fielded many ill-informed questions, while Jenny Woodward edited the manuscript rigorously and amiably. A generous grant from the Searle Freedom

Trust helped Encounter bring this volume to the attention of prospective readers.

The book is dedicated to my family, whose support and forbearance made it possible.

NOTES

FOREWORD

1. Kenneth Minogue, *The Liberal Mind* (Indianapolis: Liberty Fund, 2004 [originally published London: Methuen, 1963), p. 1.

INTRODUCTION

1. Franklin D. Roosevelt, Address at Madison Square Garden, New York City, 31 October 1936; John T. Woolley and Gerhard Peters, *The American Presidency Project* [online]. Santa Barbara, CA: University of California (hosted), Gerhard Peters (database). Available from World Wide Web: http://www.presidency.ucsb.edu/ws/?pid=15219.
2. "Not Enough," *The Nation*, 4 January 1964, p. 2.
3. Merton C. Bernstein, "What Future for Social Security?," *The New Republic*, 9 January 1965, p. 10.
4. "The Poor in Their Place," *The New Republic*, 20 November 1965, pp. 3–4.
5. United States. Kerner Commission, *Report of the National Advisory Commission on Civil Disorders* (Washington: U.S. Government Printing Office, 1968), Introduction, on "History Matters," http://historymatters.gmu.edu/d/6545/.
6. Leon Wieseltier, "Climates," *The New Republic*, 6 August 2007; http://www.tnr.com/columnists/story.html?id=908491de-b0d0-4d2b-8b1e-7bcaofb8bed8&p=1.
7. Paul Waldman, "The Failure of Antigovernment Conservatism," *The American Prospect*, 8 August 2007, http://www.prospect.org/cs/articles?article=the_failure_of_antigovernment_conservatism.
8. Theodore H. White, *The Making of the President, 1964* (New York: Atheneum, 1965), p. 365.
9. Steven F. Hayward, *The Age of Reagan: The Fall of the Old Liberal Order, 1964–1980* (Roseville, CA: Prima Publishing, 2001), p. x.

10. Sidney M. Milkis and Jerome M. Mileur, editors, *The Great Society and the High Tide of Liberalism* (Amherst: University of Massachusetts Press, 2005).

11. Jonathan Rieder, *Canarsie: The Jews and Italians of Brooklyn Against Liberalism* (Cambridge: Harvard University Press, 1985), p. 4.

12. James Q. Wilson, "Why Reagan Won and Stockman Lost," *Commentary*, August 1986, p. 21.

CHAPTER 1

1. Ann Lewis and Max B. Sawicky, "The Rights of Bill," *The American Prospect*, 2 July 2004; http://www.prospect.org/cs/articles?article=the_rights_of_bill.

2. Lewis and Sawicky, "The Rights of Bill."

3. Ronald Reagan Inaugural Address, 20 January 1981; http://www.presidency.ucsb.edu/ws/index.php?pid=43130.

4. Remarks by Pres. Reagan to the annual meeting of the American Bar Association on 1 August 1983 in Atlanta; http://www.reagan.utexas.edu/archives/speeches/1983/80183a.htm.

5. Franklin D. Roosevelt, "Commonwealth Club Address," 23 September 1932; http://www.americanrhetoric.com/speeches/fdrcommonwealth.htm.

6. Alan Brinkley, *The End of Reform: New Deal Liberalism in Recession and War* (New York: Vintage Books, 1995), p. 43.

7. Brinkley, *The End of Reform*, pp. 4–5, 65–66, 84–85.

8. James MacGregor Burns, *Roosevelt, the Soldier of Freedom* (New York: Harcourt, Brace, Jovanovich, 1970), p. 121.

9. Lewis and Sawicky, "The Rights of Bill;" Office of Management and Budget, *The Budget for Fiscal Year 2009, Historical Tables*, p. 135 (Table 8.2—Outlays by Budget Enforcement Act Category in Constant (FY 2000) Dollars, 1962–2013).

10. Seymour Martin Lipset, *American Exceptionalism: A Double-Edged Sword* (New York: Norton, 1996), p. 17.

11. OECD *Factbook 2008*: Economic, Environmental and Social Statistics; http://lysander.sourceoecd.org/vl=3320116/cl=21/nw=1/rpsv/fact2008/; "Comparative Real Gross Domestic Product Per Capita and Per Employed Person: 16 Countries, 1960–2007,"

U.S. Department of Labor, Bureau of Labor Statistics, Office of Productivity and Technology, 7 July 2008.

12. OECD *Factbook 2008*; http://lysander.sourceoecd.org/vl=1535264/cl=17/nw=1/rpsv/factbook/100202.htm.

13. George F. Will, "French Welfare State Built on Cultural Contradictions," *Washington Post*, 20 May 2007; http://www.realclearpolitics.com/articles/2007/05/french_welfare_state_built_on.html.

14. OECD *Factbook 2008*, "Total Tax Revenue," http://masetto.sourceoecd.org/vl=16909447/cl=13/nw=1/rpsv/factbook/100401.htm.

15. Robert Samuelson, "The End of Europe," *The Washington Post*, 15 June 2005, p. A25.

16. 2008 Democratic Party Platform; http://www.presidency.ucsb.edu/ws/index.php?pid=78283.

17. Matt Bai, "The Money Issue: The Poverty Platform," *The New York Times Magazine*, 10 June 2007; http://www.nytimes.com/2007/06/10/magazine/10edwards-t.html.

18. John Cassidy, "Relatively Deprived," *The New Yorker*, 3 April 2006; http://www.newyorker.com/fact/content/articles/060403fa_fact.

CHAPTER 2

1. Hendrik Hertzberg, "Like, Socialism," *The New Yorker*, 3 November 2008; http://www.newyorker.com/talk/comment/2008/11/03/081103taco_talk_hertzberg.

2. Robert Kuttner, "Friendly Takeover," *The American Prospect*, April 2007; http://www.prospect.org/cs/articles?articleId=12573.

3. Quoted in Olaf Gersemann, "Europe's Not Working," *The American Enterprise*, October – December 2005; http://www.taemag.com/issues/articleID.18719/article_detail.asp.

4. Jonah Goldberg, "Governments and Cultures," *National Review*, 10 April 2007; http://corner.nationalreview.com/post/?q=NjZmNGQxNWNmODk5NWQ4NjUrNDlhNjhlNjA2NDJjNGE=.

5. Lipset, *American Exceptionalism*, pp. 109, 35–38.

6. Seymour Martin Lipset and Gary Marks, *It Didn't Happen Here: Why Socialism Failed in the United States* (New York: Norton, 2000), pp. 22–23.

7. Ronald J. Pestritto, ed., *Woodrow Wilson: The Essential Political Writings* (Lanham, MD: Lexington, 2005), p. 173.
8. *The Federalist Papers*, No. 51; The Avalon Project of the Lillian Goldman Law Library at Yale Law School; http://avalon.law.yale.edu/18th_century/fed51.asp.
9. Pestritto, ed., *Woodrow Wilson: The Essential Political Writings*, p. 167.
10. James W. Ceaser, "True Blue vs. Deep Red: The Ideas That Move American Politics," a discussion paper for the Hudson Institute's 2006 Bradley Symposium, p. 9; http://www.bradleyfdn.org/pdfs/framingessay.pdf.
11. Ronald J. Pestritto, *Woodrow Wilson and the Roots of Modern Liberalism* (Lanham, MD: Rowman & Littlefield, 2005), p. 6.
12. Calvin Coolidge, "Speech on the Occasion of the One Hundred Fiftieth Anniversary of the Declaration of Independence," 5 July 1926; http://teachingamericanhistory.org/library/index.asp?document=41.
13. *The Federalist Papers*, No. 10; The Avalon Project; http://avalon.law.yale.edu/18th_century/fed10.asp.
14. Ceaser, "True Blue vs. Deep Red," pp. 9–10.
15. Pestritto, *Woodrow Wilson and The Roots of Modern Liberalism*, p. 6.
16. Richard Hofstadter, *The American Political Tradition: And the Men Who Made It* (New York: Vintage, 1973), p. 21.
17. C.S. Lewis, *The Screwtape Letters* (New York: MacMillan, 1961), p. 118.
18. Richard Rorty, *Contingency, Irony, and Solidarity* (Cambridge: Cambridge University Press, 1989), p. 86.
19. *Trop v. Dulles*, 356 U.S. 86 (1958).
20. Ceaser, "True Blue vs. Deep Red," p. 12.
21. Pestritto, ed., *Woodrow Wilson: The Essential Political Writings*, p. 221.
22. Quoted in Charles R. Kesler, "Woodrow Wilson and the Statesmanship of Progress," in Thomas B. Silver and Peter W. Schramm, eds., *Natural Right and Political Right: Essays in Honor of Harry V. Jaffa* (Durham, NC: Carolina Academic Press, 1984), pp. 123–124.

23. Michael Tomasky, "Jackboots and Whole Foods," *The New Republic*, 12 March 2008, http://www.tnr.com/toc/story. html?id=d6977c2f-4788-468e-8f63-2e92109320fe.
24. Sidney M. Milkis, "Roosevelt and the New Politics of Presidential Leadership," in Sidney M. Milkis and Jerome M. Mileur, eds., *The New Deal and the Triumph of Liberalism* (Amherst: University of Massachusetts Press, 2002), pp. 39–40.
25. V.O. Key, *The Responsible Electorate* (Cambridge: Harvard, 1966), p. 31.
26. Sidney M. Milkis, *The President and the Parties: The Transformation of the American Party System Since the New Deal* (New York: Oxford, 1993), p. 48.
27. Richard E. Neustadt, *Presidential Power: The Politics of Leadership from FDR to Carter* (New York: Wiley, 1980), p. 119.
28. Franklin D. Roosevelt, Address Accepting the Democratic Presidential Nomination, 2 July 1932, John T. Woolley and Gerhard Peters, *The American Presidency Project* [online]. Santa Barbara, CA: University of California (hosted), Gerhard Peters (database). Available from World Wide Web: http://www. presidency.ucsb.edu/ws/?pid=75174.
29. Roosevelt, 1932 acceptance speech.
30. Milkis, "Roosevelt and the New Politics of Presidential Leadership," p. 35.
31. Franklin D. Roosevelt, "Commonwealth Club Address."
32. Roosevelt, "Commonwealth Club Address."
33. Roosevelt, "Commonwealth Club Address."
34. Arthur M. Schlesinger, Jr., *The Politics of Upheaval* (Boston: Houghton Mifflin, 1960), p. 581.
35. 1936 Democratic Party Platform, in John T. Woolley and Gerhard Peters, *The American Presidency Project* [online]. Santa Barbara, CA: University of California (hosted), Gerhard Peters (database). Available from World Wide Web: http://www.presidency.ucsb. edu/ws/?pid=29596.
36. 1936 Republican Party Platform, in John T. Woolley and Gerhard Peters, *The American Presidency Project* [online]. Santa Barbara, CA: University of California (hosted), Gerhard Peters (database). Available from World Wide Web: http://www.presidency.ucsb. edu/ws/?pid=29639.

37. Roosevelt, "Commonwealth Club Address."
38. David Kennedy, *Freedom From Fear: The American People in Depression and War, 1929–1945* (Oxford: Oxford University Press, 1999), pp. 184–5.
39. Schlesinger, *The Politics of Upheaval*, pp. 284–285; William E. Leuchtenburg, *The Supreme Court Reborn: The Constitutional Revolution in the Age of Roosevelt* (Oxford: Oxford University Press, 1995), p. 90.
40. *A.L.A. Schechter Poultry Corp. v. United States*, 295 U.S. 495.
41. *Schechter*, 295 U.S. 495, 551–553.
42. Milkis, "Roosevelt and the New Politics of Presidential Leadership," p. 42.
43. Schlesinger, *The Politics of Upheaval*, p. 285.
44. 1936 Democratic Party Platform.
45. Kennedy, *Freedom From Fear*, p. 326.
46. Kennedy, p. 326.
47. Kennedy, p. 333.
48. Kennedy, pp. 336–337.
49. Bernard Schwartz, *The Supreme Court: Constitutional Revolution in Retrospect* (New York: Ronald Press, 1957), p. 27; Peter M. Shane, "In Whose Best Interest? Not the States'," *The Washington Post*, 21 May 2000; http://www.cir-usa.org/articles/113.html.
50. Theodore J. Lowi, *The End of Liberalism: The Second Republic of the United States*, second edition (New York: Norton, 1979), p. 93.
51. Richard A. Epstein, *How Progressives Rewrote the Constitution* (Washington, DC: Cato Institute, 2006), pp. 71, 75.
52. Epstein, p. 8.
53. Epstein, p. 119. The decision is *Wickard v. Filburn*, 317 U.S. 111.
54. Robert G. McCloskey, *The American Supreme Court* (Chicago: University of Chicago, 1960), p. 185.
55. Richard A. Epstein, "The Mistakes of 1937," *George Mason University Law Review*, vol. 11, no. 2, pp. 13–20.
56. Leuchtenburg, *The Supreme Court Reborn,* p. 236.
57. Gerald Ford, Address to a Joint Session of Congress, 12 August 1974: John T. Woolley and Gerhard Peters, *The American Presidency Project* [online]. Santa Barbara, CA: University of California (hosted), Gerhard Peters (database). Available from World Wide Web: http://www.presidency.ucsb.edu/ws/?pid=4694.

58. G. Edward White, *The Constitution and the New Deal* (Cambridge: Harvard University Press, 2000), pp. 198–236.

59. Franklin D. Roosevelt, Acceptance Speech at the Democratic National Convention, 27 June 1936; John T. Woolley and Gerhard Peters, *The American Presidency Project* [online]. Santa Barbara, CA: University of California (hosted), Gerhard Peters (database). Available from World Wide Web: http://www.presidency.ucsb.edu/ws/?pid=15314.

60. *United States v. Carolene Products Company*, 304 U.S. 144 (1938).

61. Epstein, *How Progressives Rewrote the Constitution*, p. 113.

62. *Carolene Products*, 304 U.S. 152.

63. *Carolene Products*, n. 4.

64. Ceaser, "True Blue vs. Deep Red," pp. 11–12.

65. *Shapiro v. Thompson*, 394 U.S. 618.

66. *Roe v. Wade*, 410 U.S. 113.

67. Alexander Bickel, *The Least Dangerous Branch* (New York: Bobbs-Merrill, 1962), p. 16.

68. Franklin D. Roosevelt, State of the Union Message to Congress, 11 January 1944; John T. Woolley and Gerhard Peters, *The American Presidency Project* [online]. Santa Barbara, CA: University of California (hosted), Gerhard Peters (database). Available from World Wide Web: http://www.presidency.ucsb.edu/ws/?pid=16518.

69. Roosevelt, 1944 State of the Union address.

70. Roosevelt, 1944 State of the Union address.

71. Roosevelt, 1944 State of the Union address.

72. Roosevelt, 1944 State of the Union address.

73. Roosevelt, 1944 State of the Union address.

74. Quoted in James T. Kloppenberg, *Uncertain Victory: Social Democracy and Progressivism in European and American Thought, 1870–1920* (New York: Oxford University Press, 1986), p. 203.

75. Roosevelt, 1936 Acceptance Speech.

76. Wilson W. Wyatt, Address to Americans for Democratic Action national convention, ADA press release, 21 February 1948. The Wisconsin Historical Society holds the ADA archives; this citation is from Series 4 of their collection. Wilson Wyatt, in addition to being one of ADA's founders, was mayor of Louisville, Lieutenant Governor of Kentucky, and manager of Adlai Stevenson's presidential campaign in 1952.

77. Cass Sunstein, *The Second Bill of Rights: FDR's Unfinished Revolution and Why We Need It More than Ever* (New York: Basic Books, 2004), p. 87.
78. Universal Declaration of Human Rights, Adopted by the United Nations General Assembly, 10 December 1948; http://www.un.org/Overview/rights.html.
79. Milkis, "Roosevelt and the New Politics of Presidential Leadership," pp. 57–59; Roosevelt, 1944 State of the Union Address.
80. Sunstein, pp. 1–4.
81. Sunstein, pp. 152–154.
82. R. Shep Melnick, "The Price of Rights," *The Claremont Review of Books*, Fall 2004; http://www.claremont.org/publications/crb/id.1372/article_detail.asp; "Correspondence," *The Claremont Review of Books*, Winter 2004/05; http://www.claremont.org/publications/crb/id.1368/article_detail.asp.

CHAPTER 3

1. James Q. Wilson, "American Politics, Then and Now," *Commentary*, February 1979, p. 41, quoted in R. Shep Melnick, *Between the Lines: Interpreting Welfare Rights* (Washington, DC: The Brookings Institution, 1994), p. 25.
2. "The Liberal Agenda," *The American Prospect*, 20 January 2005; http://www.prospect.org/cs/articles?article=the_liberal_agenda. The winning entry was, "Liberals believe our common humanity endows each of us, individually, with the right to freedom, self-government, and opportunity; and binds all of us, together, in responsibility for securing those rights." Dorian Friedman, the director of external relations for the magazine, kindly provided me with this information after changes in the *Prospect's* website had made it difficult to retrieve.
3. Michael Tomasky, "Party in Search of a Notion," *The American Prospect*, May 2006, http://www.prospect.org/cs/articles?article=party_in_search_of_a_notion_041606.
4. James W. Ceaser, "True Blue vs. Deep Red," p. 5.
5. Kenneth Baer and Andrei Cherny, "A Message to Our Readers," *Democracy*, Summer 2006; http://www.democracyjournal.org/article.php?ID=6465.

6. Jonathan Chait, "Why Big Ideas Won't Save Liberalism," *The New Republic*, 26 June 2006, http://www.tnr.com/doc. mhtml?i=w060626&s=chait060626.

7. Rorty, *Contingency, Irony and Solidarity*, p. 86.

8. Franklin D. Roosevelt, Address at Oglethorpe University, 22 May 1932; Reprinted in *The Public Papers and Addresses of Franklin D. Roosevelt, Vol. 1, 1928–32*, (New York: Random House, 1938), p. 639; http://newdeal.feri.org/speeches/1932d.htm.

9. Chait, "Big Ideas."

10. Alan Brinkley, *Liberalism and Its Discontents* (Cambridge, MA: Harvard University Press, 1998), pp. 18, 37.

11. Chait, "Big Ideas"; Hofstadter, *The American Political Tradition*, p. 411; Robert Lekachman, "Fashions in Liberalism," *The Nation*, 26 November 1977, p. 62.

12. Charles R. Kesler, "The New Freedom and the New Deal," in Robert Eden, ed., *The New Deal and Its Legacy: Critique and Reappraisal* (New York: Greenwood, 1989), pp. 160–161.

13. Roosevelt, "Commonwealth Club Address."

14. Milkis, "Roosevelt and the New Politics of Presidential Leadership," pp. 41, 53, 47.

15. Chait, "Why Big Ideas Won't Save Liberalism."

16. Sunstein, *The Second Bill of Rights*, pp. 5, 233.

17. Sunstein, pp. 234, 3.

18. Arthur M. Schlesinger, Jr., "The Perspective Now," *Partisan Review*, May-June 1947, pp. 231, 242; quoted in Thomas B. Silver, *Coolidge and the Historians* (Durham, NC: Carolina Academic Press, 1982), pp. 98–99.

19. Bruce Ackerman and Todd Gitlin, "We Answer to the Name of Liberals," *The American Prospect*, November 2006, pp. 24–25.

20. Robert H. Wiebe, *Self-Rule: A Cultural History of American Democracy* (Chicago: University of Chicago Press, 1995), p. 239.

21. The 1972 Democratic Party platform, for example, says, "We are determined to make economic security a matter of right." (http://www.presidency.ucsb.edu/ws/index.php?pid=29605).

22. Fair Housing Act Amendments of 1988, 42 U.S.C. §§ 3601–3619; http://www.usdoj.gov/crt/housing/fairhousing/about_fairhousingact.htm.

23. Lisa W. Foderaro, "Protests of Housing Plan Lead to HUD Inquiry, and Debate," *The New York Times*, 1 September 1994; http://www.nytimes.com/1994/09/01/nyregion/protests-of-housing-plan-lead-to-hud-inquiry-and-debate.html?pagewanted=all; Heather MacDonald, "Big Brother HUD," *City Journal*, Autumn 1994; http://www.city-journal.org/article01.php?aid=1378.

24. Foderaro, *The New York Times*, 1 September 1994; Gayle M.B. Hanson, "Activists Attract HUD Thought Police," *Insight on the News*, 19 September 1994, pp. 6–9.

25. Chester Hartman, "Shelterforce Interview; Roberta Achtenberg," *Shelterforce Online*, January/February 1995; http://www.nhi.org/online/issues/79/achtenberg.html; Foderaro, *The New York Times*, 1 September 1994.

26. Hartman, Achtenberg Interview; Roberta Achtenberg, "Sometimes on a Tightrope at HUD," *The Washington Post*, 22 August 1994, p. A17.

27. Harry S. Truman, Democratic Convention Acceptance Speech, July 15, 1948; http://presidency.ucsb.edu/ws/index.php?pid=12962.

28. Mario Cuomo, "A Tale of Two Cities," delivered July 16, 1984, at the Democratic convention in San Francisco; http://www.americanrhetoric.com/speeches/cuomo1984dnc.htm.

29. Quoted in Brinkley, *The End of Reform*, p. 155.

30. Alan Ryan, *John Dewey and the High Tide of American Liberalism* (New York: W.W. Norton, 1995), p. 25.

31. John Dewey, "Democracy and Educational Administration" (1937), in John Dewey, *The Later Works (1925–1953)* (Carbondale, IL: Southern Illinois University Press), vol. 11, pp. 217–218. See David Fott, *John Dewey: America's Philosopher of Democracy* (Lanham, MD: Rowman and Littlefield, 1998), pp. 65–66.

32. Wiebe, *Self-Rule*, p. 5.

33. Sidney M. Milkis, "New Deal Party Politics, Administrative Reform, and the Transformation of the American Constitution," in Robert Eden, ed., *The New Deal and Its Legacy*, p. 129.

34. Schlesinger, "The Perspective Now," quoted in Silver, *Coolidge and the Historians*, p. 98.

35. Nathan Glazer, *Affirmative Discrimination* (New York: Basic Books, 1978), p. 56.

36. Terry Eastland, *Ending Affirmative Action: The Case for Colorblind Justice* (New York: Basic Books, 1996), pp. 106–107.

37. John F. Kennedy, "Radio and Television Report to the American People on Civil Rights," 11 June 1963; John T. Woolley and Gerhard Peters, *The American Presidency Project* [online]. Santa Barbara, CA: University of California (hosted), Gerhard Peters (database). Available from World Wide Web: http://www.presidency.ucsb.edu/ws/?pid=9271.

38. Paul Craig Roberts and Laurence M. Stratton, *The New Color Line: How Quotas and Privilege Destroy Democracy* (Washington, DC: Regnery, 1995), pp. 69, 75, 77–78.

39. Lyndon B. Johnson, Commencement Address at Howard University, "To Fulfill These Rights," 4 June 1965; John T. Woolley and Gerhard Peters, *The American Presidency Project* [online]. Santa Barbara, CA: University of California (hosted), Gerhard Peters (database). Available from World Wide Web: http://www.presidency.ucsb.edu/ws/?pid=27021.

40. Roberts and Stratton, p. 91.

41. Roberts and Stratton, pp. 88–95.

42. *United Steelworkers of America v. Weber*, 443 U.S. 193, 195; Roberts and Stratton, pp. 106–107.

43. William J. Clinton, Remarks at the National Archives and Records Administration, 19 July 1995; John T. Woolley and Gerhard Peters, *The American Presidency Project* [online]. Santa Barbara, CA: University of California (hosted), Gerhard Peters (database). Available from World Wide Web: http://www.presidency.ucsb.edu/ws/?pid=51631.

44. *Grutter v. Bollinger*, 539 U.S. 306 (2003).

45. Scott Jaschik, "Doomed to Disappoint Justice O'Connor," *Inside Higher Ed*, 26 March 2008; http://insidehighered.com/news/2008/03/26/bakke.

46. Jaschik, "Doomed to Disappoint Justice O'Connor."

47. Thomas Sowell, "'Affirmative Action': A Worldwide Disaster," *Commentary*, December 1989, p. 26.

48. Clinton address of 19 July 1995; *Steelworkers v. Weber*, 443 U.S. 193, 195.

49. 443 U.S. 193, 195.

50. Alicia Montgomery, "Oops, She Did It Again," *Salon*, 16 August 2000; http://dir.salon.com/story/politics/feature/2000/08/16/black_caucus/index.html.
51. Roberts and Stratton, p. 78.
52. Matthew Yglesias, "The Demerits of Democracy," *The American Prospect*, 31 January 2006; http://www.prospect.org/cs/articles?articleId=11031.
53. Yglesias, "The Demerits of Democracy;" John Rawls, *A Theory of Justice* (Cambridge, MA: Harvard University Press, 1971), p. 432.
54. Gareth Davies, *From Opportunity to Entitlement: The Transformation and Decline of Great Society Liberalism* (Lawrence: University Press of Kansas, 1996), pp. 229, 232.
55. Jill Nelson, "Apocalypse Now," *The Nation*, 26 August 1996, p. 10.
56. Timothy Egan, "As Idaho Booms, Prisons Fill and Spending on Poor Lags," *New York Times*, April 16, 1998, p. 1.
57. Fred Siegel, *The Future Once Happened Here: New York, D.C., L.A. and the Fate of America's Big Cities* (New York: Free Press, 1997), pp. 46–61. See also, Vincent J. Cannato, *The Ungovernable City: John Lindsay and His Struggle to Save New York* (New York: Basic Books, 2001).
58. Christopher Jencks, "The Moynihan Report," *The New York Review of Books*, 14 October 1965, p. 39.
59. Robert Scheer, "Clinton Ended Welfare, Not Poverty," *The Nation*, 26 August 2006; http://www.truthdig.com/report/item/20060829_robert_scheer_clinton_welfare/.
60. William J. Clinton, The President's Radio Address, 19 May 1996; John T. Woolley and Gerhard Peters, *The American Presidency Project* [online]. Santa Barbara, CA: University of California (hosted), Gerhard Peters (database). Available from World Wide Web: http://www.presidency.ucsb.edu/ws/?pid=52834.
61. Matthew Yglesias, "Welfare Reform as Politics," *The American Prospect*, 24 August 2006, http://www.prospect.org/weblog/2006/08/.
62. "Fared Well," *The New Republic*, 4 September 2006; http://www.tnr.com/article/fared-well.
63. Tomasky, "Party in Search of a Notion."
64. Tomasky.
65. Tomasky.

66. Ceaser, "True Blue vs. Deep Red," pp. 13–14.
67. Elizabeth Anderson, "Social Insurance and Self-Sufficiency," Left2Right.com, 5 February 2005, http://www-personal.umich. edu/~eandersn/blogpoliticaleconomy.html.
68. E.L. Doctorow, "The Rise of Ronald Reagan: Dream Candidate," *The Nation*, 19 July 1980; http://www.thenation.com/ doc/19800719/doctorow.
69. "Is the Common Good Good?," *The American Prospect*, July 2005; http://www.prospect.org/web/page.ww?section=root&name=View Print&articleId=11663.
70. Joseph Cropsey, "Conservatism and Liberalism," in Robert A. Goldwin, ed., *Left, Right and Center: Essays on Liberalism and Conservatism in the United States* (Chicago: Rand McNally, 1965), pp. 52–53.
71. Catherine Bauer, "The Middle Class Needs Houses Too," *The New Republic*, 29 August 1949, p. 19.
72. Arthur M. Schlesinger, Jr., *The Politics of Hope* (Boston: Houghton Mifflin, 1963), p. 91.
73. Irving Sarnoff, "Bad Boys, Bad Times," *The New Republic*, 18 January 1960, p. 14.
74. Franklin D. Roosevelt, Radio Address to the Young Democratic Clubs of America, 24 August 1935; http://www.presidency.ucsb. edu/ws/index.php?pid=14925.
75. "Forgotten in Abundance?," *The Nation*, 1 February 1965, p. 97.
76. Clive Crook, "John Kenneth Galbraith Revisited," *National Journal*, 12 May 2006; http://www.theatlantic.com/doc/200605u/ nj_crook_2006-05-09.
77. Arthur M. Schlesinger, Jr., "Liberalism," *Saturday Review*, 8 June 1957, pp. 11–12.
78. Richard H. Pells, *The Liberal Mind in a Conservative Age: American Intellectuals in the 1940s and 1950s* (New York: Harper and Row, 1985), p. 248.
79. Rawls, *A Theory of Justice*, p. 442.
80. James T. Patterson, *Grand Expectations: The United States, 1945–1974* (Oxford: Oxford University Press, 1996), pp. 337–342.
81. Alan Ehrenhalt, *The Lost City: Discovering the Forgotten Virtues of Community in the Chicago of the 1950s* (New York: Basic Books, 1995), pp. 211–213.

82. Roosevelt, 1944 State of the Union Address.
83. Lyndon B. Johnson, Remarks at the University of Michigan, 22 May 1964, *Public Papers of the Presidents of the United States: Lyndon B. Johnson, 1963–64; Volume I,* entry 357, pp. 704–707. Washington, DC: Government Printing Office, 1965; http://www.lbjlib.utexas.edu/johnson/archives.hom/speeches.hom/640522.asp.
84. Johnson, Remarks at the University of Michigan.
85. "Is the Common Good Good?," *The American Prospect,* July 2005.
86. Clifford Orwin, "Moist Eyes—From Rousseau to Clinton," *The Public Interest,* Summer 1997, pp. 5–6.
87. Al Gore speech to the 1992 Democratic National Convention, http://www.al-gore-2004.org/gorespeeches/1992convention.htm; George H.W. Bush speech to the 1988 Republican National Convention, http://www.presidency.ucsb.edu/ws/index.php?pid=25955.
88. Thomas Sowell, "Race: Affirmative Action Around the World," *Hoover Digest,* 2004, No. 4, http://www.hoover.org/publications/digest/3010426.html; Sowell, "The Grand Fraud: Part III," *Jewish World Review,* 3 April 2003, http://www.jewishworldreview.com/cols/sowell040303.asp.
89. Richard H. Sander, "A Reply to Critics," 57 *Stanford Law Review* (2005), pp. 1964–1965.
90. Joanne Hou and Audrey Kuo, "Critiquing Affirmative Action," *UCLA Daily Bruin,* 6 November 2007; http://dailybruin.ucla.edu/stories/2007/nov/6/critiquing-affirmative-action/; Gail Heriot, "Affirmative Action Backfires," *OpinionJournal.com,* 26 August 2007, http://www.opinionjournal.com/editorial/feature.html?id=110010522.
91. Roosevelt, 1936 Acceptance Speech.
92. Roosevelt, 1936 Acceptance Speech.
93. Jean-Jacques Rousseau, *Emile* or *On Education,* Book Four (trans. Allan Bloom [New York: Basic Books, 1979], p. 235n); Jean Bethke Elshtain, "Sense and Sensibility," *The New Republic,* 30 September 1996, p. 29.
94. Mickey Kaus, "Up From Altruism: The Case Against Compassion," *The New Republic,* 15 December 1986, pp. 17–18.

95. Orwin, "Moist Eyes," p. 12.

96. Robert D. Putnam, "*E Pluribus Unum*: Diversity and Community in the Twenty-first Century; The 2006 Johan Skytte Prize Lecture," *Scandinavian Political Studies,* Volume 30, Issue 2 (June 2007); doi:10.1111/j.1467-9477.2007.00176.x.

97. Cropsey, p. 54.

98. Noam Scheiber, "Individual Rights v̇. The Common Good: Vision Problems," *The New Republic,* 28 April 2006; http://www.tnr.com/doc.mhtml?i=w060424&s=scheiber042806.

99. "Is the Common Good Good?," *The American Prospect,* July 2005.

100. "Is the Common Good Good?," *The American Prospect,* July 2005; Robert Kuttner, *The Life of the Party: Democratic Prospects in 1988 and Beyond* (New York: Elisabeth Sifton Books; Viking, 1987), pp. 170–171.

101. Buck Wolf, "Great Shakes: 'Hands Across America' Twenty Years Later," ABCNews.com, 23 May 2006; http://abcnews.go.com/Entertainment/WolfFiles/story?id=2044810&page=1.

102. William James, "The Moral Equivalent of War," lecture delivered in 1906; http://www.des.emory.edu/mfp/moral.html; William Galston, "Is the Common Good Good?," *The American Prospect,* July 2005.

103. Arthur M. Schlesinger, Jr., *The Vital Center: The Politics of Freedom* (Boston: Houghton Mifflin, 1949), p. 186.

104. James Ceaser, "Alive and Kicking," *The Weekly Standard,* 25 February 2009; http://www.weeklystandard.com/Content/Public/Articles/000/000/016/196msdeq.asp.

105. Noam Scheiber, "Individual Rights v. The Common Good," *The New Republic,* 28 April 2006; http://www.tnr.com/doc.mhtml?i=w060424&s=scheiber042806; Jeffrey Goldberg, "Central Casting," *The New Yorker,* 29 May 2006; http://www.newyorker.com/archive/2006/05/29/060529fa_fact2?currentPage=all.

106. Chait, "Why Big Ideas Won't Save Liberalism."

107. Theodore Lowi, *The Personal President* (Ithaca, NY: Cornell University Press, 1985), pp. 154–156.

108. Jonathan Chait, "The Anti-Dogma Dogma," *The New Republic,* 28 February 2005, http://www.tnr.com/doc.mhtml?pt=EGc8sNwd1QGmAjr7FY7r%2Bh%3D%3D.

109. Chris Edwards, "Spender vs. Spender," *National Review*, March 29, 2004; http://www.nationalreview.com/comment/edwards200403290835.asp.
110. Kuttner, *The Life of the Party*, p. 171.
111. Charles Murray, *Losing Ground: American Social Policy, 1950–1980* (New York: Basic Books, 1984), p. 47.
112. *The Federalist Papers*, No. 62; The Avalon Project, Lillian Goldman Law Library, Yale Law School; http://avalon.law.yale.edu/18th_century/fed62.asp.
113. *The Federalist Papers*, No. 62.
114. Michael Kinsley, "The Shame of the Democrats," *The New Republic*, 25 July 1981, pp. 14–16.

CHAPTER 4

1. Lyndon B. Johnson, Remarks at the Civic Center Arena in Pittsburgh, 27 October 1964; John T. Woolley and Gerhard Peters, *The American Presidency Project* [online]. Santa Barbara, CA: University of California (hosted), Gerhard Peters (database). Available from World Wide Web: http://www.presidency.ucsb.edu/ws/?pid=26674.
2. Michael Tomasky, "The Pathetic Truth," *The American Prospect*, 13 September 2004; http://www.prospect.org/cs/articles?article=the_pathetic_truth.
3. Tomasky, "The Pathetic Truth."
4. See Robert Weissberg, *Polling, Policy, and Public Opinion: The Case Against Heeding The "Voice of the People"* (New York: Palgrave Macmillan, 2002).
5. Harold Malmgren, "The Economy: A Case for Efficient Planning," *The New Republic*, 7 November 1964, p. 47.
6. Peter Schrag, *Paradise Lost: California's Experience, America's Future* (Berkeley: University of California Press, 1999), pp. 34–35.
7. David O. Sears and Jack Citrin, *Tax Revolt: Something for Nothing in California* (Cambridge, MA, Harvard University Press, 1982), p. 251; quoted in Schrag, pp. 156–157.
8. "Nixon's Affluence," *The New Republic*, 30 August 1969, p. 8.
9. "Me First," *The New Republic*, 17 June 1978, p. 5; Peter Connoly, "The Voice of Raw Greed," *The Nation*, 22 July 1978, p. 77.

10. Jonathan Cohn, "Neoliberal Utopia Awaits," *The New Republic*, January 15, 2007; http://www.tnr.com/article/neoliberal-utopia-awaits.
11. Carter Dougherty, "High Income Taxes in Denmark Worsen a Labor Shortage," *The International Herald Tribune*, 5 December 2007; http://www.iht.com/articles/2007/12/05/business/labor.php?page=2.
12. Jonathan Cohn, "Tax Alternative," *The New Republic*, 28 March 2005.
13. "A Federal Oil Firm," *Time*, 24 February 1975; http://www.time.com/time/magazine/article/0,9171,917122,00.html?iid=chix-sphere.
14. "A Federal Oil Firm," *Time*, 24 February 1975.
15. Paul Starr, "Liberalism After Socialism," *The American Prospect*, September 1991, http://www.prospect.org/cs/articles?article=liberalism_after_socialism.
16. Brian Morton, *Starting Out in the Evening* (New York: Harcourt, 1998), p. 313.
17. Richard Rorty, *Achieving Our Country: Leftist Thought in Twentieth Century America* (Cambridge, MA: Harvard University Press, 1998), pp. 103–105.
18. Starr, "Liberalism After Socialism."
19. Joseph Heath and Andrew Potter, *A Nation of Rebels: Why Counterculture Became Consumer Culture* (New York: Harper Business, 2004), pp. 325–326.
20. Cass Sunstein, "A Brave New Wikiworld," *The Washington Post*, 24 February 2007, p. A19.
21. Brinkley, *The End of Reform*, p. 5; Freda Kirchwey, "Old Liberties for a New World," *The Nation*, 10 February 1940, quoted in Brinkley, p. 290.
22. Brinkley, *The End of Reform*, pp. 6–7.
23. Patterson, *Grand Expectations*, p. 61.
24. Arthur M. Schlesinger, Jr., "Which Way for the Democrats?" *Reporter*, 20 January 1953, p. 32.
25. Edwin Dale, "Confessions of a One-Time Conservative," *The New Republic*, 29 May 1961, pp. 9–10. Italics in the original.

26. Daniel Patrick Moynihan, *Maximum Feasible Misunderstanding: Community Action in the War on Poverty* (New York: The Free Press, 1969), pp. 28–29.

27. Jonathan Cohn, "Tax Alternative," *The New Republic*, 28 March 2005, p. 6.

28. Michael Barone, *Our Country: The Shaping of America From Roosevelt to Reagan* (New York: The Free Press, 1990), p. 414.

29. Arthur M. Schlesinger, Jr., *A Life in the 20th Century: Innocent Beginnings, 1917–1950* (New York: Houghton Mifflin Harcourt, 2000), p. 124.

30. Arthur M. Schlesinger, Jr., *Robert Kennedy and His Times* (New York: Houghton Mifflin Harcourt, 2002), pp. 803–804.

31. Schlesinger, *Robert Kennedy*, p. 824.

32. Tom Geoghegan, "Miami and the Seeds of Port Huron," *The New Republic*, 2 September 1972, pp. 16–18.

33. David Burnham, "Schlesinger Calls Violence a U.S. Trait," *The New York Times*, 6 June 1968; http://partners.nytimes.com/books/00/11/26/specials/schlesinger-violence.html.

34. William Schneider, "JFK's Children: The Class of '74," *The Atlantic Monthly*, March 1989, p. 35.

35. Charles Peters, "A Neoliberal's Manifesto," *The Washington Monthly*, May 1983, pp. 9–18.

36. Arthur M. Schlesinger, Jr., "Requiem for Neoliberalism," a review of *A New Democracy*, by Gary Hart, *The New Republic*, 6 June 1983, pp. 28–30.

37. E.J. Dionne, "Rob Reiner: Ceaseless in California," *The Washington Post*, 3 March 2006, p. A17, http://www.washingtonpost.com/wp-dyn/content/article/2006/03/02/AR2006030201205.html.

38. E.J. Dionne, "Lessons for Liberals in California," *The Washington Post*, 9 June 2006, p. A23, http://www.washingtonpost.com/wp-dyn/content/article/2006/06/08/AR2006060801669.html.

39. Democratic Presidential Candidates Debate, Philadelphia, 16 April 2008; http://abcnews.go.com/Politics/DemocraticDebate/Story?id=4670271&page=3.

40. Jason Furman and Austan Goolsbee, "The Obama Tax Plan," *The Wall Street Journal*, 14 August 2008, p. A13; http://online.wsj.com/public/article_print/SB121867201724238901.html.

41. Ezra Klein, "Being Rich," *The American Prospect*, 12 March 2008; http://www.prospect.org/csnc/blogs/ezraklein_archive?month=03&year=2008&base_name=being_rich#104982.
42. Table HINC-06. Income Distribution to $250,000 or More for Households: 2007; U.S. Census Bureau, Current Population Survey, 2008; http://www.census.gov/hhes/www/macro/032008/hhinc/new06_000.htm
43. Bertrand de Jouvenel, *The Ethics of Redistribution*, (Indianapolis: Liberty Press, 1989), pp. 24, 28. Originally published by Cambridge University Press in 1952.
44. Jouvenel, pp. 28–29.
45. These percentages are derived from the U.S. Census Bureau, Current Population Survey, 2008 Annual Social and Economic Supplement; Table HINC-06, "Income Distribution to $250,000 or More for Households, 2007," http://pubdb3.census.gov/macro/032008/hhinc/new06_000.htm.
46. Congressional Budget Office, *Historical Effective Federal Tax Rates, 1979 – 2005*, December 2007, Appendix, Table 1C; http://www.cbo.gov/ftpdocs/88xx/doc8885/Appendix_wtoc.pdf. I'm grateful to Ed Harris of the CBO Tax Analysis Division for explaining these numbers to me.
47. Jared Bernstein, "Economic Opportunity and Poverty in America," Economic Policy Institute Viewpoints, 13 February 2007; http://www.epi.org/content.cfm/webfeatures_viewpoints_econ_oppty_and_poverty.
48. Furman and Goolsbee.
49. Furman and Goolsbee.
50. Evan Thomas, "The Left Starts to Rethink Reagan," *Newsweek*, 3 May 2008; http://www.newsweek.com/id/135382.
51. Congressional Budget Office, *Historical Effective Federal Tax Rates, 1979 to 2005*, December 2007.
52. Rawls, *A Theory of Justice*, p. 302.
53. Robert Nozick, *Anarchy, State and Utopia* (New York: Basic Books, 1974), pp. 160–164.
54. Nozick, p. 163.
55. Jouvenel, *The Ethics of Redistribution*, pp. 23–25.
56. Jonathan Chait, "Envy Them? No. Tax Them? Oh Yeah," *The Los Angeles Times*, 10 June 2005; http://www.latimes.com/

news/opinion/commentary/la-oe-chait10jun10,0,2245814.
column?coll=la-news-comment-opinions.

57. David M. Kennedy, *Freedom From Fear*, p. 282.

58. Jim Webb, "Class Struggle," *The Wall Street Journal*, 15 November 2006; http://www.opinionjournal.com/editorial/feature. html?id=110009246.

59. AFL-CIO Executive PayWatch Database; http://www.aflcio. org/corporatewatch/paywatch/ceou/; Fortune Global 500, 2008; http://money.cnn.com/magazines/fortune/global500/2008/ full_list/; Jon Heyman, "Yankees Reach Agreement With Teixeira on 8-Year, $180 Million Deal," *SI.com*, 23 December 2008; http:// sportsillustrated.cnn.com/2008/baseball/mlb/12/23/teixeira/index. html.

60. George F. Will, "Folly and the Fed," *The Washington Post*, 16 August 2007, p. A15.

61. Irving Kristol, *Two Cheers for Capitalism* (New York: Basic Books, 1978), p. 211.

62. James Tobin, "Barry's Economic Crusade," *The New Republic*, 24 October 1964, p. 16.

63. Christopher Jencks, "Paying for Education-II," *The New Republic*, 1 February 1964, p. 14.

64. William F. Buckley, Jr., *Up From Liberalism*, 2nd ed. (Briarcliff Manor, NY: Stein and Day, 1984), p. 162.

65. Speech by Sen. John Edwards to the Democratic National Convention, 28 July 2004, reprinted in *The Washington Post* (http://www.washingtonpost.com/wp-dyn/articles/A22230-2004Jul28.html).

66. Keith Love and Karen Tumulty, "Top Democrat Stirs Fuss on Social Security," *The Los Angeles Times*, 18 April 1985; http:// articles.latimes.com/1985-04-18/news/mn-23533_1_social-security.

67. Chris Suellentrop, "George W. Bush, Philosopher-King," *Slate*, 17 January 2005 (http://www.slate.com/id/2112357/).

68. Jonathan Cohn, "The Urgency of Ted Kennedy's Message," *The New Republic*, 26 August 2008; http://blogs.tnr.com/tnr/blogs/ the_plank/archive/2008/08/26/160919.aspx.

69. Starr, "Liberalism After Socialism."

70. Quoted in C. Eugene Steuerle and Jon M. Bakija, *Retooling Social Security for the 21st Century: Right and Wrong Approaches* (Washington, DC: The Urban Institute Press, 1994), p. 16.

71. Sandra Tsing Loh, "The Rantings of a P.T.A. Mom," *The New York Times*, 9 September 2008; http://campaignstops.blogs.nytimes.com/2008/09/09/the-rantings-of-a-pta-mom/?ref=opinion.

72. Mickey Kaus, "Let's Not Save Social Security," *Slate*, 5 May 2005; http://www.slate.com/id/2118109/.

73. Ramesh Ponnuru, "A Social Security Puzzle," *National Review*, 27 September 2007; (http://corner.nationalreview.com/post/?q=MWE1OGQ1ZmI5NTZjM2VjMjRkYWRiZjE1MTk0MmNiZDg=).

CHAPTER 5

1. Ramesh Ponnuru, "Conservatism on the Couch," *National Review*, 20 November 2006; http://nrd.nationalreview.com/article/?q=MTEwNWRjNDE4NzU1YTI3OGNiZjZjJA1ZjVlZTY0OWI=.

2. "Romney Reaches for Reagan Touch," *The Boston Globe*, 25 November 2006; http://www.boston.com/news/local/articles/2006/11/25/romney_reaches_for_reagan_touch/.

3. Carl Campanile, "Rudy Suggests Bush is No Ronald Reagan," *The New York Post*, 15 June 2007; http://www.nypost.com/seven/06152007/news/nationalnews/rudy_suggests_bush_is_no_ronald_reagan_nationalnews_carl_campanile.htm.

4. "McCain on the Superhighway, Attempts to Appeal to Reagan Conservatives," *We Need to Blog*, 18 February 2007; http://weneedtoblog.blogspot.com/2007/02/mccain-on-superhighway-attempts-to.html.

5. U.S. Census Bureau, "Table 7. Resident Population by Age and Sex: 1980 to 2070," Current Population Reports, P25-1095; "Table US-EST90INT-04—Intercensal Estimates of the United States Resident Population by Age Groups and Sex, 1990–2000: Selected Months"; published 13 September 2002; <http://www.census.gov/popest/archives/EST90INTERCENSAL/US-EST90INT-04.html>; and "Annual Estimates of the Population by Sex and Five-Year Age

Groups for the United States: April 1, 2000 to July 1, 2007 (NC-EST2007-01)"; release date: May 1, 2008 <http://www.census.gov/popest/national/asrh/NC-EST2007/NC-EST2007-01.xls>.ctof.

6. Milkis, "Roosevelt and the New Politics of Presidential Leadership," p. 41.
7. Social Security Administration, Research Note #23, "Luther Gulick Memorandum re: Famous FDR Quote," http://www.ssa.gov/history/Gulick.html.
8. Bob Woodward, *The Agenda: Inside the Clinton White House* (New York: Simon and Schuster, 2005), p. 161.
9. Major Garrett, *The Enduring Revolution: How the Contract With America Continues to Shape the Nation* (New York: Crown Forum, 2005), p. 130.
10. Garrett, pp. 128–129.
11. Garrett, p. 248.
12. 1996 Republican Party Platform: http://www.presidency.ucsb.edu/ws/index.php?pid=25848.
13. Garrett, p. 248.
14. Lowi, *The End of Liberalism.*
15. Jacob S. Hacker, "Reviving the Social Safety Net," *The New Republic*, 4 July 2005; http://www.tnr.com/doc.mhtml?i=2005070 4&s=hacker070405.
16. A.V. Dicey, *Law and Public Opinion in England*, (London: Macmillan, 1914), pp. 257–8; quoted in Milton Friedman, *Capitalism and Freedom* (Chicago: University of Chicago Press), p. 201.
17. Wilson, "Why Reagan Won and Stockman Lost," pp. 18–19.
18. Ronald Reagan, Farewell Address, 11 January 1989; http://www.reaganlibrary.net/.
19. Friedman, *Capitalism and Freedom*, p. 6.
20. See, for example, Epstein, *How Progressives Rewrote the Constitution*, pp. 14–51.
21. Matthew Yglesias, "Libertarians and Democracy," *The Atlantic*, 22 January 2008; http://matthewyglesias.theatlantic.com/archives/2008/01/human_nature.php#comments.
22. Tyler Cowen, "The Paradox of Libertarianism," *Cato Unbound*, 11 March 2007; http://www.cato-unbound.org/2007/03/11/tyler-cowen/the-paradox-of-libertarianism/.

23. Louis Menand, "He Knew He Was Right: The Tragedy of Barry Goldwater," *The New Yorker*, 26 March 2001; http://www.newyorker.com/archive/2001/03/26/010326crbo_books.
24. Cowen, "The Paradox of Libertarianism."
25. William F. Buckley, "Murray Rothbard, RIP," *National Review*, 6 February 1995, p. 19.
26. Ronald Reagan, Inaugural Address, 20 January 1981.
27. Ronald Reagan, "Address Accepting the Presidential Nomination at the Republican National Convention in Detroit," 17 July 1980; http://www.presidency.ucsb.edu/ws/index.php?pid=25970.
28. Timothy Noah, "David Stockman, Working Class Hero," *Slate*, 4 September 2003; http://slate.msn.com/id/2087957/.
29. David Frum, *Dead Right* (New York: Basic Books, 1994), pp. 34–35.
30. Cropsey, "Liberalism and Conservatism," pp. 46–47.
31. "The Election," *National Review*, 28 November 1980, p. 1435.
32. "Budget: The Real Issue," *National Review*, 20 February 1981, pp. 136–137.
33. The data for Tables 16, 17 and 18 are derived from OMB's historical table 1.2, "Summary of Receipts, Outlays, and Surpluses or Deficits (–) as Percentages of GDP: 1930–2013," and the Census Bureau's historical population estimates in the *Statistical Abstract*, Table HS-1.
34. Daniel Patrick Moynihan, "Reagan's Bankrupt Budget," *The New Republic*, 31 December 1983, p. 19.
35. Wilson, "Why Reagan Won and Stockman Lost," p. 19.
36. Bruce Bartlett, "'Starve the Beast': Origins and Development of a Budgetary Metaphor," *The Independent Review*, Summer 2007, pp. 5–26.
37. Frum, *Dead Right*, p. 50.
38. Frum, p. 35.
39. Moynihan, "Reagan's Bankrupt Budget," pp. 18–19.
40. Bruce Bartlett, "A Taxing Experience," *National Review*, 29 October 2003, http://www.nationalreview.com/nrof_bartlett/bartlett200310290853.asp.
41. Quoted in "The Achievement of the New Deal," by William E. Leuchtenburg, in Harvard Sitkoff, ed., *Fifty Years Later: The New*

Deal Evaluated (Philadelphia: Temple University Press, 1985), pp. 220–221.

42. Glenn C. Loury, "The Return of the 'Undeserving Poor,'" The Atlantic Monthly, February 2001; http://www.theatlantic.com/doc/200102/loury.

43. Jared Bernstein, "Taxes and Interdepend," The American Prospect, 15 April 2005; http://www.prospect.org/web/page.ww?section=root&name=ViewWeb&articleId=9520.

44. The data for Tables 19–22 are derived from the CBO report, "Historical Effective Federal Tax Rates: 1979 to 2005," published in December 2007. CBO's appendix tables present the statistics for the top quintile in aggregated form: the top 1, 5, 10 and 20 percent. I used some spreadsheet algebra to disaggregate the numbers for the ninth decile, 91st through 95th percentiles, and 96th through 99th percentiles. Recall from Chapter Four that CBO defines income expansively, including such things as employer-paid health insurance and the employer's portion of payroll taxes.

45. CNN, "U.S. President National Exit Polls;" http://www.cnn.com/ELECTION/2004/pages/results/states/US/P/00/epolls.0.html.

46. Thomas Byrne Edsall, "The Changing Shape of Power: A Realignment in Public Policy," in Steve Fraser and Gary Gerstle, editors, The Rise and Fall of the New Deal Order, 1930–1980 (Princeton: Princeton University Press, 1989), p. 283.

47. Mickey Kaus, The End of Equality (New York: Basic Books, 1992), pp. 64–65.

48. "The Frayed Knot," The Economist, 26 May 2007, p.22.

49. Kaus, The End of Equality, pp. 18, 77.

50. Joseph A. Pechman, "The Future of the Income Tax," The American Economic Review, vol. 80, no. 1, March 1990, p. 4.

51. Kaus, The End of Equality, pp. 61–62.

52. 1976 Democratic Party Platform; http://www.presidency.ucsb.edu/ws/index.php?pid=29606.

53. Jim Webb, "Class Struggle: American Workers Have a Chance to Be Heard," The Wall Street Journal, 15 November 2006; http://www.opinionjournal.com/editorial/feature.html?id=110009246.

54. E.J. Dionne, "Reagan Democrat," *The Washington Post*, 25 January 2007, p. A25; http://www.washingtonpost.com/wp-dyn/content/article/2007/01/24/AR2007012401649.html.

55. Joan Walsh, "The New Great Communicator . . . Isn't," *Salon*, 6 February 2009; http://www.salon.com/opinion/feature/2009/02/04/obama/index.html.

56. Kaus, *The End of Equality*, pp. 63–71.

57. Peter Beinart, "Simple Life," *The New Republic*, 15 May 2006; http://www.tnr.com/article/simple-life.

58. David A. Stockman, *The Triumph of Politics: How the Reagan Revolution Failed* (New York: Harper and Row, 1986), p. 113.

59. Stockman, pp. 123, 376, 391, 394.

60. Wilson, "Why Reagan Won and Stockman Lost," pp. 17–21.

61. Wilson, "Why Reagan Won," p. 17.

62. Garrett, *The Enduring Revolution*, pp. 13–14.

63. Wilson, "Why Reagan Won," p. 21.

64. David A. Stockman, "The Social Pork Barrel," *The Public Interest*, 39, Spring 1975, pp. 3–28.

65. Wilson, pp. 18, 20.

66. Stockman, "The Social Pork Barrel," pp. 22–24.

67. Stockman, "The Social Pork Barrel," pp. 28–29.

68. Stockman, "The Social Pork Barrel," pp. 29–30.

69. Paul Pierson, *Dismantling the Welfare State? Reagan, Thatcher and the Politics of Retrenchment* (Cambridge: Cambridge University Press, 1994), p. 6.

70. Irving Kristol, "Two Parties in Search of Direction," *The Wall Street Journal*, 12 May 1993, p. A14.

71. Wilson, "Why Reagan Won," p. 20.

72. William F. Buckley, Jr., "God Bless Godlessness," *National Review*, 30 January 2001; http://www.nationalreview.com/buckley/buckley013001.shtml.

73. Michael Tanner, "We Are All Democrats Now?", *National Review*, 8 December 2008; http://corner.nationalreview.com/post/?q=ZW EoMjdkMjMxY2E2MGJlZDZhZmJkNmRhZjU2ZDJiZWY=.

74. Frum, *Dead Right*, p. 28.

75. U.S. Census Bureau, "2008 National Population Projections," released August 2008, <http://www.census.gov/population/

www/projections/2008projections.html>. it; Table 10. Resident
Population Projections by Sex and Age: 2010 to 2050.

76. Congressional Budget Office, *The Long Term Budget Outlook*,
December 2007, Table 1.2, p. 5; www.cbo.gov/ftpdocs/88xx/
doc8877/12-13-LTBO.pdf.

77. William Galston, "How Big Government Got Its Groove Back,"
The American Prospect, 9 June 2008; http://www.prospect.org/cs/
articles?article=how_big_government_got_its_groove_back.

78. Matt Miller, "What Is the Democrats' Secret Number?", *Fortune*,
23 February 2005; http://www.mattmilleronline.com/democrats_
number.php.

79. Miller, "Secret Number."

80. Wilson, "Why Reagan Won," p. 18.

81. Frum, *Dead Right*, p. 8.

82. "Correspondence," *The Claremont Review of Books*, Winter 2007,
p. 4.

83. Steven M. Gillon, *The Pact: Bill Clinton, Newt Gingrich, and the
Rivalry That Defined a Generation* (Oxford: Oxford University
Press, 2008), p. xv.

84. Gillon, pp. 218–221, 266–267.

85. Josh Patashnik, "Back to the Future?" *The New Republic*,
10 June 2008; http://blogs.tnr.com/tnr/blogs/the_plank/
archive/2008/06/10/back-to-the-future.aspx#comments.

86. Gillon, pp. 197, 203.

87. Gillon, p. 279.

88. Gillon, p. 268.

89. Quoted in Lipset and Marks, *It Didn't Happen Here*, p. 16.

90. Patashnik, "Correspondence," *The Claremont Review of Books*,
Winter 2007, p. 4.

91. Robert C. Pozen, "A Win-Win Proposition," *The Wall Street
Journal*, 3 May 2005; http://www.opinionjournal.com/editorial/
feature.html?id=110006639.

92. Ramesh Ponnuru, "Social Security on the First Date," *The
New York Times*, 30 January 2008; http://www.nytimes.
com/2009/01/30/opinion/30ponnuru.html?_r=1&ref=opinion.

93. Gillon, p. xv.

94. Irving Kristol, "A Conservative Welfare State," *The Wall Street Journal*, 14 June 1993, p. A14.

95. "Correspondence," *The Claremont Review of Books*, Winter 2008/09, p. 4.

96. Richard A. Epstein, "The Mistakes of 1937," *The George Mason University Law Review*, 1988–89, p. 5.

97. Michael S. Greve, "How to Think About Constitutional Change, Part I: The Progressive Vision," *The Federalist Outlook*, No. 23 (1), June 2005, p. 2.

98. William F. Buckley, Jr., "Publisher's Statement," *National Review*, 19 November 1955; http://www.nationalreview.com/flashback/buckley200406290949.asp.

99. Robert A. Levy and William Mellor, *The Dirty Dozen: How Twelve Supreme Court Cases Radically Expanded Government and Eroded Freedom* (New York: Sentinel, 2008), p. 2.

100. Levy and Mellor, pp. 19–36.

101. Greve, "Constitutional Change," p. 2, footnote 11.

102. Levy and Mellor, pp. 19–20.

103. Sunstein, *Second Bill of Rights*, pp. 196–197.

104. Greve, p. 4.

CONCLUSION

1. Cropsey, "Liberalism and Conservatism," pp. 42–43.

2. W.S. Gilbert and Arthur Sullivan, "Iolanthe," Gilbert and Sullivan Archive, Boise State University; http://math.boisestate.edu/GaS/iolanthe/web_op/iol14.html.

3. Ceaser, "True Blue vs. Deep Red," p. 5.

4. Ceaser, p. 15.

5. Alan Wolfe, *The Future of Liberalism* (New York: Alfred A. Knopf, 2009), p. 25.

6. Wolfe, p. 19.

7. Ceaser, pp. 17–22.

8. James Fallows, "Markets Can't Do Everything," *The Washington Monthly*, January/February 1996, p. 27.

9. Quoted in Aaron Wildavsky, *The Beleaguered Presidency* (New Brunswick, NJ: Transaction, 1994), p. 81.

10. Abraham Lincoln, Message to the Special Session of Congress, 1861, in Richard N. Current, ed., *The Political Thought of Abraham Lincoln* (Indianapolis: Bobbs-Merrill, 1967), p. 181.
11. Simon Schama, *Citizens: A Chronicle of the French Revolution* (New York: Knopf, 1989), p. xiii.
12. David Brooks, "What Life Asks of Us," *The New York Times*, 26 January 2009; http://www.nytimes.com/2009/01/27/opinion/27brooks.html.

INDEX

abortion rights, 85, 146–47

Achtenberg, Roberta, 108–10

Ackerman, Bruce, on liberalism, 104

"adequate social investment," 57

adhocracy, 145–48, 151–53

affirmative action, 112–22, 136–42
  and college admissions, 117–19, 137–41
  and compassion, 136–42
  and liberalism, 117, 121–22, 137
  and the Supreme Court of the United States, 116–17, 119–21

Affluent Society, The (Galbraith), 132–33, 160, 170

AFL-CIO, 190

aggregate demand, 168–72

Aid to Families with Dependent Children (AFDC), 124–27, 149, 200

American Enterprise Institute, 266

American labor movement, 58

American Prospect, The, 15, 144
  on the common good, 126–30
  on liberalism, 96, 104
  on socialism, 166–67
  on tax ceilings, 178
  on the welfare state, 198
  on welfare state expansion, 207, 255

Americans for Democratic Action, 90

Anarchy, State and Utopia (Nozick), 186–87

Anderson, Elizabeth, on Social Security, 128–29

Archer, Bill, 259

Argentina, 278

Aristotle, 103

AT&T, 190

athletes, salaries of, 189–91

Australia, Public Social Expenditures of, 43–49

baby boomers, 253–55

Baer, Kenneth, on liberalism, 97

Bai, Matt, on poverty relativity, 53

Bank of America, 190

Barber, Benjamin, 102

Barone, Michael, on the Great Society, 173

Bartlett, Bruce, 228

Begala, Paul, 260

Beinart, Peter, on estate taxes, 243

Belgium, Public Social Expenditures of, 43–49

Bernstein, Jared
  on redistribution of wealth, 182–83
  on the welfare state, 231

Bickel, Alexander, on majority rule, 86

Biden, Joseph, 182, 199

156–57, 162–63, 188, 193, 231,
248–49, 256
and public opinion, 158–59, 215
reconstruction of, 247–48, 250
stigma of, 228–29
West Coast Hotel Co. v. Parrish,
82, 271
White House Conference
on Equal Employment
Opportunity, 115
Wiebe, Robert H.
on rights, 105
on the welfare state, 112
Wilentz, Sean, on income tax
rates, 183, 243
Will, George F., on victimization
of the many, 192
Wilson, James Q.
on big government, 95, 246
on conservatism, 213
on David Stockman, 244–47
on tax cut legislation, 222
on the welfare state, 250,
256–57

Wilson, Woodrow, 78, 87
critique of the U.S.
Constitution, 60–61
and faction, 65
on leadership, 68
and progressivism, 97
Wolfe, Alan, on liberalism, 275
Works Progress Administration,
229
workweeks, mandating, 49
Wyatt, Wilson, on government's
responsibility, 90

Yglesias, Matthew, 242
on Aid to Families with
Dependent Children, 126
on spontaneous order, 214
on welfare rights, 122–23

Zhou En-lai, on the French
Revolution, 277